First World War
and Army of Occupation
War Diary
France, Belgium and Germany

37 DIVISION
63 Infantry Brigade
Duke of Cambridge's Own (Middlesex Regiment)
4th Battalion
1 July 1916 - 28 February 1919

WO95/2528/2

The Naval & Military Press Ltd
www.nmarchive.com
Published in association with The National Archives

Published by

The Naval & Military Press Ltd

Unit 10 Ridgewood Industrial Park,

Uckfield, East Sussex,

TN22 5QE England

Tel: +44 (0) 1825 749494

www.naval-military-press.com

www.nmarchive.com

This diary has been reprinted in facsimile from the original. Any imperfections are inevitably reproduced and the quality may fall short of modern type and cartographic standards.

© **Crown Copyright**
Images reproduced by permission of The National Archives, London, England, 2015.

Contents

Document type	Place/Title	Date From	Date To
Heading	WO95/2528/2 4 Bn Middx Regt July 1916-Feb 1919		
Heading	4th Bn Middlesex Regt Jly 1916-Feb 1919		
Heading	War Diary of 4th Bn. Middlesex Regiment. For July 1916		
War Diary		01/07/1916	31/07/1916
Miscellaneous	Q Office. 37th Division.	01/09/1916	01/09/1916
War Diary		01/08/1916	01/08/1916
War Diary	Maisnil Bouche	26/08/1916	02/09/1916
War Diary	Frevillers	03/09/1916	16/09/1916
War Diary	Ablain St Nazaire	17/09/1916	27/09/1916
War Diary	Souchez I	25/09/1916	30/09/1916
Miscellaneous	Q Office 37th Division	01/11/1916	01/11/1916
War Diary	Ablain St Nazaire	01/10/1916	06/10/1916
War Diary	Souchez I	07/10/1916	09/10/1916
War Diary	Houlette Wood	10/10/1916	16/10/1916
War Diary	Hermin	17/10/1916	17/10/1916
War Diary	Villers	18/10/1916	18/10/1916
War Diary	Brulin	19/10/1916	19/10/1916
War Diary	Berlencourt	20/10/1916	20/10/1916
War Diary	Amplier	21/10/1916	21/10/1916
War Diary	Raincheval	22/10/1916	29/10/1916
War Diary	Beauval	30/10/1916	31/10/1916
Miscellaneous	Memorandum		
Miscellaneous	4 Middlesex Regt Vol XXI		
War Diary	Beauval	01/11/1916	01/11/1916
War Diary	Doullens	08/11/1916	08/11/1916
War Diary	Lucheux	10/11/1916	10/11/1916
War Diary	Lealvillers	12/11/1916	30/11/1916
War Diary	Raincheval	01/12/1916	03/12/1916
War Diary	Beauval	04/12/1916	11/12/1916
War Diary	Beauval to Amplier	13/12/1916	13/12/1916
War Diary	Amplier to Barly	14/12/1916	14/12/1916
War Diary	Barly to Vacquerie	15/12/1916	15/12/1916
War Diary	Vacquerie to Troisvaux	16/12/1916	16/12/1916
War Diary	Troisvaux to Raimbert	17/12/1916	17/12/1916
War Diary	Lillers	19/12/1916	21/12/1916
War Diary	Vielle Chappelle	22/12/1916	29/12/1916
War Diary	Locon	30/12/1916	31/12/1916
Heading	War Diary 4th Middlesex Jan 1917 Vol 30		
War Diary	Locon	01/01/1917	03/01/1917
War Diary	Neuve-Chappelle	04/01/1917	09/01/1917
War Diary	Croix Barbee	10/01/1917	14/01/1917
War Diary	Locon	15/01/1917	31/01/1917
War Diary	Le Touret	01/02/1917	01/02/1917
War Diary	Beuvry	02/02/1917	11/02/1917
War Diary	Support Trenches near Loos	12/02/1917	12/02/1917
War Diary	14 Bus Sector Loos	13/02/1917	14/02/1917
War Diary	Loos Salient 14 Bis Rgt Sector	15/02/1917	18/02/1917
War Diary	Mazingarbe	19/02/1917	28/02/1917
War Diary	(13 Bis) Loos	01/03/1917	03/03/1917

Type	Location	Start	End
War Diary	Mazingarbe	04/03/1917	04/03/1917
War Diary	Bethune	05/03/1917	05/03/1917
War Diary	Bas Rieux	06/03/1917	06/03/1917
War Diary	Ligny Les Aire	07/03/1917	09/03/1917
War Diary	Bethonval Conteville	10/03/1917	10/03/1917
War Diary	Houvin Houigneul	11/03/1917	05/04/1917
War Diary	Beaufort	06/04/1917	09/04/1917
War Diary	Arras	09/04/1917	09/04/1917
War Diary	Near Arras	09/04/1917	11/04/1917
War Diary	Arras	12/04/1917	12/04/1917
War Diary	Duisans	13/04/1917	13/04/1917
War Diary	Abnez-Les-Doisans	14/04/1917	14/04/1917
War Diary	Manin	15/04/1917	18/04/1917
War Diary	Gouves	19/04/1917	19/04/1917
War Diary	Arras	20/04/1917	22/04/1917
War Diary	Near Arras	22/04/1917	29/04/1917
War Diary	Manin	30/04/1917	30/04/1917
War Diary		05/04/1917	28/04/1917
War Diary	Manin	01/05/1917	18/05/1917
War Diary	Simencourt	19/05/1917	19/05/1917
War Diary	Achicourt	20/05/1917	28/05/1917
War Diary	Tilloy	29/05/1917	31/05/1917
Miscellaneous	War Diary 4th Middlesex June 1917 Vol 35		
War Diary	Manin	01/06/1917	07/06/1917
War Diary	Matringhem	08/06/1917	22/06/1917
War Diary	Auchy-Au-Bois	23/06/1917	23/06/1917
War Diary	Thiennes	24/06/1917	24/06/1917
War Diary	Caestre	25/06/1917	25/06/1917
War Diary	Nr. Kemmel	26/06/1917	01/07/1917
War Diary	Mont Kemmel	02/07/1917	06/07/1917
War Diary	Kemmel	07/07/1917	11/07/1917
War Diary	Trenches	12/07/1917	19/07/1917
War Diary	Blaire Camp Mt Kemmel	20/07/1917	20/07/1917
War Diary	Beaver Camp	21/07/1917	25/07/1917
War Diary	In The Line	26/07/1917	26/07/1917
War Diary	Beaver Camp	27/07/1917	29/07/1917
War Diary	In the line	30/07/1917	31/07/1917
Miscellaneous	War Diary 4th Middx Regt August 1917 Vol 37		
War Diary	In The Line	01/08/1917	01/08/1917
War Diary	Dranoutre	03/08/1917	08/08/1917
War Diary	Beaver Corner	09/08/1917	25/08/1917
War Diary	Butterfly Farm	26/08/1917	28/08/1917
War Diary	Bois Confluent	29/08/1917	29/08/1917
War Diary	O.5.a.3.0	30/08/1917	31/08/1917
Heading	War Diary 4 Middlesex Sept 1917 Vol 38		
War Diary		01/09/1917	06/09/1917
War Diary	N.15.c.9.9	07/09/1917	09/09/1917
War Diary	Mont Kokereele	10/09/1917	27/09/1917
War Diary	S.E. of Ypres	27/09/1917	30/09/1917
War Diary	S.E. of Ypres	01/09/1917	10/09/1917
War Diary	Mont Kokereele	11/09/1917	18/09/1917
War Diary	S. Of Ypres	19/09/1917	20/09/1917
War Diary	Mont Kokereele	21/09/1917	30/09/1917
Heading	War Diary 4th Middlesex Oct 1917 Vol 39		
War Diary		01/10/1917	14/10/1917
War Diary	Mont Kokereele	15/10/1917	21/10/1917

War Diary	Meteren	21/10/1917	31/10/1917
War Diary	Ypres	01/11/1917	07/11/1917
War Diary	Meteren	08/11/1917	10/11/1917
War Diary	Beggars Rest. Camp	11/11/1917	17/11/1917
War Diary	Curragh Camp	17/11/1917	25/11/1917
War Diary	In the Line	25/11/1917	31/12/1917
Heading	4th Battalion The Middlesex Regiment. January 1918		
War Diary	In The Field	01/01/1918	31/01/1918
Heading	4th Battalion The Middlesex Regiment. February 1918		
War Diary	In The Field	01/02/1918	14/02/1918
War Diary	La Belle Hotesse	14/02/1918	14/02/1918
War Diary	Dickebusch	15/02/1918	15/02/1918
War Diary	Mount Sorrel	16/02/1918	21/02/1918
War Diary	In The Field	22/02/1918	28/02/1918
Heading	4th Battalion The Middlesex Regiment. March 1918		
War Diary	In The Field	01/03/1918	31/03/1918
Heading	4th Battalion The Middlesex Regiment. April 1918		
War Diary	In The Field	01/04/1918	30/04/1918
Heading	4th Battalion The Middlesex Regiment. May 1918		
War Diary	In The Field	01/05/1918	31/05/1918
Heading	4th Battalion The Middlesex Regiment. June 1918		
War Diary	In The Field	01/06/1918	22/06/1918
War Diary	Couin	23/06/1918	25/06/1918
War Diary	In The Field	26/06/1918	30/06/1918
Heading	4th Battalion The Middlesex Regiment. July 1918		
War Diary	In The Field	01/07/1918	06/07/1918
War Diary	Essarts	07/07/1918	11/07/1918
War Diary	In The Field	12/07/1918	12/07/1918
War Diary	Souastre	13/07/1918	17/07/1918
War Diary	In The Field	18/07/1918	31/07/1918
Heading	4th Battalion The Middlesex Regiment. August 1918		
War Diary	In The Field	01/08/1918	31/08/1918
Miscellaneous	4th Battalion Middlesex Regiment. Account of Operations- 21.8.18 to 25.8.18		
Heading	4th Battalion The Middlesex Regiment. September 1918		
War Diary	In The Field	01/09/1918	30/09/1918
Heading	4th Battalion The Middlesex Regiment. October 1918		
War Diary	In The Field	01/10/1918	31/10/1918
War Diary	Ref. Sheet 57B N.E. 1/20,000	12/10/1918	12/10/1918
Heading	4th Battalion The Middlesex Regiment. November 1918		
War Diary	In The Field	01/11/1918	30/11/1918
Heading	4th Battalion The Middlesex Regiment. December 1918		
War Diary	In The Field	01/12/1918	01/12/1918
War Diary	Haussy		
War Diary	Villers-Pol	02/12/1918	13/12/1918
War Diary	In the Field Louvignies	14/12/1918	14/12/1918
War Diary	Sous-Le-Bois	15/12/1918	16/12/1918
War Diary	Grand-Reng	17/12/1918	17/12/1918
War Diary	Ressaix	18/12/1918	18/12/1918
War Diary	Courcelles	19/12/1918	20/12/1918
War Diary	Reves	21/12/1918	31/01/1919
Miscellaneous	63rd Inf Bde	03/03/1919	03/03/1919
War Diary	Reves	01/02/1919	28/02/1919

WO95/2528/2

4 BN. MIDDX REGT

July 1916 — Feb 1919

37TH DIVISION
63RD INFY BDE

4TH BN MIDDLESEX REGT
JLY 1916-FEB 1919

From 21 Div 63 Bde

63/37

Bn. transferred
Bde to 37th
Div. 7.7.16.

War Diary

of

4th Bn. Middlesex Regiment

for

July 1916.

Feb 19

WAR DIARY or INTELLIGENCE SUMMARY

Army Form C. 2118.

July 4 Middlesex Regt

Vol 24

Place	Date	Hour	Summary of Events and Information	Remarks and references to Appendices
	1st July	6.25 am	The intense preliminary bombardment commenced at 6.25 AM: this caused some retaliation by the enemy's artillery which caused considerable casualties among the two companies occupying the front line, especially A Coy. The leading Platoons attempted to throw its trenches at 7.20 AM in accordance with instructions, but suffered severely from machine gun fire shot to get back. Two men were reported to 7.28 AM on our right near the German TAMBOUR. The leading Platoons left the front trenches again slightly before 7.30 AM, the actual hour of assault, were met by intense rifle machine gun fire. The remainder of A & B Companies followed in line of Platoons at 100 yards distance; C. Coy. followed them in two lines, two Platoons in each line, at the same distance. D. Coy. in the same formation, but the rear line carrying the Batts. reserve of ammunition & grenades. Troops had practised moved with the rear line of C. Coy.	
		7.30 am	The leading Companies reached & passed over the German front line. By this time all the officers with the exception of 2nd Lieutenant, and most of the N.C.O's had been hit; the survivors pushed on in small groups beyond the support line; between this line the SUNKEN ROAD in front of redan Fighting they were able to maintain themselves until the arrival of the Supporting Platoons. They attached themselves to the 2nd Lincoln Regt. on their arrival & remained with them until the morning of 3rd July when they were brought back to Bn. Hd Qrs by Sgt. Millinood C.D Company Batts Hd Qrs. suddenly lost very heavily from machine gun	

WAR DIARY or INTELLIGENCE SUMMARY

Army Form C. 2118.

Place	Date	Hour	Summary of Events and Information	Remarks and references to Appendices
	1st July		fire in crossing "No Man's Land" by the time they reached it had established themselves in the German front line trench were reduced to a strength of from Officers & about one hundred other ranks. Owing to the failure of the 50th Inf. Bde on the right to take the German trenches in front of FRICOURT the right flank of the Battn. was exposed considerable parties of the enemy with machine guns were able to work up between the remnants of the leading Companies & the support Companies from the direction of FRICOURT. At this time the situation was extremely critical the leading Coys. were disorganized & had lost the whole of their Officers; the supporting Coys. were holding & had only partly consolidated their position in the German front line trench. At this time most valuable service was rendered by Capt. Walker and 2/Lt. Loftus and Tarrant also by Sgt. Hardy's, Sgt. Wright & Sgt. Northwood. About this time several bombing attacks were made by the enemy from the right all of which were repulsed. It was noticed that owing to the severe losses & strong opposition of the enemy that any attempt to advance further without support would be impossible; it was decided to consolidate & a message was sent to Brigade Hd. Qrs.	
		8.15am	The ground won & at 8.15am a message to this effect was sent to Brigade Hd. Qrs.	

WAR DIARY or INTELLIGENCE SUMMARY

Army Form C. 2118.

Place	Date	Hour	Summary of Events and Information	Remarks and references to Appendices
	1st July	9.15 am	At about 9.15 AM the supporting Battns. began to arrive: the 10th York & Lancaster Regt. pushed through the left of the Battn. where the enemy from his supporting lines noted they occupied and the 8th Lincolns went through the 8.5. Somersets & reinforced LOZENGE ALLEY and eventually the SUNKEN ROAD.	
		11 AM	At about 11 AM. twelve men arrived from Brigade to protect the right flank of the Brigade as the York & Lancaster & Lincoln Regt. were going to make a further advance. The bombing posts which had already been established were strengthened & Lewis guns added and all enemy trenches leading to FRICOURT were blocked. So far the defensive flank stretched the whole length of the Battn. and this position was held till 1st and day 3rd July. The Lewis guns were able to bring a most effective fire to bear on the enemy in FRICOURT & inflicted severe casualties on parties seen moving about.	
	2nd July		The Battn. continued to hold this position which was subjected at intervals to heavy shelling by guns of large calibre which however did little harm. During the afternoon K.O.O.'s who had been left behind as a reinforcement joined the Battn. soon after day break (all available men were employed at nothing comprising at ammunition & supplies to 62nd Inf Bde dugouts in adverse wing up the	
	3rd July		The Battn. remained in the same position till after noon day. During the morning the bodies of all the officers who had been killed were collected and a	

2449 Wt. W14957/M90 750,000 1/16 J.B.C. & A. Forms/C.2118/12.

Place	Date	Hour	Summary of Events and Information	Remarks and references to Appendices

3/7/16 — Given day but owing to heavy shelling the work could not be completed. A heavy shell fell in the trench killing 2Lt. Rannik and Sgt. Millward + Pressley, all of whom had rendered most conspicuous good service during the action, besides killing + wounding about 20 other ranks.

At noon orders were received to move to LOZENGE ALLEY and take up a position there in Brigade Reserve facing North. In the new position, T the Brigade were on the forward trenches further North covering the left flank of the Division.

4/7/16 — At 3 a.m. the Batn. were relieved by a Batn. of 17th Division and marched to DERNACOURT, providing later by train and march to VAUX about 12 Kilometres N.W of AMIENS.

Casualties in operations 1st – 3rd July.

Officers killed. Capt. O.R.F. Johnston. Lt. A. Soplet. Lt. G.L.E. Ridgate, 2Lt. A. Branch. 2Lt. A.G. Chambers
2Lt. A.H. Johnston. 2Lt. S.F. Chudfield. 2Lt. A.H. Winne-Sampson. 2Lt. W.J. Wood. 2Lt. E. Peyton.
2Lt. E.M. Whitby. 2Lt. A.F.C. Panton. 2Lt. G.R. Avery. 2Lt. P. Barrett.

Officers Wounded. Capt. B.C.L. Rowley (died 2 July). 2Lt. P. Leigh-Pemberton. 2Lt. A.J. Brennan.
2Lt. F.E. Coomber. 2Lt. R.T.C. Cary.

Other Ranks. killed   131
              wounded   337
              missing believed killed 15
              missing   18

Army Form C. 2118.

WAR DIARY
or
INTELLIGENCE SUMMARY

(Erase heading not required.)

Place	Date	Hour	Summary of Events and Information	Remarks and references to Appendices
	7th July		The Battn. were resting at VAUX till their orders arrived for the Brigade to be transferred to the 37th Division. It paraded at 3.45 P.M. and marched with the remainder of the Brigade to TALMAS, arriving at 8.P.M.	
	8th July		Battn. marched to HALLOY. A message from Brig. Gen. Campbell, a copy of which is attached, was received on leaving the 37th Division.	
	11th July		Battn. marched to HUMBERCAMP when they had dinners and later to BIENVILLERS when they took over reserve billets, the remainder of the Brigade occupying the front line trenches at HANNESCAMP. Battn. supplied working parties to the front trenches which took all available men. An accident occurred in the transport lines; while being moved a horse of grenades exploded killing four men wounding four others as well as 12 horses.	
	12th July		Maj. Odling left to assume command of 6th Bn. North Stafford Regt. During the time in BIENVILLERS the village was frequently shelled but the Battn. had no casualties.	

2449 Wt. W14957/M90 750,000 1/16 J.B.C. & A. Forms/C.2118/12.

Army Form C. 2118.

WAR DIARY
or
INTELLIGENCE SUMMARY
(Erase heading not required.)

Place	Date	Hour	Summary of Events and Information	Remarks and references to Appendices
	14 July		Working parties supplied in the morning. At 4 P.M. the Batt. moved to POMMIER. The Division being relieved by 56th Division.	
	15 July		Batt. marched at 7.30 am to HOUVIN – HOUVIGNEUL.	
	16 July		Batt. marched to VILLERS – BRULIN.	
	18 July		Batt. marched to MAISNIL – BOUCHÉ. Message received that body of 2 Lt G.A. St. John Jones, reported "missing believed killed" on 14 July, had been found near the Guinnan TAMBOUR. F.3.a.4.1. MONTAUBAN.	
	19 July		Following Officers joined for duty:– Lieuts S.A.H. Irwin, and R. Ustwhile. 2 Lieuts O.C. Trindle, E.M.M. Williams, P.M. Cannon, L.C. Thompson, O.H. Martin, S.C.L. Murray, O.G. Johnston, P.W. Smith, R.M. Hilton, A.N. MacLeod, S.A.G. Hutchell, O.S. Pennnan, M.E. Stockly. Batt. classified for grants of Service Proficiency Pay. Following Officers joined for duty:– 2 Lieuts F.N. Schofield, A.D. Hooker, R.C. Hotherns, A.D. Troswell, R.J.T. Brown.	
	20 July			

Army Form C. 2118.

WAR DIARY
or
INTELLIGENCE SUMMARY
(Erase heading not required.)

Instructions regarding War Diaries and Intelligence Summaries are contained in F. S. Regs., Part II. and the Staff Manual respectively. Title Pages will be prepared in manuscript.

Place	Date	Hour	Summary of Events and Information	Remarks and references to Appendices
	22nd July		The Battn. 1st Line Transport was inspected by the Divisional Commander Maj. Gen. Ernest G'Hunter.	
	24th July		Coy. Officers & Company Commanders reconnoitred the trenches, BERTHONVAL Section, VIMY RIDGE to be taken over by the Battn.	
	25th July		Battn. relieved 1/17th London Regt. 47th Division, in trenches in sub-section BERTHONVAL(A) 2Lt. Lopte proceeded on bombing course. 2Lt. H.M. Williams proceeded on Physical training course.	
	27th July		Lieut. S.W. Milbourne and three Sergeants joined.	
	28th July		Draft of 45 other ranks joined. Lt. R. Underhill proceeded on Physical Training course. Lt. E.A.G. Mitchell proceeded on Trench Warfare course. 2Lt. H.P. Rowson proceeded on Sniping course. 2Lt. S. Ainsworth proceeded on Lewis Gun course.	
	29th July		2Lt. H.M. Williams rejoined.	
	30th 31st July		Battn. relieved in trenches by 8th Somerset Light Inf. after very quiet tour during which there were no casualties and returned to 8th Lincoln Regt. in support lines at CABARET ROUGE.	

F. Pickworth. Lt Col.
Comg. a/Middx. Regt.

To

    "Q" Office,

        37th Division.
        ....

            Herewith original War Diary of this Battalion for month of August, 1916.

            Kindly acknowledge receipt.

                                      2/Lieut for Lieut-Colonel,

Commanding, 4th Battalion, Middlesex Regiment.
....

<u>1st Sept. ,1916.</u>

Army Form C. 2118

(3/37)
4 In of divis.

Vol 2 s.

WAR DIARY
or
INTELLIGENCE SUMMARY
(Erase heading not required.)

Place	Date	Hour	Summary of Events and Information	Remarks and references to Appendices
	Aug 1st		Awarded Military Medal for Operations at FRICOURT on July 1st— No: 355 Cpl. Clarke. W. D. Company 1207 Cpl. Ingram. W. D. Company 1679 Sgt. Wright. C. A. Company 7852 Pte. Page. F. A. Company 14599 " Folkes. R. A. Company 7792 Sgt. Westbrook. R. (Attached T.M. Battery). date of award 23-7-16. Awarded D.C.M. 11092. C.S.M. Worboys. A. date of award 29-7-16. S. Latches Capt.	

WAR DIARY
INTELLIGENCE SUMMARY
(Erase heading not required.)

Army Form C. 2118.

Place	Date	Hour	Summary of Events and Information	Remarks and references to Appendices
MAILLY	26/6/16		H/Q, Snipers & Scouts returned from Bos Bourn at DESTRAYELLE; 2/Lt Jones & party returned to Battalion Bivouac St CAMIERS & 2/Lt Harris from Physical Training School Rigby. Draft to PERNES. 2/Lt Schofield joined Snipers Bourn et PERNES. Specialist training.	
	28/6/16		Draft of 5 Sgts also 1/2 Lewis Gunners & Bombers arrived from Bases. Training continued. Normal standard.	
BOIS DES ALLEUX	29/6/16		2/Lt Harris posted to 63rd Trench Mortar Battery. Major R M Heath D.S.O. joined to take over command duties of 2nd in Command.	
	30/6/16		Working party (under Lt Melbourne) joined Battalion from BOIS DES ALLEUX. 2/Lt L.W. Anderson posted to Battalion for 63rd T.M. Battery. 2/Lt Stocks returned from France hospital. 2/Lt Sutherson from Lewis Guns Bourn PERNES.	
	31/6/16		& 2/Lt Leaman Bourn PERNES, & 2/Lt Maitland joined & proceeded down to et CHARRUED. Battalion training. 2/Lt Maitland joined 2/Lt Rouse at ???	

togo.

J. Ruhle,
LIEUT-COLONEL
COMMDG. 4/ MIDDLESEX RGT.

WAR DIARY or INTELLIGENCE SUMMARY

Army Form C. 2118.

Vol 96 / 4 MIDDLESEX
SEPT 1916

Place	Date	Hour	Summary of Events and Information	Remarks and references to Appendices
MONTAY BRUAY	SEPT 1st		Battalion Training	
	2nd		2/Pr Brown & 21 OR detached as working party, Maître-mte-Mines Au-Bois, under 11 Sussex C.O. & Army 33.	
	3rd	10 am	Battalion proceeded to FREVILLERS. Halt E. L. Sussex Brigade Reserve for 153 Bgd.	
	4th		Coy training. 19 O.R. joined Battalion from drafts to various amounts of 10/R.Hants Rgt Battalion training. 2/Lt Senn appointed Div Asst Instructor for Scouts for Division.	
	5th		Battalion training	
	6th		"B" Coy inspected in Marching Order by G.O.C. 152nd Brigade. Battalion training	
	7th		Battalion Route March. Capt H.R. Willis joined Battalion from Base	
	8th		Battalion training. 2/Lt Murray rejoined Battalion from Base	
	9th		Battalion training. 2/Lt Scales rejoined from Base. 2/Lts Currie, Merrie S, Lt B.P. Jones 2/Lt W.E. Hart & E.J. Murr joined Battalion from Base on posting	

JS Griffiths

Army Form C. 2118.

WAR DIARY
INTELLIGENCE SUMMARY.
(Erase heading not required.)

Instructions regarding War Diaries and Intelligence Summaries are contained in F. S. Regs., Part II. and the Staff Manual respectively. Title pages will be prepared in manuscript.

Place	Date	Hour	Summary of Events and Information	Remarks and references to Appendices
FRÉVIN-CAPELLE	SEPTR. 10TH		Sunday. C.O. M/Sgt Catan + C. boy proceed to Officers School of Sig.	
	11TH		2/C. Mitchell proceed to join Bombing School at PERNES. Battalion Training	
	12TH		Battalion Rest March + Cl. Maillard rejoined Battalion for one week's course Battalion training. Reinforcement 21 O.R. joined Battalion in the 17 have Grimer.	CARQUES.
	13TH		I new Lewis m/gr. D.A.M. otherwise up to strength.	
	14TH		Battalion training. Company bombers proceed to CARENCY to reconnoitre.	
	15TH		Battalion training.	
	16TH		Battalion training.	
ABLAIN ST NAZAIRE	17TH	2 PM.	Battalion marched to ABLAIN ST NAZAIRE relieving HOOD BN. in support of RNaval Division in SOUCHEZ Section. Dispositions :- "A" Coy on right, covering ABLAIN-SOUCHEZ Road. "C" Coy centre; "D" Coy on left (at LORETTE SPUR). "B" Coy in reserve MAESTRE LINE. Both sides ended of quiet. BnH.Qrs. in ABLAIN ST NAZAIRE. Transport parks at COURANT; ON/C Stores at HERSIN. Divl. Second Echelon only before H.Q. Williame proceed to HERSIN to join Brigade officers there while Brigade in line. Thy exception of desultory sniping + occasional enemy gunfire, Generally of defensive nature, it	

2353 Wt W2544/1454 700,000 5/15 D. D. & L. A.D.S.S./Forms/C. 2118.

Army Form C. 2118.

WAR DIARY
or
INTELLIGENCE SUMMARY.
(Erase heading not required.)

Instructions regarding War Diaries and Intelligence Summaries are contained in F. S. Regs., Part II. and the Staff Manual respectively. Title pages will be prepared in manuscript.

Place	Date	Hour	Summary of Events and Information	Remarks and references to Appendices
	SEPT.			
AIX-NOULETTE	18th		in SOUCHEZ Section. 8th Somerset L.I. occupying trenches in SOUCHEZ I, 8th Lincolns Sgt. Maj. in SOUCHEZ II, 10th K.R.R.C. in reserve at BOIS DE NOULETTE. Brigade H.Q. Army at AIX-NOULETTE. Both sides still inactive.	
	19th		Still very quiet. Bad weather prevents aeroplanes reconnaissance for full 24 hours before the attack.	
ST. MARIE CAPPELLE	20th 21st		Considerable artillery activity on both sides. Weather bright. Enemy large numbers of troops seen on VIMY RIDGE. Batteries followed up on both sides directing practice. German front line heavy aeroplane patrols on our line 9.30 - 11.30 on G.H.Q. line in parts without result. Six new Quickfire Batteries 300 yds. nw of Br. N.Cn. very active during the day. formed. Heavy artillery fire with others. 12 enemy T.M.L. posts at 63rd S.M. Battery. Quiet day.	
	22nd			
	23rd 24th	8pm	Battalion relieved by Somerset L.I. in front line, SOUCHEZ I. Sub-Section. "A" Coy in right "B" Coy centre "C" Coy left of line. "D" Coy in support in SUNKEN ROAD; the day also occupying SOUCHEZ PIT with Pt off. + 10 B.R. + 1 then 6pm & day and Artillery trench Ruins SOUCHEZ by night. Relief completed 11.35 pm. 10 yds. of these on right left in SOUCHEZ I. Very quiet. Our Artillery very active. German artillery very dormant. No casualties.	
SOUCHEZ I.	25th			

2353 Wt. W2544/1454 700,000 5/15 D. D. & L. A.D.S.S./Forms/C. 2118.

WAR DIARY

Army Form C. 2118.

Vol 26

INTELLIGENCE SUMMARY
(Erase heading not required.)

4. Middlesex

Place	Date	Hour	Summary of Events and Information	Remarks and references to Appendices
	Sept 26th / 27th		Enemy immensely busy. No damage. Our aeroplane active. No casualties. A Coy had to hold up by enemy trench mortars. Retaliation to ½ by our Stokes Mortar. One slight casualty - name sent to adjt. 2/O Wilkinson joined 37th Divn. Salvage officer.	
	28th		Artillery active on both sides. Enemy more active with machine gun than usual at night. Our machine guns fired 2 guns on support & C.T. at intervals from 9.30 p.m. 65th Divn Battery fired 175 rounds during afternoon seriously damaging enemy front line trenches and support line. Site of hostile T.M. Battery located - first of two, [illegible] not known.	
	29th		Very quiet day, mainly owing to weather. Nightly training. at Platoon of 20 men under 2/O Dowell detailed for duty with 32 [illegible] Bde will leave early at AIX NOULETTE	
	30th	8 pm	No casualties. Battalion relieved by 2/Somerset L.I. & proceeded to Loos [illegible] Sere (B.Coy at ADAM STRAZAINE) disposition of Snipers & coops as detailed 17th inst.	

[signature] F. Mitchell
Commanding 4 Middlesex Regt.

[signature] Kialt Stone
Sgt.

To

"Q" Office,

37th Division.

      I attach herewith original War Diary of the Battalion under my command for the month of October.

      Kindly acknowledge receipt.

                                [signature] Lieut-Colonel,

Commanding, 4th Battalion, Middlesex Regt.

1st November, 1916.

WAR DIARY or INTELLIGENCE SUMMARY

Army Form C. 2118.

Vol 27

Place	Date	Hour	Summary of Events and Information	Remarks and references to Appendices
Bois de la Haie	1/7/16		Very quiet. Nothing to report. Confusion busy wiring & draining trenches.	
St Pierre	4/7/16		2nd Lt. Mr T.R. Williams proceeded to School of Instruction.	
AMES	5/7/16		Still most quiet. 2/Lt Col. O. Johnson admitted to Field Ambulance.	
			2nd Lt Col. Pickett assumed command of 63rd Infty Bgde. Capt & Adjt A.L. Grantham sent Major M.S. Abbot-Bowen in command of Batt.	
SOUCHEZ	6/7/16	6 pm	Stokes' Mewed & Somerset R.I. in SOUCHEZ trenches. Inspected Bgde "A" Coy on right of out. station — "C" Coy on left — "B" Coy in SOUCHEZ "C"+"D" Bay of support. Trenches in very bad condition owing to recent bombardments — communication in some part of front line impossible. Very quiet night though. Enemy most active with minenwerfer. One of our Stokes guns buried No casualties. Quiet at night.	
SOUCHEZ	7/7/16		Violent bombardment all day. Little retaliation possible owing to atmospheric conditions. Our Sgt & 6 men temporarily cut off from Coy (11 Coy) owing to portion of trench decay than	
	8/7/16		enemy. M.P. wounded. Still very active. Our trenches blown in as fast as we re-build them	
	9/7/16		Little or no retaliation by our artillery	

Army Form C. 2118.

WAR DIARY
or
INTELLIGENCE SUMMARY.
(Erase heading not required.)

Instructions regarding War Diaries and Intelligence Summaries are contained in F. S. Regs., Part II. and the Staff Manual respectively. Title pages will be prepared in manuscript.

Place	Date	Hour	Summary of Events and Information	Remarks and references to Appendices
HOULETTE	10/7		1 Man wounded by trench mortar. Draft of 5 Sgts arrived.	
	11/7		2 men killed & 4 wounded by T.M.F. Relieved at 7 P.M. by 6th Bn Lincolnshire Regt & proceeded to HOULETTE WOOD in Bivouac Bivouac.	
"	12/7 to 14/7		Nothing to report. Working available men on working parties.	
"	15/7		Draft of 133 O.R. joined Battalion	
"	16/7		2/Lt Gibbons D.S.O. rejoined Batt. Battalion relieved by 25th Bn Somerset Infantry & proceeded to HERMIN where accommodated in Billet	
HERMIN	17/7		Major A. I. Webb Gowan posts to command of 8/Bat hours Regt.	
VILLERS BRULIN	18/7		Batt. proceeded to VILLERS BRULIN HQ Coy & A.B Coys billetted there C & D Coys at QUESTREVILLE.	
	19/7		Nothing to report	
BERLENCOURT	20/7		Parades to Billet at BERLENCOURT. Coy & Bn Coy proceeded to ENGELBEMER to reconnoitre	
AMPLIER	21/7		March to AMPLIER - quarters in Billet there	
RAINCHEVAL	22/7		" RAINCHEVAL Billets	
"	23/7		Battalion practised cutting Zone in	
"	24/7		Nothing to report.	

Army Form C. 2118.

WAR DIARY
INTELLIGENCE SUMMARY.
(Erase heading not required.)

Instructions regarding War Diaries and Intelligence Summaries are contained in F. S. Regs., Part II. and the Staff Manual respectively. Title pages will be prepared in manuscript.

Place	Date	Hour	Summary of Events and Information	Remarks and references to Appendices
RITIEVAL	25/6 26/6 27/6 28/6 29/6		Nothing to record. Battalion fortour the attack in each day. Draft of 110 O.R. (all transfers from G.H.Q. Base Dpt.) joined Bn. Draft of 36 O.R. (from 20th Bn Middx Regt) joined Bn: Lieut G. Grove & 2/Lt joined Bn from England + assumed duties of and in command Draft of 6 O.R. (all late of this Batt – recently wounded) joined Lt S.H. Melbourne departed to England	
BEAUVAL	30/6 31/6	1.40pm	Battalion proceeded to BEAUVAL & are in billets. Artillery formation + intervals & order of return by Battn.	

J.Tickner
Lt Colonel
Commanding 4th Bn Middx Regt.

Army Form C. 348.

MEMORANDUM.

From Officer Commanding
4ᵗʰ Middlesex Regt

To "Q" Office
37ᵗʰ Division.

From

To

ANSWER.

In the Field.
2ⁿᵈ January 1917.

Herewith original War Diary of this Battalion for month of December.

Will you kindly acknowledge receipt.

J. D. Mashieo

Major.
Commanding 4ᵗʰ Middx Regt.

191 .

3/21

4 Middlesex Regt

Vol XXI

Army Form C. 2118.

WAR DIARY
or
INTELLIGENCE SUMMARY.
(Erase heading not required.)

4 Middlesex Regt
Vol 28

Instructions regarding War Diaries and Intelligence Summaries are contained in F. S. Regs., Part II. and the Staff Manual respectively. Title pages will be prepared in manuscript.

Place	Date	Hour	Summary of Events and Information	Remarks and references to Appendices
BEAUVAL	1/11/16		Battalion in billets, training, remained here till 8/11/16.	
DOULLENS	8/11/16	6.30 PM	Battn. marched to DOULLENS. A.B. & C. Companies billetted in the Citadel in Gaukins. D. Company in the town. Hd. Qrs at HOTEL de VILLE. Battn. remained here till 10/11/16.	
LUCHEUX	10/11/16	2 PM	Battn. marched to LUCHEUX. remained there till 12/11/16	
LEALVILLERS	12/11/16	8 AM	Marched to LEALVILLERS. Blankets, packs & rations collected preparatory to active operations; ordered to be ready to move at short notice; remained till 14/11/16	
	14/11/16	11 AM	Marched to HEADAUVILLE, arriving about 3 PM. had dinners and marched again at 6 PM. to position of assembly, 1 mile S.E. of ENGLEBELMER. arriving about 8 PM. Marched again at 10 PM. to take up position in Brigade reserve at STATION ROAD, EAST of HAMEL. arrived there about 2 AM. Brigade disposed as follows. 10th York & Lancs holding right of front line. Brigade Sector, 8th Lincolns holding left of front line. 8th Somerset L.I. in support	

WAR DIARY
or
INTELLIGENCE SUMMARY.
(Erase heading not required.)

Army Form C. 2118.

Instructions regarding War Diaries and Intelligence Summaries are contained in F. S. Regs., Part II. and the Staff Manual respectively. Title pages will be prepared in manuscript.

Place	Date	Hour	Summary of Events and Information	Remarks and references to Appendices
	18/11/16		just EAST of STATION ROAD. On arrival in this position half of each Company was in STATION TRENCH half in the valley. Battn. remained here till morning of 18th furnishing carrying & working parties. STATION TRENCH and the Valley were heavily shelled at intervals the Battn. had 40 casualties.	
	18/4/16		The weather was bitterly cold there being hard frosts at night, some snow.	
	18/11/16	8.30 A.M.	At 8.30 A.M. a message was received from Brigade stating that the II Corps, SOUTH of the ANCRE, would attack GRANDCOURT at 8.10 A.M. and that the 37th Division were to be prepared to capture PUSIEUX and RIVER TRENCHES NORTH of the ANCRE. The 8th Somerset L.I. supported by E. Middlesex would be prepared to attack there in order to form junction with MIRAUMONT ALLEY at 11 A.M.	
		10.20 A.M.	At 10.20 A.M. a message was received that this attack would commence at 11 A.M. The Battn. immediately left for BEAUCOURT to be in position to support the attack. The going was very bad the mud in places being knee deep & the road was being heavily shelled; the Battn. reached the Hd. Qrs. of the 8/Somerset L.I. about 800 yards East of BEAUCOURT without	

WAR DIARY or INTELLIGENCE SUMMARY

Army Form C. 2118.

Place	Date	Hour	Summary of Events and Information	Remarks and references to Appendices
		11.5 a.m.	Casualties at 11.5 a.m. On receipt from the O.C. 8/Somerset L.I. stated that owing to non-receipt of the orders his Battn. was not yet assembled for an attack in a position to commence the attack. It was decided therefore to inform the Brigade that the two Battns would be ready to attack by 1.30 p.m. to ask for a new barrage. This was done. At the same time the 8/Somerset L.I. were to send patrols towards the Southern end of PUSIEUX TRENCH. Three patrols managed to get into the trench followed by one Company of the 8/Somerset L.I. C Company was sent forward to support them: on doing so Lt Underhill was killed and 2/Lt Bund & Mackeod wounded. The Company suffered severely. D Company was therefore sent to reinforce them: this company also suffered severely & 2/Lt Loyd was wounded.	
		3 p.m.	About 3 p.m. orders were received for the 4/Middlesex to relieve the 8/Somerset L.I.: the latter Battn. withdrew leaving C & D Companies holding PUSIEUX TRENCH between the ANCRE and the MIRAUMONT ROAD. the enemy holding the remainder. This situation continued till the evening of 19th Nov. when the attack on GRANDCOURT having failed to make progress it was decided to	

Army Form C. 2118.

WAR DIARY
or
INTELLIGENCE SUMMARY.
(Erase heading not required.)

Instructions regarding War Diaries and Intelligence
Summaries are contained in F. S. Regs., Part II.
and the Staff Manual respectively. Title pages
will be prepared in manuscript.

Place	Date	Hour	Summary of Events and Information	Remarks and references to Appendices
	19th		withdraw from PUSIEUX TRENCH. As soon as it was dark A Company commenced to dig a new line from BOIS D'HOLLANDE to the ANCRE and when this was nearly complete C & D Companies withdrew. They thinned the trench straight back all the time & got back without casualties.	
	20th	9 P.M.	On this date the Battn. was relieved by 8th South Staffords and withdrew to a position in the old 3rd German line pressing through heavy barrage with only three casualties. The Battn. remained here till the 22nd Nov. providing working & carrying parties from around to the old German front line.	
	22nd		The Battn. remained in this position still providing working parties till 25th Nov.	
	25th			
	26th	6.30 am	On the 26th Nov. the relief of the Division was completed the Battn. moved to billets at MAILLY MAILLET. During these operations the casualties amounted to 2 Officers killed & 3 wounded, about 140 O.R. killed and wounded. The weather conditions were however exceptionally trying and the losses due to cold wet and exposure were heavy.	

Army Form C. 2118.

WAR DIARY
or
INTELLIGENCE SUMMARY.

(Erase heading not required.)

Place	Date	Hour	Summary of Events and Information	Remarks and references to Appendices
	29/11/16		Battn. moved the huts in MAILLY WOOD.	
	30/11/16		moved to huts in ACHEUX WOOD	
			Whitmile	
			Lieu Colonel	
			Comma 2nd d Inniskin Regt	

Army Form C. 2118.

4 Middlesex Rgt
Vol 29

WAR DIARY
or
INTELLIGENCE SUMMARY.
(Erase heading not required.)

Place	Date	Hour	Summary of Events and Information	Remarks and references to Appendices
RAINCHEVAL	1/12/16		Battalion marched to RAINCHEVAL. Billets good but scattered.	TBBcapt
— " —	2/12/16		Remained at Raincheval time devoted to inspection etc.	TBBcapt
— " —	3/12/16		Wet day, little could be done. Orders received in the evening to march to billets at BEAUVAL	TBBcapt
— " —	4/12/16		Bn marched off at 9.am via BEAUQUESNE to BEAUVAL. Billets here exceptionally good. Settled in billets at about 1.30.pm.	TBBcapt
BEAUVAL	5/12/16		On "cleaning up" of arms & equipment inspection etc. LT. Colonel BICKNELL & CAPT. WILLIS proceed on leave for 28 days & 10 days respectively	TBBcapt
— " —	6/12/16		Rifle & football grounds & sites for training grounds & range were selected. Programme of work submitted to Bde. Major J D MATHEW of the DENBIGH HUSSARS (YEOMANRY) took over temporary command of Battalion. Capt Ellis admitted to field Ambulance	TBBcapt

Army Form C. 2118.

WAR DIARY
or
INTELLIGENCE SUMMARY.
(Erase heading not required.)

Instructions regarding War Diaries and Intelligence Summaries are contained in F. S. Regs., Part II. and the Staff Manual respectively. Title pages will be prepared in manuscript.

Place	Date	Hour	Summary of Events and Information	Remarks and references to Appendices
BEAUVAL	7/12/16		Battalion training. Notification received that the Corps Commander LT. GEN. FANSHAW would shortly inspect the Battalion. CAPT E. J. DONALDSON joined the Bn & assumed command of "A" Coy. LTS. G. GROGAN, J.K. GREGSON & H.M. MONK joined Bn. — T.B.Bept.	
	8/12/16		Battalion training & inspection by Company Officers in Drill, musketry. Orders 2 LIEUT. HEFFER & 2 LT THOMSON appointed Temporary Captains T.B.Bept.	
	9/12/16		Notification that the Corps Commander would inspect the Battalion today was received late last night. The Bn therefore paraded at 11.30 AM. The turnout was good but owing to the above orders not quite up to standard. Rain during the inspection. CAPT W. G. LARGIE (C.F.) joined Bn T.B.Bept.	
	10/12/16		Voluntary Church Parade Service at the MAIRIE. Training also carried out & Inspection of kit & men by Division Officers T.B.Bept.	
	11/12/16		Training though hampered by rain still progressing. Transport improving. by Company Officers T.B.Bept.	

Army Form C. 2118.

WAR DIARY
or
INTELLIGENCE SUMMARY.
(Erase heading not required.)

Instructions regarding War Diaries and Intelligence Summaries are contained in F. S. Regs., Part II. and the Staff Manual respectively. Title pages will be prepared in manuscript.

Place	Date	Hour	Summary of Events and Information	Remarks and references to Appendices
BEAUVAL to AMPLIER	13/12/16		Orders have been received for the Division to join the 1st Army. The first stage of journey commenced to-day. Bn paraded & marched off to AMPLIER to billet for the night. Arrived in billets about 1pm. Men in huts. Billets fair. T.S.Beapt	
AMPLIER to BARLY	14/12/16		Bn paraded & marched via DOULLENS. Bn halt continued to BARLY. Marched into BARLY. Arrived Billets about 2pm. Fairly good march. Well driven. T.S.Beapt	
BARLY to VACQUERIE	15/12/16		Marched to VACQUERIE. Wet roads. Heavy marching. About 15 feet out in line of march but again after Bn arrived at VACQUERIE. Billets very poor. Company officers held a conference at the MAIRIE at 8pm & referred to the "maintenance of discipline on the march which have not been good during the morning march." T.S.Beapt	
VACQUERIE to TROISVAUX	16/12/16		Marched to TROISVAUX & BELVAL via ST. POL. Division is now in 1st Army. Marching better. T.S.Beapt	

Army Form C. 2118.

WAR DIARY
or
INTELLIGENCE SUMMARY.
(Erase heading not required.)

Instructions regarding War Diaries and Intelligence Summaries are contained in F. S. Regs., Part II. and the Staff Manual respectively. Title pages will be prepared in manuscript.

Place	Date	Hour	Summary of Events and Information	Remarks and references to Appendices
TROISVAUX to RAIMBERT	17/12/16		Battalion marched to RAIMBERT via VALHUON & PERNES arrived in excellent health at 2.30 pm. Though billets were restricted & uncomfortable night was spent, march Discipline much better. TBBeap	
	18/12/16		Resumed march at 11am via LILLERS to LA MIQUELLERIE & LE CORNET BOURDOIS 3 kilometres from LILLERS. Good billets but scattered.	
LILLERS	19/12/16		On resting. Inspections carried out & platoon training on the second day. A draft of 1 Officer - Lt J.E. LYALL joined the Battalion. Capt HEFFER & Lt AMOR proceeded on leave on the 21st. Nothing special to report. TBBeap	
	20/12/16			
	21/12/16			
VIELLE CHAPPELLE	22/12/16		Battalion marched to VIELLE CHAPPELLE arriving about 3 pm. Difficulty in billetting but 4pm some very difficulties were overcome. Battalion is very scattered. This village is very much	

T.134. Wt. W708—776. 500000. 4/15. Sir J. C. & S.

WAR DIARY
or
INTELLIGENCE SUMMARY.
(Erase heading not required.)

Army Form C. 2118.

Place	Date	Hour	Summary of Events and Information	Remarks and references to Appendices
VIEILLE CHAPELLE	22/12/16		Very interesting to the Battalion for it was here that some very heavy fighting took place in October 1914 when the 5th Div and the 3rd Division. T.B.Boyd	
—	23/12/16		Bull Baxter. Preparation for Xmas. Men bring moss for the Bath also removing lime probably for the white wash. T.B.Boyd	
—	24/12/16		So attended Divine Service at 11 am in the Y.M.C.A hut. A Quiet day. T.B.Boyd	
—	25/12/16		Xmas day. Divine Service was held at the Y.M.C.A & Dinners were served in Coys at 3 pm. A real good dinner was served by utilizing Canteen funds & gifts of pudding from home the whole Bn were very happy. The Commy Officers Bn is Commanded 2 Adjt waited all day during this hour. There were no exercises & Parades were held in the evening. A very happy day was spent. Lt General C.P.A. HULL who commanded this Battalion	

T2134. Wt. W708—776. 500000. 4/15. Sir J. C. & S.

Army Form C. 2118.

WAR DIARY
or
INTELLIGENCE SUMMARY.
(Erase heading not required.)

Instructions regarding War Diaries and Intelligence Summaries are contained in F. S. Regs., Part II. and the Staff Manual respectively. Title pages will be prepared in manuscript.

Place	Date	Hour	Summary of Events and Information	Remarks and references to Appendices
NEUVE CHAPPELLE	25/12/16		Before the outbreak of hostilities & during the prior few months the men visited the Bn during the morning. T.S.Beauf.	
- -	26/12/16		Coys at disposal of Coy Commdrs for Training. T.S.Beauf.	
- -	27/12/16		Bn training in morning & inspection by Commdg Officer in the afternoon. T.S.Beauf.	
- -	28/12/16		GENERAL SIMPSON the frist Commdg Officer of this Bn inspected the Bn during morning. Usual training programme carried out. T.S.Beauf.	
- -	29/12/16		The Commdg Officer & Staff reviewed the new scheme of the line to be taken over by the Bn on the 2nd January. Bn forming Working Parties remainder training moving Coy Commdrs. T.S.Beauf.	

Place	Date	Hour	Summary of Events and Information	Remarks and references to Appendices
LOCON	30/12/16		new LOCON On move to new billeting area Billets given but approaches are very wet the roads being inundated to the depth of 1 foot. have been overseen by 1 p.m. & every effort made to make them more expensive so it is believed that this will be our permanent area during the remainder of the winter. CAPT A.C. DAWSON T.O Coy joined Battn.	
	31/12/16		All day Officers visited their section of the new line, in the NEUVE CHAPPELL Sector Trenches are rather wet & need a lot of work to keep them in a good defensive state. They are nearly breastworks & can only be conveted to Trenches during summer as the water-level is about 18" below the surface of the ground. With time & attention to drainage it will be possible to make this sector fairly comfortable. The Enemy does not appear to be very aggressive at present. T.O Coy —	

S. Hughes.
Major
Commanding 1st Canadian Rgt

WAR DIARY.

Vol 30

4th Machine [Gun]

Jan 1917

Army Form C. 2118.

WAR DIARY
or
INTELLIGENCE SUMMARY.
(Erase heading not required.)

Instructions regarding War Diaries and Intelligence Summaries are contained in F. S. Regs., Part II. and the Staff Manual respectively. Title pages will be prepared in manuscript.

Place	Date	Hour	Summary of Events and Information	Remarks and references to Appendices
LOCON	1/1/17		Corps Training. Officers newer seen to be taken over on 2nd inst. Section known as "NEUVE CHAPPELLE RIGHT". The New Year Gazette contains following honors: Lieut-Col Birtwell D.S.O. — mentioned in Despatches Capt. & Adjt T.L. BODEN — MILITARY CROSS Lieut & Q'mr E.H. AMOR — mention in Despatches Co. Sergt. A. ANDREWS — MERITORIOUS S. MEDAL Arm Staff Sgt. F. EMBERSON — mention in Despatches TBB capt	
"	2/1/17		To relieve the 13th Bn K.R.R. in Trenches. Relief complete at 12 noon. No casualties. Capt. P. GROVE-WHITE proceeded to ALDERSHOT for senior Officers Course. 2 Lieut H.G. FLUCK joined Batt, also 6 other ranks. TBB capt	
"	3/1/17		Trenches quiet. Nothing to report. Trenches very poor condition & wet. TBBcapt	

Army Form C. 2118.

WAR DIARY
or
INTELLIGENCE SUMMARY.
(Erase heading not required.)

Instructions regarding War Diaries and Intelligence Summaries are contained in F. S. Regs., Part II. and the Staff Manual respectively. Title pages will be prepared in manuscript.

Place	Date	Hour	Summary of Events and Information	Remarks and references to Appendices
NEUVE - CHAPPELLE	4/1/17		2nd Lt. H.G. FLUCK ordered to return to England. Much noise done on our front. No casualties. Nothing special to report. T.B.Blagr	
-	5/1/17		Enemy quiet, nothing to report. T.B.Blagr	
-	6/1/17		Quiet day. No casualties. Lt. Col. Behrens rejoins Battalion. T.B.Blagr	
-	7/1/17		Capt. G.C. MORAN rejoins from some officers course. Nothing to report. No casualties. T.B.Blagr	
-	8/1/17		Bn relieved by 6th SOMERSET L. Infantry. Bn move to support at CROIX BARBEE. The whole turn of the trenches being completed without casualties. Relief completed by 4 pm. Working Parties of 200 from B Bn. T.B.Blagr	
-	9/1/17		Capt. B.C. Moore assumes command of B Coy. Working Parties from B Battalion. T.B.Blagr	

WAR DIARY
or
INTELLIGENCE SUMMARY.
(Erase heading not required.)

Army Form C. 2118.

Place	Date	Hour	Summary of Events and Information	Remarks and references to Appendices
CROIX BARBEE	10/7/15		Bn chiefly employed on R.E. Working parties. The anniversary of the retreat was very interesting for it was here that this Bn detrained in October 1914. Many graves of the comrades are here. - Nothing special to report. 10.30pm	
	11/7/15		Nothing special to report. Major J.D. MAYHEW returns to join the 10th LOYAL NORTH LANCS for temporary command. 10.30pm	
	12/7/15		Nothing special to report. 10.30pm	
	12/7/15		2 Officers & 100 Other Ranks proceeded to HAVERSKERQUE for work on Divisional Rifle Range. Nothing special to report. 10.30pm	
	13/7/15		2 Officers & 100 O.Ranks proceeded to HAVERSKERQUE for duty on Gunnery Bn relieved by 13th Bn Rifle Bde & proceeded to billets at LOCON. No casualties. March complete by 9pm. 10.30pm	

Army Form C. 2118.

WAR DIARY
or
INTELLIGENCE SUMMARY.
(Erase heading not required.)

Instructions regarding War Diaries and Intelligence Summaries are contained in F.S. Regs., Part II. and the Staff Manual respectively. Title pages will be prepared in manuscript.

Place	Date	Hour	Summary of Events and Information	Remarks and references to Appendices
LOCON	15/1/17		Bn billeted in LOCON. General cleaning up. T.B.Beap	
	16/1/17		Training carried out as far as possible under scarcity conditions. Brown in endeavour to work away to cultivation. Nothing special to report. T.B.Beap	
	22/1/17			
	23/1/17		Divisional Commander inspected Bn in marching order. The turn out of the Bn was fairly good. T.B.Beap	
	24/1/17		Coy Training. T.B.Beap	
	25/1/17		Lieut D. CUTBUSH awarded Military Cross for work during operations Sergt. T. Sewell "D.C.Medal" on the ANCRE in November 1916. Coy Training nothing to report. T.B.Beap	

T2134. Wt. W708—776. 500000. 4/15. Sir J.C. & S.

WAR DIARY
or
INTELLIGENCE SUMMARY.
(Erase heading not required.)

Army Form C. 2118.

Place	Date	Hour	Summary of Events and Information	Remarks and references to Appendices
LOCON	25/1/17		Training - nothing special to report. B. Beauf	
	26/1/17			
	27/1/17			
	28/1/17			
	29/1/17		Bn relieved the 8th EAST LANCS REGT in reserve billets at LE TOURET, being in support to Right Bn in FERME - DE Bois sector of the line. Bn to be ready to move off at one hours notice with one Coy ready "standing to". B. Beauf	
	30/1/17		Nothing special to report. Weather very cold. B. Beauf	
	31/1/17		Bn orders to be ready to move back to H.Q. Reserve tomorrow. B. Beauf	

B. Beauf
Lieut. Colonel,
Commanding 4/Bn. Middlesex Regiment.

Army Form C. 2118.

WAR DIARY
or
INTELLIGENCE SUMMARY.
(Erase heading not required.)

4 Middlesex
Vol 31

Place	Date	Hour	Summary of Events and Information	Remarks and references to Appendices
LE TOURET	1/2/17		Battalion in reserve by 1st B. CHESHIRE REGT of the 5th Division & proceeded to billets at BEUVRY. The whole of this Division was moving out of the line & becoming G.H.Q. reserve. Billets good all arrived by 3 p.m. No casualties. T.H.Shepp.	
BEUVRY.	2/2/17		Battalion to be ready to move out 6 hours notice from any time. General cleaning up of Arms & Equipment. T.H.Shepp.	
—	3/2/17		Boys at disposal of Bty Commanders nothing special to report. T.H.Shepp.	
—	4/2/17		So to be ready to move at any time with 12 hours notice. Two Coys for work near R.E. superanum reserves attached "Divn Servis". All officers available attended lecture at BETHUNE on the "French Organisation for attack" which organisation in miniature form is to be adopted by the British Army. T.H.Shepp.	
—	5/2/17		Bn with transport route march in period of 3 hours. 2 Lt L. BARTLETT & E.B. SLADE joined Bn on return in their respective coys. T.H.Shepp.	

WAR DIARY
or
INTELLIGENCE SUMMARY.

(Erase heading not required.)

Army Form C. 2118.

Place	Date	Hour	Summary of Events and Information	Remarks and references to Appendices
BEUVRY	6/9/17		Reorganisation of Coys on Platoon basis on instructions issued by Division are carried out. Under this system a platoon becomes a complete unit of all Infantry arms. J.B. Leaf	
	7/9/17		The Bn continues organisation & in the afternoon were formed up in the new attack formation by the Company Officers. Details of this formation are attached. J.B. Leaf	
	8/9/17		Orders received that Bn are to move to take over a new Sector in the line. The C.O. and 2/Coy Commanders proceeded to reconnoitre the 14 B I S Sector at LOOS which is to be taken over by the Brigade at an early date. J.B. Leaf	
	9/9/15		Training carried out under Coy Commanders. Chiefly to instruct all N.C.O.'s the new attack formation communication. J.B. Leaf	
	10/9/15			
	11/9/15		Hockey & practice to wire. J.B. Leaf	

WAR DIARY or INTELLIGENCE SUMMARY

Army Form C. 2118.

Place	Date	Hour	Summary of Events and Information	Remarks and references to Appendices
Support Trenches near LOOS	12/2/17		Bn. marched from BOUVRY and SAILLY-LABOURSE to Reserve Trenches in the 14 Bis SECTOR. LOOS relieving 1st O. Regt Fusiliers. The line taken over is known as the VILLAGE LINE. Relief complete by 3 pm. Q'Mr Stores & Transport are at LES BREBIS about 8 Kilometres away. No casualties. T.B.Bapt.	
14 Bis SECTOR LOOS	13/2/17		Bn. relieved the 3rd O. Rifles Bde. in 14 Bis Right SECTOR. The C.T.s are in very good condition & so also the front line & Supports but it is evident that when the thaw has completely started everything will be in a wet weather state. The right of our sector is formed by the CRASSIER, a long bank of rubble from the mines of LOOS & is not held except by a post from the Bde on our right. Relief was completed by 2.30 pm. No casualties during relief & a very quiet day. T.B.Bapt.	
	14/2/17		Minenwerfers were chief annoyance during the 24 hours but their effect is more moral than anything else. One Grenadier wounded & relieved then. T.B.Bapt. Dummies hill.	

T PHILOSOPHE

Army Form C. 2118.

WAR DIARY
or
INTELLIGENCE SUMMARY.
(Erase heading not required.)

Instructions regarding War Diaries and Intelligence Summaries are contained in F. S. Regs., Part II. and the Staff Manual respectively. Title pages will be prepared in manuscript.

Place	Date	Hour	Summary of Events and Information	Remarks and references to Appendices
LOOS SALIENT	15/9/17		Quiet day but enemy very active on our Right and TMs at 10 p.m. We annexe two casualties both wounded by Rifle Grenades. T.B.Sept.	
14 Bn Right Sector	16/9/17		A quiet day but Enemy as usual very active at night & by 5 p.m. is almost incessant. TMs on the greatest annoyance on this front. Have to be silenced by our Stokes mortar bomb. 1 Killed & 2 Wounded by T.M. fire. T.B.Sept.	
—	17/9/17		Quiet day. There has not in 3 months no annoying enemy't rounds. Wiring parties for road & supper line continues by Reserve Support Coy. About 80 coils put on. Casualties 1 Killed T.B.Sept.	
—	18/9/17		Quiet day. Lieut Col Belmer D.S.O. proceeds to ordinary School for Entrance of Commr Officers. T.B.Sept. (Capt A.G. Dawson assumes Command B. T.B.S.C.y.)	
MAZINGARBE	19/9/17		Relieved by 8th Somerset Light Infantry & proceeds to billets in MAZINGARBE. Relief complete by 3 p.m. No casualties. Billets good. T.B.Sept.	
—	20/9/17		Quiet day. Enemy trying in vain to continue owing to Rain & then stop 3 days. Men employed cleaning CTs nightly. Bn is employed about 1/2 were employed cleaning streets of Town Wee. T.B.Sept.	

Army Form C. 2118.

WAR DIARY
or
INTELLIGENCE SUMMARY.
(Erase heading not required.)

Instructions regarding War Diaries and Intelligence Summaries are contained in F. S. Regs., Part II. and the Staff Manual respectively. Title pages will be prepared in manuscript.

Place	Date	Hour	Summary of Events and Information	Remarks and references to Appendices
MALINCARBE	21st to 25th/9/17		Bn Employed nightly in repair of Communication Trenches etc & in carrying parties for Trench Mortars etc. During the period nothing special to report. TBSepr	
	26/9/17		Bn relieved 8th Somerset L.I. & Dorsets in Sector as hereinunder on the night of Relief by night & completed by 4 AM 27th inst. No casualties. TBSepr	
	27/9/17		Quiet day. A Dummy raid was carried out on Sept Bn front by Artillery but little retaliation provoked. Casualties 2 Wounded by Rifle Grenades. Lt Col Pickwell rejoined. Artillery Active & both sides during day & at night. Bn Bde on our left discharged Gas. The Artillery bombardment & M. Guns also caused. Apparently the above was very good & Enemy retaliation heavily with M Go & T.Ms but very little reply from the enemies. he some material damage. TBSepr	
	28/9/17			

F. Pickwell Lt.Col

T2134. Wt. W708-776. 500000. 4/15. Sir J. C. & S.

Army Form C. 2118.

WAR DIARY
or
INTELLIGENCE SUMMARY.
(Erase heading not required.)

4 Middlesex

No 32

Place	Date	Hour	Summary of Events and Information	Remarks and references to Appendices
(13 Bis) LOOS	1/3/15		Nothing special to report. Enemy quiet except for an occasional Trench Mortar. Trenches are very bad & owing to thaw very much work is entailed to keep communication trenches at all passable. No casualties. T.J.Seap.	
—	2/3/15		Our artillery were active during the day but very little enemy retaliation. Minnenwerfer are the chief annoyance. Casualties 1 killed. 2nd Lieut F. H. STEELE joined Bn on return T.J.Seap.	
—	3/3/15		Bn relieved by two Bns of the 6th Division. 2nd Bn Durham Light Infantry to 1st Bn The BUFFS. Relief complete by 3.30 p.m. Bn billeted in MAZINGARBE T.J.Seap. No casualties.	
MAZINGARBE	4/3/15		Battalion paraded & marched to BETHUNE via NOEUX-LE-MINES where billeted for one night in Tobacco Factory. T.J.Seap.	
BETHUNE	5/3/15		Marched to BAS RIEUX via CHOCQUES. Arrived Billets 1.30 p.m. 5.3. Marched were well along & falling out T.J.Seap.	

WAR DIARY
or
INTELLIGENCE SUMMARY.
(Erase heading not required.)

Army Form C. 2118.

Place	Date	Hour	Summary of Events and Information	Remarks and references to Appendices
BAS RIEUX	6/3/17		Marched via LILLERS & ST HILAIRE to LIGNY-LES-AIRE. Billets 2p.m. close. 3 fell out on line of march but rejoined. TSBeap	
LIGNY-LES AIRE	7/3/17		Bn resting & generally cleaning up for 1st day. 2nd day Bn Run organised & carried out and good results. Weather cold. TSBeap	
" "	8/3/17			
" "	9/3/17		Bn paraded at 9.30 a.m. & marched to BETHONVAL & CONTEVILLE being billeted in both places for one night. TSBeap	
BETHONVAL & CONTEVILLE	10/3/17		Bn marched via ST POL to HOUVIN – HOUVINAL. This is to be the training area for the forthcoming Offensive. Billets for men are good. Officers close billeting. TSBeap	
HOUVIN HOUIGNEUL	11/3/17		Inspection of Arms Equipment etc & Voluntary Church Service held. Training Area reconnoitred. TSBeap	

Place	Date	Hour	Summary of Events and Information	Remarks
HOUVIN HOUVIGNEUL	12/3/17		Training commenced with a route march for about 10 miles in two transport accompanying the Battalion. Lieut Colonel Bicknell who has been in command of this Battalion for 18 months ordered to proceed to the Senior Officers School Aldershot as an instructor. Major A.G. DAWSON took over command of the Battalion. Brigadier General E.R. HILL who has been in command of the 63rd Bde of which this Bn is a part ordered to proceed to England. His command is to be taken over by Brig General F.L. CHALLONER D.S.O. Alterations in the lower commands of the Bn also took effect from this morning Lieut D.J. CUTBUSH M.C. took over command of A Coy & Lieut E.G. GROGAN took over command of B. Senior Gun Officer, T.B.Self	
	13/3/17		Battalion Bathed & went on site for Rifle Range were started in conjunction with the 10th York & Lancs. T.B.Self	

Army Form C. 2118.

WAR DIARY
or
INTELLIGENCE SUMMARY.
(Erase heading not required.)

Instructions regarding War Diaries and Intelligence Summaries are contained in F.S. Regs., Part II. and the Staff Manual respectively. Title pages will be prepared in manuscript.

Place	Date	Hour	Summary of Events and Information	Remarks and references to Appendices
HOUVIN HOUVINEUL	14/3/17		Training continued. The Ground allotted to the Battalion is very limited & though training is carried out by coys & for a while until ground becomes available it will not be possible to practise the Bn. as a whole in war attack formation. Subjects are as follows. Physical training, Drill, Musketry, Bombing, Bayonet fighting, Gas Helmet Drill, Lectures etc as are carried out. Working hours from 8.30 A.M — 12.30 p.m 2 — 4 p.m Two route marches per week (one 5? 2 in Bayonet) & two afternoons for Recreation training are to be carried out. T/J/Slay? Bayonet Route march about 16 miles. T/J/Slay?	
	15/3/17			
	16/17/3/17		Training as usual. Lieut A C TERRELL proceeded on a General Course at the Divisional School. Lt SLADE proceeded on Bombing Course T/J/Slay?	

Army Form C. 2118.

WAR DIARY
or
INTELLIGENCE SUMMARY.
(Erase heading not required.)

Instructions regarding War Diaries and Intelligence Summaries are contained in F.S. Regs., Part II. and the Staff Manual respectively. Title pages will be prepared in manuscript.

Place	Date	Hour	Summary of Events and Information	Remarks and references to Appendices
HOUVIN HOUVINEUL	19/3/17		Divine Service was held in the afternoon the Bn football team played the 11th Bn Hussars Regt at IZEL LEZ HAMEAU securing a win by 5 to 1 goals. (This Bn is commanded by Lieut Colonel T.S. WOLLOCOMBE who relinquishes the Adjutancy of this 4th Bn in September 1915) Lieut Colonel W.I. WEBB-BOWEN joined & assumed command of this Squadron T.S.Bcap.	
	19/3/17		Bn Route march. Lieut F.W. Schofield rejoined Bn from employment as Divisional Camouflage Officer & resumed his previous duties as Bn Sniping & Intelligence Officer T.S.Bcap.	
	29/3/17		Orders received to be ready to move at 6 hours notice. The Divisional Officer visited the ARRAS Sector today. Lieut R.G. WILLIAMS left Bn to report for duty as Divisional Dump Officer T.S.Bcap	
	9/3/17		Usual Training. T.S.Bcap	

WAR DIARY
or
INTELLIGENCE SUMMARY

Army Form C. 2118.

Place	Date	Hour	Summary of Events and Information	Remarks and references to Appendices
HOUVIN	22/3/17		Bn marched to Corps training area near DENIER. The weather Sleet & snow impeded training & Bn arrived to billets by 2 h. T.B.Coyt	
HOUVINEUL	23/3/17		Bn training. The Army Commander Sir Edmund Allenby presented medal ribbons to the Survivors on the Bn football ground. Capt H.E. Heffer was in command of the Guard of Honour of the 60 Du Bose. Regt Qm Sergt A ANDREWS received the meritorious Service medal & S/Cpl S. CASS received his military medal. T.B.Coyt	
	24/3/17		Training in arms & Bn Orders. T.B.Coyt	
	25/3/17		Divine Service in football field. Football match with 10th Yr Lancs & lost 3-2. Lieut L.C. THOMPSON proceeded on course at the Div Army School. T.B.Coyt	

T.B.Coyt

WAR DIARY
or
INTELLIGENCE SUMMARY.
(Erase heading not required.)

Army Form C. 2118.

Place	Date	Hour	Summary of Events and Information	Remarks and references to Appendices
HENIN	26/3/17		Batt. Route march. Capt E.J. DONALDSON rejoined from Corps School	
HOUVINEUL	27/3/17		Usual training. 1 Bombing Officer per day attending a demonstration at Divisional School with a new percussion Grenade called the "HUMPHREYS".	
	28/3/17		Usual Training. Nothing special to report.	
	29/3/17		Brigade Route march. Distance 10 miles. Very wet day.	
	30/3/17		Training as usual. Brigade Transport Competition. Events in classes. 1 Cooker, 1 Water Cart, 1 Limber, 1 Mess Cart, 2 Pack mules. So won 1st prize in the 1st & 3rd items & 2 seconds in the last never had anything turn out.	

W. J. M_____ Lieut. Colonel,
Commanding 4/Bn. Middlesex Regiment.

WAR DIARY or INTELLIGENCE SUMMARY

Army Form C. 2118.

4 Middlesex Regt

Vol 33

Place	Date	Hour	Summary of Events and Information	Remarks and references to Appendices
HOUVIN-HOUVIGNEUL	1-4-17		Divine Service was held in open air. Battalion Training Resumed. Remainder of the day was spent in Recreational Training. A boxing Tournament of the Battalion versus the York & Lancs Regt was postponed through inclement weather. Draft of 20 O.R. joined.	
	2-4-17		Route March was carried out by Battalion via MAGNICOURT, MAZIERES, TERNAS, BONEVILLE, MONCHEAUX to WILLET. Remainder of the day spent in lectures and inspections. Boxing competition cancelled.	
	3-4-17		Usual Training Programme of Physical Training, Platoon, and Company Drill, Bayonet fighting, etc was carried out during morning. Afternoon devoted to continuing Inter-Company football and cross country runs.	
	4-4-17		Battalion expected to carry out Training on Bn's Training Area at DENIER, but owing to bad weather, the scheme was cancelled. The Adjutant gave a lecture to N.C.O.s and conferred with officers on future platoon operations. The afternoon was made a holiday for all ranks. Draft of 12 O.R. joined. Captain P. GROVE-WHITE joined from Senior Officers Course at ALDERSHOT. Lieut. L.A.H. FENN proceeded to GOUY-EN-TERNOIS to assume duty of TOWN MAJOR.	
	5-4-17		Battalion proceeded to BEAUFORT to billet. Obstacle races for all ranks, good jollity	

Army Form C. 2118.

WAR DIARY
or
INTELLIGENCE SUMMARY.
(Erase heading not required.)

Place	Date	Hour	Summary of Events and Information	Remarks and references to Appendices
BEAURAINS	6.4.17		Battalion was to have moved, and O.O. for such had been prepared but were cancelled at 12 mid-night. This day was therefore given to Training under Brigade arrangements.	
	7.4.17		Battalion moved to NOYELLETTE. Killed Capt. P. GROVE-WHITE left to assume duty of Second-in-Command of 11th R. Warwickshire Regt.	
	8.4.17		Battalion moved to DOISANS, where it was billeted in huts. Bombs, Tools, Iron Rations, &c were drawn and issued with the exception of The Bombs. Orders were received from Brigade that zero hour would be at 5:30 a.m. and that the Battalion would move to the place of assembly of that hour.	
	9.4.17		Battalion moved off at 5:30 a.m. Very heavy rain fell. The Brigade column was delayed for an hour and a half by traffic on the St Pol - ARRAS road between DAINVILLE and ARRAS. At 11 a.m. the Battalion reached ARRAS Station, where a large ammunition dump exploded and blew up. Lt. Col. W. I. Webb-Bowen was wounded. Several other casualties occurred, but the Battalion had a remarkably narrow escape as the dump was only 200 yds. away. Left in Capt. T.L. BODEN. M.C.	

Army Form C. 2118.

WAR DIARY
or
INTELLIGENCE SUMMARY.
(Erase heading not required.)

Instructions regarding War Diaries and Intelligence Summaries are contained in F. S. Regs., Part II. and the Staff Manual respectively. Title pages will be prepared in manuscript.

Place	Date	Hour	Summary of Events and Information	Remarks and references to Appendices
ARRAS	9.4.17	11 am	Took over Temporary command. Major A.B. DAWSON left the Transport lines. He Took over command.	

WAR DIARY
or
INTELLIGENCE SUMMARY

Army Form C. 2118.

Place	Date	Hour	Summary of Events and Information	Remarks and references to Appendices
Miraumont	9-4-17	12.30 PM	Battalion in Assembly Trenches with Battalion Headquarters at junction of IVY STREET + DUPLICATE RESERVE LINE.	Map references S.I.B. N.W. S.I.B. S.W. 1/20,000
		2.15 PM	Orders from Brigade to send out Officers Patrols to reconnoitre the route taken by 111th Brigade	
		3.35 PM	Orders received to proceed to BATTERY VALLEY in accordance with instructions previously issued.	
		5.—PM	In position in BATTERY VALLEY deployed on right of 8th SOMERSET L.I.	
		7.15 PM	Verbal orders from Brigade that the Brigade would advance on ORANGE HILL with 8th SOMERSET L.I. + 8th LINCOLNSHIRE REGT in front (Right + Left respectively) with 4th MIDDLESEX REGT in support to both Battalions with 10th YORK + LANCS REGT in reserve	
		7.30 PM	Moved as above	
		9—PM	Battalion digging cover in road H.27.c.8.4. to H.27.b.2.2. with patrols pushed forward in touch with 8th S.L.I. + 8th LINCOLNS.	
		11.15 PM	Orders from Brigade received that when 2 Battalions of 111th Brigade arrive to support 63rd Brigade the 4th MIDDLESEX REGT are to be prepared to prolong the left of line as held by 8th S.L.I. + 8th LINCOLNS if possible along SUNKEN ROAD in H.29.b. Should Enemy	
	10-4-17	12.30 AM	Orders from Brigade via 8th S.L.I. to move up on to the left of LINCOLNS as above. The YORK + LANCS are to move up on MIDDLESEX left as soon as two Battalions of 111th Brigade arrive.	

WAR DIARY or INTELLIGENCE SUMMARY

Army Form C. 2118.

Place	Date	Hour	Summary of Events and Information	Remarks and references to Appendices
Near Arras	10-4-17	12.30 AM	Patrols on arrival at this front are to be sent out along SCARPE VALLEY joining up with CAVALRY POST at H.23.a.9.7.	
		2 AM	Battalion moved off to take up position as above. Moved up on left of LINCOLNS who were WEST of SUNKEN ROAD. The left of this Battalion (MIDDLESEX) resting near ruin approximate position H.28.b.7.d. Patrols were sent out, but did not gain touch with Cavalry Post along SCARPE VALLEY.	
		5 AM	Battalion in position as above.	
		10.30 AM	Verbal orders received that the Brigade would advance to LONE COPSE VALLEY with 8 L.I on right, then LINCOLNS, MIDDLESEX, YORK YLANCS on left	
		11.30 AM	Moved as above. The enemy put up a very heavy barrage on ORANGE HILL with Artillery & Machine Gun fire, the latter coming from direction of FAMPOUX. This fire was so well directed that at 3.30 PM the following only had arrived in LONE COPSE VALLEY :— 2 Companies 8th S.L.I. (on right), 2 Companies LINCOLNS next & 2 Company MIDDLESEX Eff. The 10 & YORK & LANCS had apparently been held up by the intense barrage, therefore the left of the MIDDLESEX was exposed to fire from FAMPOUX from an expected counter-attack from that direction.	
		6 PM	The line of 8th LINCOLNS had advanced beyond LONE COPSE VALLEY, to practically the 90° contour	

WAR DIARY
or
INTELLIGENCE SUMMARY.
(Erase heading not required.)

Army Form C. 2118.

Place	Date	Hour	Summary of Events and Information	Remarks and references to Appendices
Near Arras	10-4-17	6 P.M.	800 yds N.W. of MONCHY-LE-PREUX but were met with severe artillery somewhere gunfire their left being somewhat exposed they withdrew to the LONE COPSE VALLEY in conjunction with 8th S.L.I. our right & MIDDLESEX on left consolidated a line running along the crest of ridge at LONE COPSE VALLEY approximately right to left H.36.a.3.3. to H.30.d.3.5. This line being exposed from left a defensive flank was formed by the MIDDLESEX on left across valley. A half hearted attempt to counter-attack by the enemy took place at about 6.30 P.M., but was not pressed by them.	
		6.30 P.M.	A message was received from 13th Headquarters that the line held by remainder of Brigade was practically along the line of the SUNKEN ROAD on the Eastern slopes of ORANGE HILL.	
		7.15 P.M.	Message received from Brigade Headquarters that Heavy Artillery were bombarding MONCHY-LE-PREUX until 7.30 P.M., when the 111th Brigade, supported by 63rd Brigade would attack on our or near that line so possible.	
		7.30 P.M.	Remainder of Battalion not yet reinforced LONE COPSE VALLEY two cgns of 111th Brigade	
		8.30 P.M.	Remainder of Battalion moving into LONE COPSE VALLEY. Battalion reforming & forming a few owing to casualties.	

Army Form C. 2118.

WAR DIARY
or
INTELLIGENCE SUMMARY.
(Erase heading not required.)

Instructions regarding War Diaries and Intelligence Summaries are contained in F.S. Regs., Part II. and the Staff Manual respectively. Title pages will be prepared in manuscript.

Place	Date	Hour	Summary of Events and Information	Remarks and references to Appendices
Near Arras	11.4.17	12 midnight	The move spent very quiet. Patrols & Posts out. Enemy are apparently holding a line N.W. of MONCHY-LE-PREUX, evidently the trenches in H.36.d.	
		3 AM	Orders received as follows:- 1st Corps will advance at 5am. 3rd Division on right, 15th Division on left, 112th Brigade on right, 111th Brigade on left. The 37th Divisional boundaries as follows:- Grid lines between N.12. & N.18. Grid line between squares H & N. Starting line between 111th & 112th Brigades:- Grid line between O.1. & O.7. When the 15th Division has passed through the GREEN LINE, 63rd Brigade will advance in Divisional Reserve. Two tanks will also operate from H.36.c. operating around MONCHY. Two tanks will co-operate. 3rd Division & 15th Division advanced. Brigade shelter LONE COPSE VALLEY.	
		6.30am	Operations commenced. 3rd Division & 15th Division advanced.	
		10.40 am	Message received that 15th Division had reached KEELING COPSE & PELVES. 63rd Brigade to push on as rapidly as possible to high ground O.2.d. BOIS-DES-AUBERINES & get touch with 15th Division on their left. 111th Brigade has been ordered on same objective with 112th Brigade on their right. 10th YORK & LANCS will form the advanced guard & will move from LONE COPSE at 11.1AM on BOIS-DES-AUBÉRINES. Remainder moving in the following order:- MIDDLESEX, LINCOLNS, SOMERSETS. The MIDDLESEX will prolong the line of 10th YORK & LANCS to the left. 8th LINCOLNS in support for two Battalions. 8th SOMERSETS in Brigade Reserve	

Army Form C. 2118.

WAR DIARY
or
INTELLIGENCE SUMMARY.
(Erase heading not required.)

Place	Date	Hour	Summary of Events and Information	Remarks and references to Appendices
Nr. Arras	11-4-17	11 A.M.	The YORK & LANCS advanced but could not get forward, owing to Machine Gun fire.	
		11.30 A.M.	Battalion deployed in rear of YORK & LANCS, ready to move forward.	
		12.20 P.M.	Message from Brigade received as follows :- "4th MIDDLESEX will advance at once, moving well to the right of the YORK & LANCS, who are held up by Machine Gun fire from the left."	
		12.30 P.M.	Battalion moved Route chosen on right of YORK & LANCS along side of MONCHY ROAD running S.W. through H.3.b.c.&d. The Battalion advanced by Platoons in file. Immediately after advancing along the road, which was almost entirely devoid of cover, the enemy opened fire with artillery +M.G. fire, creating a very heavy barrage. By advancing in short rushes of 12 men lying flat, the Battalion eventually got through with comparatively small casualties. The trees went pressing greatly assisted in cover from the enemy. Bullets were a little too high.	
			On arrival of Battalion at MONCHY, the O.C. the Cavalry batto reported that the was expecting a counter-attack on his right that the Cavalry urgently required assistance. A platoon of 20 & two Lewis Guns were therefore detailed to take up a position on the right of village about C.1.c.2.4. Officers Patrol were pushed out to find the flanks of the preceding Brigade but were not successful. It was therefore decided to hold the village from any counter-attack by means of Posts of Lewis Guns & Machine Guns (some detachments of the M.G. Royal Machine Gun Company were available)	

WAR DIARY or INTELLIGENCE SUMMARY

Army Form C. 2118.

Place	Date	Hour	Summary of Events and Information	Remarks and references to Appendices
Near Arras	11-4-17	12-30 PM	The posts occupied a line approximately along track running N from MONCHY through O.1.a. South. A Machine Gun Post in wood about O.1.B.2.7 & S.W. of village at O.1.C.2.4.	
		3 PM	These Posts were established at about 3PM. Being disturbed the enemy were heavily bombing the village, thereby the arrival of definite information the men, who were not digging posts, were placed in cellars.	
		5.30 PM	An Officers' Patrol again went out & reconnoitred the whole of the village toubbists & reported that, except for the posts mentioned above, the enemy had about O.1.6.2.8, it appeared that the Brigade on the right flank had not advanced E of the village. Many scattered parties of the 115th Brigade had been found along the MONCHY ROAD, apparently consolidating a line of small isolated posts in H.36.d. Patrols were then sent to get touch with right of 8th LINCOLNS, who were known to have advanced from LONE COPSE VALLEY on our left. These patrols were unsuccessful. These troops decided to consolidate posts already held slightly approaches to the E of village. During the remainder of the night, except for intermittent shelling nothing of real happened.	
		11 PM	Battalion was relieved & proceeded to BATTERY VALLEY, where it remained until about 2 PM 12-4-17, when it returned to ARRAS.	

WAR DIARY
or
INTELLIGENCE SUMMARY.

Army Form C. 2118.

(Erase heading not required.)

Place	Date	Hour	Summary of Events and Information	Remarks and references to Appendices
ARRAS	12.4.17		The Battalion was relieved and proceeded to ARRAS. They were billeted there for the night. Hot meals were provided for the troops on arrival.	
DUISANS	13.4.17		The Battalion march to DUISANS and were billeted in huts. The remainder of the day was given to resting and cleaning up.	
AGNEZ-LES-DUISANS	14.4.17		The Battalion moved to AGNEZ-LES-DUISANS again being billeted in huts. 100 O.R. under 2/Lt. R.M. HINTON to C.C.S. for duty there.	
MANIN	15.4.17		Battalion moved to MANIN and was inspected on the march by the G.O.C. Division. The men were carried out under very inclement weather conditions.	
"	16.4.17		Companies were to dispose of Company Commanders for refitting and re-organization. Lectures and specialists. 45 O.R. joined from Lewis Training Depot, FREVENT. Training carried out, companies at the disposal of Company Commanders.	
"	17.4.17		Battalion drilled during the day. Training continued.	
GOUVES	18.4.17		Battalion proceeded to GOUVES where they were again billeted. The Commanding Officer, Adjutant, and Signal Officer proceeded to the line to reconnoitre the frontage over which returning about mid-night. 4 O.R. joined the Battalion.	

Army Form C. 2118.

WAR DIARY
or
INTELLIGENCE SUMMARY.
(Erase heading not required.)

Instructions regarding War Diaries and Intelligence Summaries are contained in F. S. Regs., Part II. and the Staff Manual respectively. Title pages will be prepared in manuscript.

Place	Date	Hour	Summary of Events and Information	Remarks and references to Appendices
ARRAS	20.4.19		Battalion paraded to ARRAS by motor lorries and was o/c booted at The WINTER GARDENS where the posts were dumped and stored. Here the battalion rested till 8 p.m. when it	MAP. 51 B. N.W. 1/20000
		3.45 p.m	moved off in fighting-order. On 3.75 p.m Company Commanders went o/c the Line to reconnoitre. Fatigue party number 2/21. R.M. HILTON rejoined from G.G.S.	
		11 p.m	the Battalion relieved The 1st R.I.F. in HONEY TRENCH and HYDERABAD WORK with Battalion "Head Quarters" in SONKEN RD. AT H.11.a.6.2. The Battalion remained here	
	22.4.19		until mid night 22.4.19	

WAR DIARY
or
INTELLIGENCE SUMMARY.

(Erase heading not required.)

Army Form C. 2118.

Place	Date	Hour	Summary of Events and Information	Remarks and references to Appendices
Mon AREA	22/4/17	Midnight	Battalion was in Assembly Trenches with Battalion Head Quarters in HYDERABAD WORK	
	23/4/17	4:50 am	Battalion attacked with three companies. The remaining company being used as a carrying party.	
	23/4/17	8:30 am	Battalion reached a point 200 yds E of the SUNKEN RD & Lynes makers, owing to both flanks being exposed, the Battalion could advance no further. Lt. Col. A.B. DAWSON was killed by a machine gun bullet, and Adjutant T.L. BODEN. M.C. Took over command.	
	23/4/17	9 am	Capt T.L. BODEN M.C. was badly wounded by snipers, & Lt. P.W. SMITH took over command of the Battalion. At this time communication with Brigade and other formations was very difficult, and operations of the position was very indefinite.	
	23/4/17	12 noon	The enemy were seen to be forming up for a counter-attack on the crest of GREENLAND HILL. They advanced down the hill in extended order and artillery formation, but this advance was checked by our rifle and Lewis Gun fire, also that of the machine guns of the 63rd M.G.C. Heavy casualties were inflicted on the enemy.	

WAR DIARY
or
INTELLIGENCE SUMMARY.
(Erase heading not required.)

Army Form C. 2118.

Place	Date	Hour	Summary of Events and Information	Remarks and references to Appendices
	2.4.17		The Battalion occupied the whole of this front in consolidating this position	
		7 h.m.	They had taken up Hostile Artillery was continually shelling throughout the day.	
	2.3.4.17	9 h.m.	Three Battalions of the 112th Brigade took over this position, and the Battalion withdrew to the SUNKEN RD at I.7.c and consolidated this line during the night.	
	24.4.17	11 p.m.	The Battalion remained in this position, which was at frequent intervals, heavily shelled, until 11 h.m. when it was relieved by 2 Companies of the 10th Royal North Lancaster Regiment, the Battalion then withdrew to HAGO TRENCH with Battalion Head Quarters in the SUNKEN RD at H.11.a.6.2. The Battalion remained here until the 27th.	
	27.4.17	11 h.m.	Two Companies moved to the Assembly Trench (CLASP TRENCH) with Battalion Head Quarters in CHILI TRENCH along with the two reserve Companies.	
	28.4.17	4.25 a.m.	Battalion attacked with two Companies in support to the 8th Somerset Light Infantry, the remaining two Companies still in reserve in CHILI TRENCH. Patrols from these two Companies were pushed out continually during the day. On account of our right flank being exposed to incessant hostile sniping they were unable to get into touch with the two front Companies.	

Army Form C. 2118.

WAR DIARY
or
INTELLIGENCE SUMMARY.

(Erase heading not required.)

Instructions regarding War Diaries and Intelligence Summaries are contained in F. S. Regs., Part II. and the Staff Manual respectively. Title pages will be prepared in manuscript.

Place	Date	Hour	Summary of Events and Information	Remarks and references to Appendices
Near ARRAS	28.4.17	10 p.m.	These two rear Companies moved up to reconnoitre CUTHBERT TRENCH. This was thought held by the enemy with machine-guns, and owing to the weakness of these two companies, it was impossible for them to go any further. They, therefore, dug themselves in in front of CUTHBERT TRENCH.	
	29.4.17	1.30 a.m.	These two Companies were withdrawn to CUBA TRENCH and were relieved by the 8th Seaforth Highlanders.	
	29.4.17	3.30 a.m.	The Battalion moved back to the Transport Lines at ST NICHOLAS, where it was conveyed by motor-lorries to MANIN.	
MANIN	30.4.17		The day was devoted to resting and general cleaning up.	
			Casualties during Monchy-le-Preux Operations	
			O.R	
			Killed 18	
			Wounded 152	
			Missing 31	
			201.	
			Casualties during Operations from 23 - 29/4/17.	
			O.R	
			Killed 21	
			Wounded 162	
			Missing 98	
			281	

Army Form C. 2118.

WAR DIARY
or
INTELLIGENCE SUMMARY.
(Erase heading not required.)

Instructions regarding War Diaries and Intelligence Summaries are contained in F. S. Regs., Part II. and the Staff Manual respectively. Title pages will be prepared in manuscript.

Place	Date	Hour	Summary of Events and Information	Remarks and references to Appendices
	5·4·17		Lt.ll. E.T. Donaldson To U.K. Sick.	
	7·4·17		Capt. R. Grove-White quitted to assume duty of Second-in-Command, 1st Royal Warwicks Regt.	
	9·4·17		Lt.Col. W.I. Webb-Bowen wounded.	
	10·4·17		Capt. G.B. Moran wounded.	
	"		2/Lt. D. Cutbush. M.G. killed.	
	"		2/Lt. A.G. Terreus wounded, died of wounds subsequently on 20·4·17.	
	"		2/Lt. W.E. Stockbey wounded.	
	"		2/Lt. A.D. Trowell wounded.	
	"		2/Lt. H.M. Williams wounded.	
	"		2/Lt. I.H. Hodgson wounded.	
	20·4·17		Capt. H.E. Heffer admitted Field Ambulance sick.	
	23·4·17		Lt.Col. A.G. Dawson killed.	
	"		Capt. & Adjt. T.L. Boden. M.G. wounded.	
	"		Capt. S.A. Willis wounded.	
	"		Lieut. E.A.M. Williams wounded.	
	"		2/Lt. R.M. Huston killed.	
	"		2/Lt. L. Bartlett wounded.	
	26·4·17		2/Lts. W.T. Farrow, A.V. Weller, H.R. Odding and J.H. Woods joined Battalion.	
	27·4·17		Lt.Col. G.A. Bridgman assumed command.	
	28·4·17		2/Lt. E.B. Slade wounded.	
	"		Lieut. B.P. Jones wounded.	
	"		2/Lt. A.D. Hooke missing.	

WAR DIARY
or
INTELLIGENCE SUMMARY

Army Form C. 2118.

4 Middlesex R / Vol 34

Place	Date	Hour	Summary of Events and Information	Remarks and references to Appendices
MANIN.	1-5-17 to 3-5-17		During this period, the Battalion rested, refitting generally.	
"	3-5-17		Training was carried out under Company arrangements. Lectures, drills, and Musketry. Specialists were trained in the different specialist subjects.	
"	4-5-17		Training carried out as yesterday. Lieut. E.A.H. Senn having rejoined the Battalion from duty as Town Major of GOUY-EN-TERNOIS, was posted to "B" Company for duty.	
"	5-5-17		The Commanding Officer judged all Companies in Field Firing and Rapid Wiring in order to select one company to represent the Battalion in the Brigade Field Firing and Rapid Wiring competitions. "A" Company was selected for Field Firing and "C" Company for Rapid Wiring.	
"	6-5-17		A Brigade Thanksgiving and Memorial Service was held; the Battalion, that its remainder of the day resting. Lieut. B.R. Newman, on joining the Battalion, was posted to "C" Company.	
"	7-5-17		The Rifle Range situated in the village was allotted to the Battalion. Two Companies used this range throughout the day. "A" Company, having been detailed to represent the 63rd Brigade in the Divisional Field Firing Battalion, was engaged in houses to LIGNEREUIL to complete. On their return the result was unknown. 2/Lts. A.C. Millar and R.F.T. Irwin were granted leave to PARIS until 11th May. 2/Lt. G. Jamieson joined Battalion and was posted to "D" Company for duty.	

Army Form C. 2118.

WAR DIARY
or
INTELLIGENCE SUMMARY.
(Erase heading not required.)

Instructions regarding War Diaries and Intelligence Summaries are contained in F. S. Regs., Part II. and the Staff Manual respectively. Title pages will be prepared in manuscript.

Place	Date	Hour	Summary of Events and Information	Remarks and references to Appendices
MANIN	8·5·17		Training was carried out under Company Commanders arrangements. Bombing was included.	
"	9·5·17 to 10·5·17		Training was carried on as usual. 7/Lt. W.T. Farror was admitted to hospital sick.	
"	11·5·17		7/Lt. J.H. Woods was admitted to hospital sick. Ration strength 539 Training was carried on with "G" Company mounted o/t to take part in the Divisional Rapid Wiring Competition. "C" Company were this competition, representing the 63rd Inf. Brigade.	
"	12·5·17		In the morning, Training was carried out under Company arrangements. The afternoon was devoted to recreational training. Nos. 11213 Sgt. Davis W, 15121 L/Sgt. Hodges T, and 27767 A/L/Cpl. Hoare, S. were awarded the Military Medal.	
"	13·5·17 and 14·5·17		Training was carried on under Company arrangements. Captain E. Belfield, upon joining the Battalion, assumed command of "D" Company. Captain M.D. Fitz-Gibbon, upon joining, assumed command of "A" Company.	
"	15·5·17		A Brigade Tactical Scheme was carried out, in the afternoon the Battalion remained in billets. Heavy rain fell all the afternoon.	
"	16·5·17		The Battalion was inspected by the G.O.C. 63rd Infantry Brigade in the morning. The remainder of the day was given to drilling and marching. Captain A.D. Sharp was admitted to hospital sick; Lieut. S.H. Ewing joined the Battalion as Medical Officer. To celebrate the occasion of ALBUHERA DAY a list of honours was issued for to every N.C.O. and man.	

WAR DIARY or INTELLIGENCE SUMMARY

Army Form C. 2118.

Place	Date	Hour	Summary of Events and Information	Remarks and references to Appendices
MANIN	17·5·17		It had been intended to carry on a Brigade Tactical Scheme, but, owing to the very bad weather, this was cancelled. The Coys. Commanders visited the Battalion in Lillers' and carried out bombing on the Rifle Range. In the afternoon the Coys. bombardier gave a lecture at Divisional Head-Quarters, at which, the Commanding Officer, and the four Company Commanders were present.	Reference sheet 51 B
"	18·5·17		The Battalion moved to Simencourt via Noyelle-Vion, Lattre St. Quentin, and Wanquetin. Here the Battalion was billeted for one night in its accommodation (as ranks were somewhat cramped up. 2/Lt. E.W. Andrew proceeded to 63rd Inf. Brigade as Brigade Sniping Officer. Division is being transferred to VI (on Centre) Corps from XIII (on Left). (Battle of ARRAS area)	
SIMENCOURT	19·5·17		The Battalion moved to ACHICOURT, a suburb of ARRAS, and was there billeted in houses and cellars. These billets were in poor condition when entered, and a great deal of cleaning up was required before they were fit for habitation.	
ACHICOURT	20·5·17		Voluntary church service took place in the mornings in the afternoon communication and bombing drill was carried out.	
"	21·5·17		Training was carried out under Company arrangements, Specialists under their specialist Officers.	
"	22·5·17		Training carried out as yesterday. The Coys. were lifted to the Battalion. The Commanding Officer and two Company Commanders proceeded to reconnoitre the front over about GUEMAPPES & Railway and weather permitted throughout the day. Major M.C.C. MIERS joined the Battalion 16th over decades of record in Command	

A5834 Wt. W4973/M687 750,000 8/16 D. D. & L. Ltd. Forms/C.2118/13.

WAR DIARY
or
INTELLIGENCE SUMMARY.
(Erase heading not required.)

Army Form C. 2118.

Place	Date	Hour	Summary of Events and Information	Remarks and references to Appendices
ACHICOURT	23-5-17		A party of a hundred men were employed in building an assault course. Otherwise training was carried on as usual	
	24-5-17		The party of one hundred men were again employed in building an assault course. A party of two NCOs & twelve men were sent out to solve Patrol Two & fought Task 30.	
	25-5-17		The above party again went out strengthened to 9 Patrol Two & various other articles. 2/Lt Tolhe & 5 O.R. joined the Battalion. 2/Lt Stebel was posted to "C" Coy. Officers Commanding "A" & "D" Coys reconnoitred the front line, which was to be occupied by the Battalion. The advance party fought in 125 Patrol Two. Lieut E.A.H. Dunn proceeded on leave to the United Kingdom	
	26-5-17			
	27-5-17		An open air Divine Parade was held in the morning. The afternoon was free for all ranks	
	28-5-17		The morning & afternoon were devoted to cleaning up billets. At 7.15.P.M the head of the Battalion moved to take relieve 13th K.R.R. in the Hindenburg line. The relief was met TILLOY and in DEVILS WOOD completed at 11.P.M. The Battalion was situated in Devils Wood at G.36.b. 153rd Brigade in right in support, 115th between 112th which goes into reserve — The Battalion in Henches & Shell Holes in Devils Wood. The day was devoted	Map 51.B
TILLOY	29-5-17		to relieving on the battle field up to 9th April 1917.	Map 51.B

WAR DIARY
or
INTELLIGENCE SUMMARY.
(Erase heading not required.)

Army Form C. 2118.

Place	Date	Hour	Summary of Events and Information	Remarks and references to Appendices
TILLOY	30-5-17		The Battalion acted as duty Battalion from midnight to midnight. At 4 A.M. the Battalion stood to until 4-45 A.M. Salving was carried out during the day with considerable success. Bathing took place in the morning. In the afternoon there was a very heavy thunderstorm, when Battalion Headquarters was flooded by about nine inches of water. The Battalion was detailed to find two hundred men for a working party on GORDON TRENCH, but the order was cancelled on account of the state of the ground after the storm. Extract from London Gazette:- "2nd Lieut. MITCHELL to be Lieut." "Lieut-Col. W. Debb Bonney, Lieut-Col. M.P.F. Bucknell, 2nd Lieut. L.C. THOMPSON to be Temp. Lieut. Capt. S.A.Willis & 2/Lt R.G. Williams were all mentioned in despatches of Sir Douglas Haig.	
TILLOY	31-5-17		The Battalion was relieved by 2nd Buckingham Regiment & proceeded to Arras to be billeted in the SCHRAMM BARRACKS. No casualties due to enemy this month.	

George Lushroner

Vol 35 War diary

4th Middlesex

June 1917

SECRET

Army Form C. 2118.

WAR DIARY
or
INTELLIGENCE SUMMARY.
(Erase heading not required.)

Instructions regarding War Diaries and Intelligence Summaries are contained in F. S. Regs., Part II. and the Staff Manual respectively. Title pages will be prepared in manuscript.

Place	Date	Hour	Summary of Events and Information	Remarks and references to Appendices
MANIN	1 June 17		The Battalion moved by motor-lorries to MANIN arriving there about 8 p.m. The Battalion was billeted there.	
	2.6.17		The battalion carried out route marches, each company commander selecting his own route. Lieut. P. W. Dunn and 2/Lt. A. D. Reid joined with 136 Other Ranks the Battalion.	
	3.6.17		There was a voluntary Divine Service held in the morning. In the afternoon companies were at the disposal of the Company Commanders for training. 3 Other Ranks joined the Battalion.	
	4.6.17		Company route marches were again carried out in the morning. Training and firing on the rifle range took place in the afternoon. 2/Lt. H. E. Hoffer awarded the Military Cross; Capt. A. D. Shaft R.A.M.C. also awarded the Military Cross.	
	5.6.17		The Battalion moved by motor-lorries to BEAUVOIS. Here to be billeted. The accommodation was rather bad, and the majority of the men slept in the open.	
	6.6.17		The Battalion marched to TANGRY to be billeted there. The billets were very good, and there was ample accommodation for all ranks.	

A 5534   Wt.W4973/M687 750,000 8/16 D. D. & L. Ltd. Forms/C.2118/13.

Army Form C. 2118.

WAR DIARY
or
INTELLIGENCE SUMMARY.
(Erase heading not required.)

Instructions regarding War Diaries and Intelligence Summaries are contained in F. S. Regs., Part II. and the Staff Manual respectively. Title pages will be prepared in manuscript.

Place	Date	Hour	Summary of Events and Information	Remarks and references to Appendices
MATRINGHEM	7.6.17		The Battalion marched to MATRINGHEM arriving there by 8 p.m. The billets were good but rather scattered.	
"	8.6.17		Company Officers and Bombing Officer reconnoitred the area for training grounds. The day was spent in cleaning up the billeting area.	
"	9.6.17		Companies were at the disposal of the Company Commanders. A working party was supplied to work on the range at HEZECQUES. 2/Lt. J. H. Hodgson, 2/Lt. F. E. Beauchamp, 2/Lt. H. McDonnell and 28 Other Ranks joined the Battalion. 2/Lt. S. S. Sutherland rejoined from 3rd Army Rest Camp; 2/Lt. D. F. Huon from 37th Divl. Depot.	
"	10.6.17		Training was carried out as per Training Programme. 2/Lt. F. L. Rogers and 10 Other Ranks joined the Battalion. Captain and Adjt. T. S. Bolton M.C. awarded a Bar to the Military Cross, Coftm P. W. Smith, 2/Lt. A. D. Hooks, 7/Lt. J. C. Boyd awarded the Military Cross. No. 125-72 9/C.S.M. C. Baillie and No. 2323 Sgt. H. E. Good awarded the D.C.M. Authorities, 6th Corps C/138/149/11/A/ dated 10-6-17 and 3rd Army H.R./475-/ dated 4.6.17	

Army Form C. 2118.

WAR DIARY
or
INTELLIGENCE SUMMARY.
(Erase heading not required.)

Instructions regarding War Diaries and Intelligence Summaries are contained in F.S. Regs., Part II. and the Staff Manual respectively. Title pages will be prepared in manuscript.

Place	Date	Hour	Summary of Events and Information	Remarks and references to Appendices
MATRINGHEM	11.6.17		Training was carried out as per programme. Major M.C.C. Mains rejoined from 63rd Rfle. school. Draft of 44 Other Ranks joined the Battalion.	
	12.6.17		Training was carried on. 2 Officers for lec. attended a lecture on "Operations on VIMY RIDGE" by Brig. Gen. P. de B. Radcliffe D.S.O.	
	13.6.17		Training was carried on with 2 Officers per Coy attended continuation of lecture on "Operations on VIMY RIDGE" by Lt. Col. Whitton. D.S.O.	
	14.6.17		Training carried on. 2/Lt. G.W. Wedgwood joined the Battalion.	
	15.6.17		Continued firing on Brigade Rifle Range, at HEZECQUES. Throughout the day. Battalion strength were held on the enemy.	
	16.7.17		Battalion carried on Training. 7 O.R. joined the Battalion.	
	17.7.17		Drill Service was held on the Training ground. 2/Lt. S. Miranos (Canadian) proceeded on leave to the U.K. until 30th inst. 2/Lt. S.S. Sutherland assumed duty as Acting Adjutant for period 17th inst to 27th inst. Captain P.W. Smith M.C. assumed command of B. Co.	
	18.7.17		Training carried on as per programme. One Officer worked on making Beyond Fighting Gallows. No. 85570 Pte. H. Jackson's sentence of 6 months I.H.L. was remitted by G.O.C. 63rd Inf. Bde. for (i) Continuous good conduct in the field. (ii) Gallantry in Action on April 24th, 1917 N. of the River Scarpe.	

Army Form C. 2118.

WAR DIARY
or
INTELLIGENCE SUMMARY.
(Erase heading not required.)

Instructions regarding War Diaries and Intelligence Summaries are contained in F. S. Regs., Part II. and the Staff Manual respectively. Title pages will be prepared in manuscript.

Place	Date	Hour	Summary of Events and Information	Remarks and references to Appendices
MATRINGHEM	19.6.17		Training was carried on as per programme. Billets were allotted to A. Bn. and Head Quarters	
—	20.6.17		Companies carried out musketry practice on the Rifle Range at HEZECQUES. Throughout the day, Inspection carried out and practice with his books under the direction of the Bombing Officer. 5. O.R. proceeded to 1st Army Rest Camp for 14 days. Battalion sports were continued in the evening.	
—	21.6.17		The day was regarded as a general holiday. Brigade Sports were held in FROSES. A presentation of medal ribbons was made by the 1st Army Commander, a detachment from "D" Coy under Lieut. A.E. Mitchell represented the Battalion in the Brigade Guard of Honour. Captain P.W. Smith. M.C. & 2nd Lt. J.C. Boyd. M.C. received medal ribbons.	
—	22.6.17		The Battalion marched to AUCHY-AU-BOIS. There to be billeted for a night. But weather allowed the march, and marching was very heavy.	
AUCHY-AU-BOIS	23.6.17		The Battalion marched to THIENNES, moving off at 5. a.m. 2/Lt. A.C. Cooks was admitted to field Ambulance.	
THIENNES	24.6.17		At 4.30 a.m. the Battalion marched to CAESTRE. Billets were very scattered there.	Reference Sheet. 28. S.W. h. Edition 5·A
CAESTRE	25.6.17		The Battalion marched to the KEMMEL area. The 2nd Army Commander inspected the Battalion on the line of march at METEREN. The Battalion was billeted at BUTTERFLY FARM.	N 19.9 – 6.7

Army Form C. 2118.

WAR DIARY
or
INTELLIGENCE SUMMARY.
(Erase heading not required.)

Instructions regarding War Diaries and Intelligence Summaries are contained in F. S. Regs., Part II. and the Staff Manual respectively. Title pages will be prepared in manuscript.

Place	Date	Hour	Summary of Events and Information	Remarks and references to Appendices
Mt. KEMMEL	26.6.17		Companies were at the disposal of the Company Commanders. The camp was in a filthy condition, great wastage lying about. It was generally cleaned up, and many articles of value, quite fit for use, were salvaged. 51 O.R. joined Battalion.	
—	27.6.17		Companies trained under arrangements of Company Commanders. The Commanding Officer and Company Commanders reconnoitred the forward area to be taken over.	Reference:— Sheet 28. S.W.
—	28.6.17		The Battalion moved off at 8 p.m. at midnight the Battalion relieved the 11th Bn. Royal Inniskilling Fusiliers in ZERO WOOD.	O.2.c.8.4
—	29.6.17		The Battalion remained in the support line. Hostile artillery was very active. Hostile M.G. was wounded.	2/Lt. J.G. Lyell
—	30.6.17	2.a.m.	The 8th Bn. Lincolnshire Regt. relieved the Battalion. The Battalion then relieved the 10th Bn. Inniskilling Fusiliers in the line. Relief completed about 3.15 a.m. C. & D. Companies were in the Front line. A. & B. Companies were in support. As much as possible, work was carried on throughout the day. During the relief our casualties were 2 Killed and 2 Wounded. Battalion Head-Quarters were at O.14.B.10.5.	
	3.15 a.m.			

Charles ...... Lieut. Colonel.
Commanding 4/Bn. Middlesex Regiment.

Army Form C. 2118.

WAR DIARY
or
INTELLIGENCE SUMMARY.
(Erase heading not required.)

Instructions regarding War Diaries and Intelligence Summaries are contained in F.S. Regs., Part II. and the Staff Manual respectively. Title pages will be prepared in manuscript.

Vol 36

Place	Date	Hour	Summary of Events and Information	Remarks and references to Appendices
				Reference
	1.7.17		The Battalion remained in the line. The day passed fairly quietly. Weather was very bad. The Casualties for the day were, 4 O.R. wounded. 2/D. J.G. Ryal and 8 O.R. proceeded to 2nd Army Rest Camp for period of 14 days – 2/Lts. R.F.T. Brown and De Wet proceeded to IX Corps School with 3 Sergeants for one monthly course.	
Mont Kemmel	2.7.17		The Battalion was relieved by the 10th Bn. Warwickshire Regt. and the 10th Bn Warwickshire Regt. and moved to camp in the DRANOUTRE – KEMMEL area at N.31.a.9.9.	Sheet 28 S.W. Edition 5ᴬ
—	3.7.17		The Battalion arrived in camp in the early hours of the morning. The day was spent in resting and cleaning up.	
—	4.7.17		Companies were placed at the disposal of Company Commanders for Kit Inspection and cleaning up of arms and equipment. A party of 200 O.R. worked on salvage of R.E. material from old trenches in the vicinity. 8 O.R. transferred to 234th Divl. Employment Co.	
—	5.7.17		In the morning Companies held inspections of arms & equipment, and cleaned up camp lines. In the evening two Companies were working on the construction of the Reserve Line. 1. O.R. attached to the 152 Field Co. R.E. was killed in action.	
—	6.7.17		Commanding Officer and two Company Commanders proceeded to reconnoitre the RIDGE defences. Two Companies were salvaging material from the old British line throughout the day.	

WAR DIARY or INTELLIGENCE SUMMARY.

Army Form C. 2118.

Place	Date	Hour	Summary of Events and Information	Remarks and references to Appendices
KEMMEL	7-7-17		Training was carried out by Two Companies. The remaining two Companies were on working parties, constructing the Reserve Line. In the afternoon the battle at DRANOUTRE were used by two Companies.	
—	8-7-17		Voluntary Services were held. The weather was very hot. One Company and a half supplied working parties for the Reserve Line. The bath at KEMMEL Chateau were used by the other Companies.	
—	9-7-17		Training was carried out by Companies, attention being devoted chiefly to Rapid Loading. Patrols to in the morning. In the afternoon specialist training was carried out.	
	10-7-17		As on the previous day training was proceeded with.	
	11-7-17		Battalion marched to the Line to relieve 8th Lincoln Regt. in support. Battalion H.Q. were situate at TORREKEN FARM (O 20 a 2 3 Ref. Wytschaete Trench Map) Relief was completed satisfactorily by 11.30 p.m. There were no casualties. Major W.C.C. McGear was camp posted to 1st Somerset Light Infantry to-day.	

Army Council 8/16 D.D. & L. Ltd. Forms/C.2118/13.

Army Form C. 2118.

WAR DIARY
or
INTELLIGENCE SUMMARY.
(Erase heading not required.)

Instructions regarding War Diaries and Intelligence Summaries are contained in F. S. Regs., Part II. and the Staff Manual respectively. Title pages will be prepared in manuscript.

Place	Date	Hour	Summary of Events and Information	Remarks and references to Appendices
Fauchez	12/3/17		Battalion was engaged upon railway work blowing up of trenches & so far as possible during daylight under direct observation of enemy. During night (up) all companies were engaged upon on working parties on the digging of Communication trenches - heavy artillery & trench mortar	
	13/3/17		Enemy artillery quiet during day. A & B Companies relieved the left & centre of Russian Bn to front to support line respectively. A Coy occupying Shell Hole & 2nd Line. The other two Companies were engaged on working parties. C Company during forward Communication trench. Enemy opened very severe barrage at 10 p.m. lasting 50 minutes - greater intensity than relief. D Company sustained more casualties than Rutter & 2 wounded	
	14/3/17		There was a heavy bombardment on front line &along Railway line to right of our sector at about 3 a.m. Enemy artillery responded including during day. Companies heavily at intervals during the night. Companies had one man wounded. Working parties to O.C. Companies were at work during night	

WAR DIARY
or
INTELLIGENCE SUMMARY

Army Form C. 2118.

Place	Date	Hour	Summary of Events and Information	Remarks and references to Appendices
Trenches	15/7/17		Raid during the evening fairly heavily. Salvage operations were proceeded with. As usual enemy artillery fairly quiet during day became very active at intervals during night. B Company had five men in on Lewis Gun Section wounded. Working parties from Res too Support Companies were continued. The work on front line communication trenches.	
	16/7/17		As usual the day passed quietly except for some considerable aerial activity. Enemy artillery was vigorous during evening on sector on right of left. During night working parties were again detailed for front line trenches from Companies in support. 2nd Lieut J.H. Hodgson reported Battalion from Reinforcement Camp at Calais & down. He had been employed as Instructor assumed duties as Transport Officer.	
	17/7/17		On our artillery was very active especially at night when a new was carried out by battalion on our left. A Company advanced the (communication trench) was thereby obtained with - Company of 6/23 & 8.4 Battalion. Shell hole line approximately 200 yards. New line ran from O.23 C.3.6 Ref. to O.23 a.8.4. 2nd Lieut J Gordon Reg. to my left. Enemy shelled fairly heavily during night especially on Close Support Company who suffered eight casualties - three killed & three wounded.	

WAR DIARY or INTELLIGENCE SUMMARY

Army Form C. 2118.

Place	Date	Hour	Summary of Events and Information	Remarks and references to Appendices
Trenches	19/9/17		In the early morning the two left for hell was noted in most companies were carrying + tidying up the area searched — the smell of the gas was too faint for any adequate use of it thereon to be given. During evening at about 9 p.m. Enemy put up heavy barrage on brigade on left sector it was shown he was counterattacking JUNCTION Buildings captured by them on previous day. During the night No 5 Platoon in close support was relieved by a platoon of C Company and the relief was carried through by a railway landing post near Sea Shells and Rotten Row.	Ref. WYTSCHAETE TRENCH MAP
	19/9/17		Battalion was relieved by 10th Loyal North Lancashires. Enemy shelled OOSTAVERNE ROAD heavily during relief which was completed by 1.30 p.m. Battalion suffered two casualties during relief.	
Bivouac Camp MT KEMMEL	20/9/17		Battalion heads arriving at Bivouac Camp during early morning. The day was spent in rest + cleaning.	

Army Form C. 2118.

WAR DIARY
or
INTELLIGENCE SUMMARY.
(Erase heading not required.)

Place	Date	Hour	Summary of Events and Information	Remarks and references to Appendices
Reserve Camp	26/4/17		Conference takes at Oxford of Company Commanders for General fitting of equipment & cleaning. 2nd Lieut. S.J. Bean joins Battalion. 2nd Lieut. A.R. Oxley proceeded to 9th Corps Signal School for six weeks' course. Lieut. Jones rejoined Battalion from a course relieving him from employment as Area Commandant (No 9 Sub Area.)	
	27/4/17		Conference takes during day beginning at 8 a.m. 2nd Lieut. R.G. Williams proceeded to 63rd Brigade School for course of instruction. 2nd Lieut. C.O. Ridgeway rejoined battalion from 63rd Brigade School. 2nd Lieut. P.H. Steele proceeded to 9th Corps Bombing & Lewis Gun School for Course of Instruction. Notification was received of the award of Cross Card for Gallantry & devotion to duty in action during Operation N. of SCARPE RIVER to C.S.M. J. Walker & Corpl. C. Burden	

Army Form C. 2118.

WAR DIARY
or
INTELLIGENCE SUMMARY.
(Erase heading not required.)

Instructions regarding War Diaries and Intelligence Summaries are contained in F. S. Regs., Part II. and the Staff Manual respectively. Title pages will be prepared in manuscript.

Place	Date	Hour	Summary of Events and Information	Remarks and references to Appendices
BEAVER CAMP.	23/7/17		The Battalion was practised in the attack in view of future operations. Battalion marched on SPY FARM at 8-15 am returning to Camp about 2-30 pm. Subsequently gas drill was carried out.	
"	24/7/17		Battalion again carried out practice of attack, returning to Camp about 1 pm. 1 Other Rank joined Battalion (specialist in Lewisry).	
"	25/7/17		Battalion proceeded to line, relieving 10th Battalion Royal North Lancashire Regt. Relief complete by 2-30 am 26/7/17.	
In the Line	26/7/17		Battalion in the line, quietness prevailed throughout the day. During afternoon orders were received that the Battalion would be relieved same took place by 13th Battalion Rifle Brigade, relief complete by 4-30 am next morning. (1 Other Rank — wounded).	

T2134. Wt. W708—776. 500000. 4/15. Sir J. C. & S.

WAR DIARY
or
INTELLIGENCE SUMMARY.
(Erase heading not required.)

Army Form C. 2118.

Place	Date	Hour	Summary of Events and Information	Remarks and references to Appendices
BEAVER CAMP	27/7		Battalion upon relief proceeded to Camp, in early hours of the morning. Hot meals were prepared for troops upon arrival. Remainder of the day was spent resting.	
"	28/7		Battalion placed at disposal of Company Commanders for general cleaning of Clothes, Equipment & arms. Owing to inclement weather the afternoon was spent in Lectures on Box Respirator & various points of interest concerning active operations. A fatigue party under Capt. E. Relyeld worked on the deepening & connecting of "Shell Hole" line with Battalion on the left. Party returning at 6-0 am next morning, no casualties occurred.	

WAR DIARY
or
INTELLIGENCE SUMMARY.
(Erase heading not required.)

Army Form C. 2118.

Place	Date	Hour	Summary of Events and Information	Remarks and references to Appendices
BEAVER CAMP	29/7		Battalion placed at disposal of Company Commanders. Inclement weather prevailed throughout the morning. Lectures were given on various points concerning active operations. Remainder of day was spent in gas drill with new box respirator extensions. Lts. A.C. Mitchell & 2/Lt. H.J. Bowles proceeded to G.H. Corps School of Instruction for Course (duration of Course 1 month).	
[Huts]	30/7		Battalion proceeded to line relieving 13th Battalion Rifle Brigade, relief being complete by about 2-0 am next morning. 2 O. Ranks killed in action.	
In the line	30/7		Battalion in the line, intermittent shelling took place on both sides. 1 Other Rank Wounded. Inclement weather prevailed throughout the day.	

Army Form C. 2118.

WAR DIARY
or
INTELLIGENCE SUMMARY.
(Erase heading not required.)

Instructions regarding War Diaries and Intelligence Summaries are contained in F. S. Regs., Part II. and the Staff Manual respectively. Title pages will be prepared in manuscript.

Place	Date	Hour	Summary of Events and Information	Remarks and references to Appendices
In the Line	31/7/17		Up to this time touch was maintained with the Company of 8th Lincolns, at JUNE & JULY FARMS. When the further advance took place the action of the Companies became distinct, so that it would be better to follow them separately. "A" Company advanced to search BAB FARM. They found two German Medical Officers and 8 Other Ranks. Almost at once a Counter-attack came up which they repelled and stood their ground waiting for more. "C" Company moved forward from RIFLE FARM to support them. About two more Counter-attacks were repelled by rifle & rifle Grenades. At this time the two Companies had machine gun fire playing on them from their left front, right front and right. Finally a Counter-attack came from the left front. The left was thrown back and extended to meet it. On it being repelled very few men were left, and they were	

Place	Date	Hour	Summary of Events and Information	Remarks and references to Appendices
In the Line	3/1/17		taken to the left by C.Sm. Worboys to join "D" Company. "D" Company meanwhile advanced till its left rested on "BEE FARM" on the South side of which were the 8th K.O.R. Lancaster Regiment. They were out of touch on the right, they reached this position about 5am, the farm was searched and about 40 prisoners taken, half of these were seen to fall, under hostile machine gun fire. Between 7am and 8am, hostile bombers approached and began to attack their right. They were met with rifle grenades, rifle and Lewis gun fire and gave no further trouble. From about 9am, when the remains of "A" and "D" joined them they were shelled heavily by 5.9" till about mid-day and suffered considerable Casualties. Hostile rifle fire was also fairly active.	

WAR DIARY
or
INTELLIGENCE SUMMARY.
(Erase heading not required.)

Army Form C. 2118.

Place	Date	Hour	Summary of Events and Information	Remarks and references to Appendices
In the Line	31/7		The best evidence is still not available. The order of advance was:- "C" Company on the Right, "A" Company on the Left, "B" Company supporting "C" and "D" Company "D" Company on the Right, "A" Company in reserve. At Zero hour the Battalion left the trenches and formed up as on parade parallel with the barrage. It was almost dark at this time. "C" Company had to form up on the East side of MAY FARM. As they passed over it, one German ran forward with hands up and surrendered. During the first advance of the barrage (up till Z plus 40) touch was at first lost with the Battalion on our left, but was regained by a divergence of "D" Company to the left. At Z plus 40, the Battalion was on the objective "C" Company RIFLE FARM. "D" Company after a gap to the left - "A" Company behind RIFLE FARM. Its left platoon had its right on the Northern enclosing hedge.	

WAR DIARY
or
INTELLIGENCE SUMMARY.
(Erase heading not required.)

Army Form C. 2118.

Place	Date	Hour	Summary of Events and Information	Remarks and references to Appendices
In the Line	31/7/17		At about 12-30 p.m, from sounds of machine guns it appeared that the King's Own was being attacked. At about 1-15 p.m a counter-attack appeared advancing on their front, and also round the left flank. The position was considered untenable by the Officers in Command, who ordered a retirement fighting on our front Shell-Hole Line. This was carried out covered by Lewis Gun fire. They retired into the front of the 19th Division having found privates of the King's Own with them. No more of the 19th Division was seen and the line was held against a possible further advance. "B" Company in reserve was in the front Shell-hole Line. This was a weak Company (40 Strong). Runners sent forward to get in touch with the leading Compa[ny] after the advance of X plus 40.	

Army Form C. 2118.

WAR DIARY
or
INTELLIGENCE SUMMARY.
(Erase heading not required.)

Instructions regarding War Diaries and Intelligence Summaries are contained in F.S. Regs., Part II. and the Staff Manual respectively. Title pages will be prepared in manuscript.

Place	Date	Hour	Summary of Events and Information	Remarks and references to Appendices
In the Line	31/7/17		No information came in. Enemy at MAY FARM, commenced sniping at about 5-30 a.m. The position was reconnoitred, and it was estimated that it contained about 50 in trenches. The Company moved out to attack them, and cleared out half of the position. The Officer Commanding called on a platoon of the 8th Lancashire Regiment, to assist on the other side. The attack was then resumed on three sides, and the place finally cleared. About 8 Germans surrendered, and the remainder were killed. The Officer Commanding the Lincoln platoon was unfortunately killed here. As soon as this was done the Officer Commanding the Battalion ordered the Company to spread out along the Shell Hole Line, to prevent a possible hostile advance. Up to this time the whole of the Battalion had been fully occupied with the enemy. Immediately after	

WAR DIARY
or
INTELLIGENCE SUMMARY.
(Erase heading not required.)

Army Form C. 2118.

Place	Date	Hour	Summary of Events and Information	Remarks and references to Appendices
	3/7/17		reinforcements of the East Lancashire Regiment, began to arrive and were sent to prepare trench on right and left. It is not apparent whether the enemy in MAY FARM, were in the trenches there, when the leading Companies passed over in the dawn or whether they were hidden in shell holes. Beyond trenches there was only one small concrete shelter there. Captain E. Belford Wounded & missing, Lieut J.W. Orr, Wounded and missing, Lieut L.C. Thompson Killed in Action, 2/Lt F. J.R. Simpson Killed in Action, 2/Lt H. McDonald Killed in Action, 2/Lt A.D. Reid Wounded in Action, 2/Lt F.E. Beauchamp Missing believed Wounded, 2/Lt S. Bean Wounded & missing, Other Ranks. Killed in Action. 15; Wounded in Action 94; Missing believed Wounded 69; Missing believed Killed 23.	

T2134. Wt. W708—776. 500000. 4/15. Sir J. C. & S.

Place	Date	Hour	Summary of Events and Information	Remarks and references to Appendices
	31/7		The following Congratulations have been received:— "The G.O.C. 34th Division, wishes to convey to the Officers, NCO's & men of this Battalion his appreciation of their steadfastness, and gallantry during the recent operations. He considers that they have fully maintained their name of "DIE HARDS". The G.O.C. 63rd Infantry Brigade thanks the Officers, NCO's & men of this Battalion for the good work they have lately performed. He fully realizes the difficulties of ground and weather that they have encountered.	Gallipoli letter Condy 4th Gurkha Rgt

War Diary
4th Middx Regt

August

WAR DIARY
or
INTELLIGENCE SUMMARY.
(Erase heading not required.)

Army Form C. 2118.

Place	Date	Hour	Summary of Events and Information	Remarks and references to Appendices
In the line	Aug 1 / Aug 2		Remained in same position as yesterday. No casualties. Battalion relieved by 13th Rifle Brigade, proceeded to BEAVER CAMP, arriving at about 3 a.m. next morning. Remainder of the day was spent resting. In the evening orders were received and Battalion proceeded to billets in DRANOUTRE, previously occupied by 11th Battalion Royal Warwickshire Regt, arriving in Camp (?) by about 7.30 p.m. Bathing was also carried out during the evening. Inclement weather prevailed throughout the day.	
DRANOUTRE	3/8/17		Companies were placed at disposal of Company Commanders for general cleaning up of equipment, clothing & arms. Remaining details of Battalion bathed during the afternoon. Kit inspections were carried out.	
DRANOUTRE	4/8/17		Companies were placed at disposal of Company Commanders for general refitting & cleaning of equipment during the morning. Remainder (of) day spent in lecturing, on use of new box respirators, attack illumination, use of anti-climbing composition etc.	

WAR DIARY
or
INTELLIGENCE SUMMARY.

Army Form C. 2118.

Place	Date	Hour	Summary of Events and Information	Remarks and references to Appendices
DRANOUTRE	5/8/17		2/Lt. C.W. WRIDGEWAY proceeded to LE TOUQUET, 2/Lt Lewis Gun Course. Companies were placed at disposal of their respective Company Commanders and carried out training during morning. Special attention being paid to Bayonet Fighting & Gas Drill. Divine Service was held in ULSTER HALL. An inspection and overhaul of Arms was carried out during the morning by the Armourer Staff Sergeant, and all repairs carried out.	
	6/8/17		Companies were placed at disposal of Company Commanders, for physical training etc. Special attention was also paid to the cleaning of Arms, owing to the continuous inclement weather. During the afternoon a thorough inspection and overhaul of Lewis Guns took place, and all necessary repairs carried out.	

Army Form C. 2118.

WAR DIARY
or
INTELLIGENCE SUMMARY.
(Erase heading not required.)

Place	Date	Hour	Summary of Events and Information	Remarks and references to Appendices
DRANOUTRE	7/6/17		Companies again carried out training under their respective Company Commanders. Company Commanders proceeded to meet the G.O.C at 10 A.M, at the MODEL TRENCHES, near LOCRE with views to discussing various points and lessons to be learnt from recent operations. The following reinforcement Officers Joined Battalion 2/LT K.B. HALLEY, 2/LT M.T. STANLEY, 2/LT E.H SWALLOW.	
	8/6/17		Companies were inspected by the Commanding Officer during the morning Dress full marching order. All available ranks attended the parade. In the afternoon 1 Officer per Company reconnoitred the new support area to the Brigade line. The Brigade Headquarters being situated at DOME HOUSE. O.9.c.0-65.	

Army Form C. 2118.

WAR DIARY
or
INTELLIGENCE SUMMARY.
(Erase heading not required.)

Instructions regarding War Diaries and Intelligence Summaries are contained in F. S. Regs., Part II. and the Staff Manual respectively. Title pages will be prepared in manuscript.

Place	Date	Hour	Summary of Events and Information	Remarks and references to Appendices
DRANOUTRE	8/8/17		During the afternoon the Battalion was relieved by the 33rd Battalion Australian Imperial Force, and proceeded thence to Camp, situated at N.15.c.99. Heavy rain fell during the night. 2/Lt. A.D. REID, died of wounds received in action, at 53 Casualty Clearing Station. 2/Lt. G.S. SUTHERLAND proceeded on leave to U.K.	
BEAVER CORNER	9/8/17		Companies were placed at disposal of Company Commanders for general cleaning & tidying up of Camp. 2 O. Ranks proceeded to 9th Corps School of Instruction for short course on Lewis Gun. Draft of 3 Other Ranks joined Battalion.	
	10/8/17		Companies carried out training during the morning, special attention being paid to physical training and musketry practice.	

Army Form C. 2118.

WAR DIARY
or
INTELLIGENCE SUMMARY.
(Erase heading not required.)

Place	Date	Hour	Summary of Events and Information	Remarks and references to Appendices
BEAVER CORNER.	10/8/17		During the evening working parties were found by the Battalion consisting of 2 Officers and 100 O.Ranks, for excavation of Communication Trench.	N.15.c.9.9
	11/8/17		Lieut-Colonel G.A. BRIDGMAN, proceeded to 63rd Brigade Headquarters, and assumed temporary Command of 63rd Infantry Brigade, during the absence of Brigadier General E.L. CHALLENOR, D.S.O. Captain B.R. NEWMAN assumed temporary command of Battalion during the absence of LIEUT-COL. G.A. BRIDGMAN. Companies carried out a scheme of training as under. Physical Training, Musketry practice, Gas helmet drill etc. 2/Lt J.P. Jamieson assumed command of "D" Company from this day. 2/Lt J.C. LYAL, M.C. was posted to "C" Company. Working parties were again found throughout the day.	
	12/8/17		Companies carried out training during the morning.	

WAR DIARY
or
INTELLIGENCE SUMMARY.
(Erase heading not required.)

Place	Date	Hour	Summary of Events and Information	Remarks and references to Appendices
BEAVER CORNER	12/6/17		Divine Service was carried out on the ground facing Battalion Headquarters. Working parties again found by Battalion during the night for carriage of material t/o Reserve Line. 2/Lt J.H. HODGSON proceeded on leave to U.K.	N15 c 9.9
	13/6/17		Companies carried out training throughout the day and found the following working parties 1 Officer and 50 Other Ranks for excavation of Communication Trench. 2 Officers and 100 Other Ranks were engaged in the carriage of material to the Reserve Line. 2/Lieut. F.W. SCHOLEFIELD and 5 Other Ranks proceeded to 2nd Army Rest Camp at AMBLETEUSE. 2/Lt. T. DE VAL and 9 Other Ranks rejoined from 2nd Army Rest Camp.	

WAR DIARY
or
INTELLIGENCE SUMMARY.

Army Form C. 2118.

Place	Date	Hour	Summary of Events and Information	Remarks and references to Appendices
BEAVER CORNER	13/5/17		2/Lt. M.T. STANLEY, and 2 Other Ranks proceeded to IX Corps School for Course, on the Lewis Gun. School situated at LA LEVERETTE. 2/Lt. C.W. WRIDGWAY, and 2 Other Ranks rejoined from Lewis Gun School, on Completion of Course.	N.15 e 9.9
		AM 11-30	A enemy aeroplane bombed our Transport Lines, at, dropping in all 4 bombs, all of which exploded causing the following Casualties. 1 Other Rank, wounded, 1 Rider Killed, 1 Charger wounded.	N 10. D
	14/5/17		Ordinary intentions were carried out as yesterday.	
	15/5/17		Training was carried on with Companies. Musketry practice was also carried out.	
	16/5/17		The Battalion moved into left support with Head Quarters at DOME HOUSE, no casualties were suffered in moving in.	J.7.c.0.7
	17/5/17 to 20/5/17		The Battalion remained in support and provided working parties each day and night	

Army Form C. 2118.

WAR DIARY
or
INTELLIGENCE SUMMARY.

(Erase heading not required.)

Instructions regarding War Diaries and Intelligence Summaries are contained in F. S. Regs., Part II. and the Staff Manual respectively. Title pages will be prepared in manuscript.

Place	Date	Hour	Summary of Events and Information	Remarks and references to Appendices
BEAVER CORNER	21.8.17		The Battalion was relieved at night by the 8th Bn. East Lancashire Regt. and proceeded to camp at BEAVER CORNER. The following officers joined the Battalion on the 17th inst. 2/Lt. A.J. Kleiboer, 2/Lt. A.S. Yates, 2/Lt. D.M. Batty; The following on the 18th inst. 2/Lt. A.S. Andrews, 2/Lt. H.M. Chaundy, 2/Lt. H. Holgate, 2/Lt. H.A. Salter, 2/Lt. D.W. Heath. Nos. 42495 Pte. Titmas, 14717 Pte. J.H. King, 10913 Pte. J. Stableborn, were awarded the Military Medal for gallantry and devotion to duty East of OOSTTAVERNE during operations on the 31st of July, 1917.	
	22.8.17		The Battalion rested and cleaned up during the day.	
	23.8.17		Physical drill was carried out by Companies during the forenoon. The Battalion was called upon to supply working parties at night - No. 11092 C.S.M. A. Worthupt was wounded. The Military [Cross] for gallantry and devotion to duty E.R. of OOSTTAVERNE on the 31st of July 1917 (Authority:- 37th Div. R.O. 2/97 dated 22.8.17)	
	24.8.17		The Battalion rested throughout the day, on account of the working parties to be supplied at night.	

Army Form C. 2118.

WAR DIARY
or
INTELLIGENCE SUMMARY.
(Erase heading not required.)

Instructions regarding War Diaries and Intelligence Summaries are contained in F.S. Regs., Part II and the Staff Manual respectively. Title pages will be prepared in manuscript.

Place	Date	Hour	Summary of Events and Information	Remarks and references to Appendices
BEAVER CORNER.	25/8/17		The Battalion rested in the day and supplied working parties at night. Lt. Col. G.A. Bridgeman was granted leave to the U.K. Captain. B.R. Newman assumed command in the absence of Lt. Col. Bridgeman.	
BUTTERFLY FARM	26/8/17		The Battalion moved to BUTTERFLY FARM at 11 a.m. Divine Service was held at 3 p.m. The working parties were supplied at night as usual.	
	27/8/17		Each Company carried out thirty minutes physical training and thirty minutes musketry. Eight O.R. proceeded to the 2nd Army Rest Camp at AMBLETEUSE for fourteen days.	
	28/8/17		Training was carried out under Company arrangements. A working-party of one Officer and thirty O.R. was employed at RAVINE WOOD throughout the day. A demonstration was held at the Regimental Canteen showing the method of cooking with small brazier and one pound of charcoal. The Commanding Officer and Company Commanders proceeded to reconnoitre the line.	
	29/8/17	8.30 a.m.	The Battalion moved off from BROLOOZE Cross-roads at 8.30 a.m. journey proceeding to Bus House via KEMMEL and VIERSTRAAT, where the Battalion de-bused and marched to BOIS CONFLUENT.	Sheet 28.S.W 1/10,000 O.1.C

WAR DIARY or INTELLIGENCE SUMMARY.

Army Form C. 2118.

(Erase heading not required.)

Instructions regarding War Diaries and Intelligence Summaries are contained in F.S. Regs., Part II. and the Staff Manual respectively. Title pages will be prepared in manuscript.

Place	Date	Hour	Summary of Events and Information	Remarks and references to Appendices
BOIS CONFLUENT	29/8/17	10·30am	Here the Battalion relieved the 16th Bn. Sherwood Foresters in reserve. The Battalion proceeded to relieve the 16th Bn. Rifle Brigade in the left sub-section.	Reference Sheet 28 S.W. 1/10,000
		8 p.m.	The weather conditions were good and the relief was completed	The Battalion
		10·45 p.m.	under quiet conditions. Battalion Head Quarters was at O·5·a·3·0	HeadQuarters from O·12·a·3·6
O·5·a·3·0	30·8·17		The Battalion remained in the line. A very quiet day was spent, about Ten rounds of 15·0 m.m. were fired at the WHITE CHATEAU (A bootrup's in support) fifty gas-shells more front	on the road, to the CANAL.
		9 p.m.	no damage was done. In the evening about fifty gas-shells were fired at the Support line. No casualties occurred.	
	31·8·17		At Battalion Head-Quarters and in the Support line, general drainage was carried out. No movement was possible by day in the shell-hole line. The weather was fine, and the enemy very quiet.	

Geoffrey Heer
Major 16th Sherwood Ft

SECRET

Vol 398 War Diary
4 Middlesex
Sept 1917

Army Form C. 2118.

WAR DIARY
or
INTELLIGENCE SUMMARY.
(Erase heading not required.)

Instructions regarding War Diaries and Intelligence Summaries are contained in F. S. Regs., Part II and the Staff Manual respectively. Title pages will be prepared in manuscript.

Place	Date	Hour	Summary of Events and Information	Remarks and references to Appendices
	1.9.17		The Battalion remained in the same position. The enemy was most active, shelling the WHITE CHATEAU and the Safford Trench. No casualties incurred.	Sheet 28 S.W. 1/20,000.
	2.9.17		The Battalion was relieved in the line by the 5th Bn. Lincolnshire Regt.	O.5.a.3.0. Sheet YPRES. 28 N.W. 1/10,000.
			The Battalion moved into support, with Battalion Head-Quarters at SPOIL BANK. Relief was completed at 10.45 p.m.	
	3.9.17		The Battalion remained here, supplying heavy working parties for the front Battalions.	
			The 1st Battalion. During the stay in the support area, two men became casualties from gas shells.	
N.15.c.9.9.	6.9.17		4 O.R. 9.A Bridgmen returned from leave to U.K.	
	7.9.17		The Battalion was relieved by the 13th Bn. Rifle Brigade, and proceeded to camp at N.15.c.9.9.9. Relief was completed at 5. p.m.	
	8.9.17		The day was spent in general cleaning up and resting. Capt. B. R. Newman and 2/Lt T. H. Stubb granted leave to U.K. until 18th September, 1917.	
			Training was carried out by Companies and Specialists. A working party of 2 Officers and 100 O.R. was supplied; this party buried cable at SPOIL BANK. 2nd Lt. H. J. Bowen proceeded to Training Reinforcement Depot, CALAIS.	
	9.9.17			

WAR DIARY
or
INTELLIGENCE SUMMARY.

(Erase heading not required.)

Army Form C. 2118.

Instructions regarding War Diaries and Intelligence Summaries are contained in F. S. Regs., Part II and the Staff Manual respectively. Title pages will be prepared in manuscript.

Place	Date	Hour	Summary of Events and Information	Remarks and references to Appendices
MONT KOKEREELE	10.9.17		The Battalion moved to MONT KOKEREELE via CANADA CORNER, WESTOUTRE, and MONT NOIR, arriving in camp at R.23.B.3.7 and R.23.B.5-8 about 4 p.m. The weather was good. The canteen-tent was not suitable.	Reference Sheet 27. S.E. 1/20,000.
— —	11.9.17		The Battalion carried out Trainings, special attention being paid to Physical Training, musketry, and rapid wiring. A working party of 4 Officers and 100 O.R. was supplied to bury cable near BOIS CONFLUENT. The party was engaged there and had to camp by motor-lorries.	
— —	12.9.17		Training was carried out as yesterday. The same working party was again supplied. 2/Lt. S. Minors appointed Acting Adjutant (Additional) (Batt. But. No. 151 - Appendices hereunder).	
— —	13.9.17		Training carried out in accordance with Battalion programme; stopped Training's Sphere, fighting, musketry, gas-drill, and bombing.	
— —	14.9.17		Training carried on with. The Rifle Range at R.22.B.5.4 was used by "B" and "C" Companies. The Lewis Guns were practised on the range also.	
— —	15.9.17		Training was carried on with.	
— —	16.9.17		The Battalion paraded for Divine Service at 9.45 a.m. The remainder of the day was spent in Recreational Training.	

WAR DIARY or INTELLIGENCE SUMMARY

Army Form C. 2118.

Place	Date	Hour	Summary of Events and Information	Remarks and references to Appendices
MONT KOKEREELE	17.9.17		The Battalion carried on with Training in accordance with programme. A working party of 2 Officers and 100 O.R. was furnished to bury cable in the neighbourhood of SPOIL BANK. The Adjutant took all Officers and N.C.O.'s for judging distance. The parade was held on the landing ground.	Reference Sheet 27. S.E. 1/20,000.
—	18.9.17		In the morning a practice contact scheme was carried out on the BOESCHEPE Training Area with troops and without an aeroplane. In the afternoon the operation was continued in co-operation with an aeroplane about	
—	19.9.17		The Battalion moved to camp at N.15-A. arriving in camp about 11 h.m. A draft of 570 O.R. joined the Battalion.	
—	20.9.17		At 4 p.m. the Battalion received orders to relieve the 10th Royal North hands. of the 112th Bde. at IRISH HOUSE, The relief was completed at 6.30 p.m. This move was completed in order that the Battalion might be in closer support to the 19th Division in active operations north of the CANAL.	
—	21.9.17		The Battalion moved back to camp at R.23.b-5-8 MONT KOKEREELE area. A draft of 9 O.R. joined the Battalion.	

Army Form C. 2118.

WAR DIARY
or
INTELLIGENCE SUMMARY.
(Erase heading not required.)

Instructions regarding War Diaries and Intelligence Summaries are contained in F. S. Regs., Part II. and the Staff Manual respectively. Title pages will be prepared in manuscript.

Place	Date	Hour	Summary of Events and Information	Remarks and references to Appendices
MONT KOKEREELE	22-9-17	Noon	The Battalion was inspected by The Commanding Officer by Companies. At 4 p.m. The Battalion was put on two hours move to move. A meeting of Company A.D.C. was sent to the parade area, but the move was cancelled at 3 p.m. Captain M.D. Stoy-Gillen appointed A.D.C. to G.O.C. 40th Division. Casualty A.G. Appointments 1343 of 17/9/17. 2/Lt. G.W. Schofield appointed Acting Captain Camp. Rd No. 15-3 of "Appointments" &c.	
—	23-9-17		Divine Service was held on the parade ground at 11.30 a.m. Afternoon spent in Recreational Training.	
—	24-9-17		Training was carried out in accordance with Battalion Programme.	
—	25-9-17		Two Companies of the Battalion took part in a Brigade Scheme; the remainder of the Battalion carried on with training. At 11.30 p.m. the Battalion was put on one hours notice to move.	
—	26-9-17		The Battalion remained under orders to move at one hours notice.	
—	27-9-17		The Battalion moved in motor-lorries at 6 p.m. to Bus House, where guides of the 1st Cambridge-shire Regt. were met. The Battalion then marched up to and relieved the 1st Cambridge-shires in the line in	

Army Form C. 2118.

WAR DIARY
or
INTELLIGENCE SUMMARY.
(Erase heading not required.)

Instructions regarding War Diaries and Intelligence Summaries are contained in F. S. Regs., Part II. and the Staff Manual respectively. Title pages will be prepared in manuscript.

Place	Date	Hour	Summary of Events and Information	Remarks and references to Appendices
S.E. of YPRES	24.9.17		Front of SHREWSBURY FOREST and East of the BASSEVILLE BEKE VALLEY A & B. Bombarded in the his. b. in support. D in Reserve. Battalion Head-Quarters were at J.26.a.1.5"	
	25.9.17		Battalion remained in the line. Enemy shelling was fairly heavy during the period but not many casualties occurred.	
	30.9.17		2/Lt H F BOWSER, reported from Training Reinforcements CALAIS 2/Lt R.A.K. STUART joined Battalion	

G.A. Sturgeon Leafer
Capt 2/5 Yorkshire Regt.

Army Form C. 2118.

WAR DIARY
or
INTELLIGENCE SUMMARY.
(Erase heading not required.)

Instructions regarding War Diaries and Intelligence Summaries are contained in F. S. Regs., Part II. and the Staff Manual respectively. Title pages will be prepared in manuscript.

Place	Date	Hour	Summary of Events and Information	Remarks and references to Appendices
S.E of YPRES	1.9.17		The Battalion remained in the same position. The enemy was more active, shelling Reforme. The WHITE CHATEAU and the Support Trench. No casualties occurred.	Ref. 28.S.W.
	2.9.17		The Battalion was relieved in the line by the 8th Lincolnshire Regt, and moved into Support with Battalion Head-Quarters at SPOIL BANK.	Sheet - YPRES 28 N.W.
	3.9.17		Working parties were supplied for the front Battalion. 5 O.R. gassed.	
	6.9.17		Lt. Col. G. A. Bridgeman returned from leave to U.K.	
	7.9.17		The Battalion was relieved by the 13th Rifle Brigade, and proceeded to camp at N.15.c.9.9	
	8.9.17		The day was spent in general cleaning up and rest. Lt. W. P. H. Steel was granted leave to U.K. until 18th inst. Lt./Lt. B.R. Newman also proceeded on leave. Training was carried out by Companies and Specialists. 2 Officers and	
	9.9.17		100 O.R. proceeded on a working-party to SPOIL BANK. 2/Lt. W. H. Bonner proceeded to Re-inforcement Training Depot, CALAIS, as instructor.	
	10.9.17		The Battalion marched to MONT KOKEREELE via CANADA CORNER - WESTOUTRE MONT NOIR arriving in camp at R.23.b.5.8 about 4 p.m. The weather was good, and the camping ground very suitable.	Sheet. 27 S.E.

Army Form C. 2118.

WAR DIARY
or
INTELLIGENCE SUMMARY.

(Erase heading not required.)

Instructions regarding War Diaries and Intelligence Summaries are contained in F.S. Regs., Part II and the Staff Manual respectively. Title pages will be prepared in manuscript.

Place	Date	Hour	Summary of Events and Information	Remarks and references to Appendices
MONT KOKEREELE	11.9.17			Reference:- Sheet 27 S.E.
	12.9.17		The Battalion carried out Training. Physical drill, musketry, and rapid wiring. 4 Officers and 100 O.R. proceeded to BOIS CONFLUENT as a working party. They were conveyed there and back by motor-lorries.	
"	"		Training was carried out as yesterday. A working party of the same strength carried on the same work. 2/Lt. S. Morans appointed A/Army Captain (Additional). Authority:- list No. 151 - Appointments and Promotions.)	
"	13.9.17		Training was continued.	
"	14.9.17		Training was continued. Two Companies utilized the Rifle Range at R.22.b.5.4.	
"	15.9.17		The Lewis Gun teams utilized the Range.	
"	16.9.17		The Battalion attended Divine Service at 9.45 a.m. The remainder of the day was spent in recreational Training.	
"	17.9.17		Training was continued. 2 Officers and 100 O.R. formed a working party and worked near BOIS CONFLUENT burying cable.	
"	18.9.17		In the morning a practice bomb Scheme was carried out. In the afternoon it was carried out and an aeroplane attacked. This was carried out on the BOESCHEPE Training Area.	

Army Form C. 2118.

WAR DIARY
or
INTELLIGENCE SUMMARY.
(Erase heading not required.)

Instructions regarding War Diaries and Intelligence Summaries are contained in F. S. Regs., Part II. and the Staff Manual respectively. Title pages will be prepared in manuscript.

Place	Date	Hour	Summary of Events and Information	Remarks and references to Appendices
S. of YPRES	19.9.17		The Battalion moved to camp at N.15.a near BEAVER CORNER. A draft of 5.O.R. joined.	
	20.9.17	4 p.m.	At 4 p.m. the Battalion received orders to relieve the 10th Royal Welch Fus.	
		6.30 p.m.	of the 112th Brigade at IRISH HOUSE. This relief was completed at 6.30 p.m. The Battalion was then in Support to the 19th Division.	
MONT KOKEREELE	21.9.17		The Battalion moved back to camp at R.23.b.5.8, MONT KOKEREELE over a draft of 9 O.R. joined.	
	22.9.17		The Battalion was inspected by the Commanding Officer. At noon, orders were received to be prepared to move at two hours notice. A billeting party proceeded to the forward area but the move was cancelled. Captain M.D. Fitzgerton was appointed A.D.C. to G.O.C. 40th Division. 2/Lt. J.W. Schofield attended Acting Captain.	
	23.9.17	11.30 a.m.	The Battalion attended Divine Service at 11.30 a.m. Recreational training was carried out in the afternoon.	
	24.9.17		Training was continued.	
	25.9.17		The Battalion was again orders to be prepared to move at an hours notice.	

Army Form C. 2118.

WAR DIARY
or
INTELLIGENCE SUMMARY.
(Erase heading not required.)

Instructions regarding War Diaries and Intelligence Summaries are contained in F.S. Regs., Part II and the Staff Manual respectively. Title pages will be prepared in manuscript.

Place	Date	Hour	Summary of Events and Information	Remarks and references to Appendices
	26.9.17		The Battalion remained under Shell orders, and stood buy.	
	27.9.17		The Battalion entrained at 6 p.m. and was conveyed to BUS HOUSE where guides of the 1st Cambridgeshire Regt. led the Battalion up to the line. The Battalion then relieved the 1st Cambridgeshire Regt. in front of SHREWSBURY FOREST and E. of the BASSEVILLE BEKE VALLEY. Battalion Head-Quarters was at J.26.9.1.5.	
	28.9.17 to 30.9.17		The Battalion remained in the line. Hostile shelling was considerable throughout this period, but few casualties occurred. 2/Lt. W.J. Bonner rejoined from CALAIS. 2/Lt. R.A.K. Short joined the Battalion. Training Re-inforcements	

R.W.Newman Capt & Lt.Col.
4th Middlesex Regt.
Commanding

2353 Wt. W2544/1454 700,000 5/15 D.D. & L.   A.D.S.S./Forms/C. 2118.

Vol 39. War Diary
4th Middlesex.
Oct 1917.

WAR DIARY
or
INTELLIGENCE SUMMARY
(Erase heading not required.)

Army Form C. 2118.

Place	Date	Hour	Summary of Events and Information	Remarks and references to Appendices
	1.10.17		The Battalion was relieved by the 8th Lincolnshire Regt and moved into Support Trenches at MONT SORREL. 2 O.R killed, 2 O.R wounded. Capt. J.P. Jamison proceeded to 2nd Army School for course. Lieut. V.S. Bower rejoined from Re-inforcement Training Camp at CALAIS.	Reference Sheet GHELUVELT 28 N.E.
	2.10.17		The Battalion remained in Support. 1 O.R. wounded.	
	3.10.17		The Commanding Officer attended a conference at Brigade Head-Quarters. In the evening, "B" & "C" companies moved up into close support of the 8th Lincolns, E. of the BASSEVILLE BEKE. Approximately 40 O.R. were evacuated from CANADA TUNNELS sick from the effects of gas poisoning.	
	4.10.17	5.45 a.m.	The 8th Lincolns attacked at 5.45 a.m., but our "B" & "C" Companies were not called upon to move forward. Battalion Head-quarters was violently shelled throughout the whole day. The rally in front of MONT SORREL being under heavy observation from ZANDVOORDE Church and The Knollings. 2 O.R. wounded.	

Army Form C. 2118.

WAR DIARY
or
INTELLIGENCE SUMMARY.
(Erase heading not required.)

Instructions regarding War Diaries and Intelligence Summaries are contained in F.S. Regs., Part II. and the Staff Manual respectively. Title pages will be prepared in manuscript.

Place	Date	Hour	Summary of Events and Information	Remarks and references to Appendices
	5.10.17		The Battalion remained in the same position. 50 O.R. from 18th Battalion Middlesex Regt. joined. 1 O.R. wounded.	Reference Sheet 28 S.W. 5 a
	6.10.17		The Battalion moved back to camp at N.15.a near HALLEBAST CORNER, being conveyed by lorries. The camp was in very poor condition, accommodation was mostly in bivouacs. Weather conditions here had. 1 O.R. killed and 2 O.R. wounded.	
	7.10.17		The Battalion remained in camp. The weather was very bad and there were many sick. Draft of 33 O.R. joined.	
	8.10.17		The Battalion remained in camp. The men bathed at SIEGE FARM and a clean change of underclothing was obtained. 16 O.R. joined.	
	9.10.17		The arms were inspected by the Armourer, and necessary repairs carried out. The Commanding Officer attended a conference at Brigade Head Quarters, 1 Officer and 1 N.C.O. proceeded to reconnoitre the forward areas. In the evening, orders were received that the Battalion should move into the line on the next day.	
	10.10.17	3 p.m.	At 3 p.m. the Battalion entrained at T track at N.8.b.2.2 in the MILKY WAY.	

Army Form C. 2118.

WAR DIARY
or
INTELLIGENCE SUMMARY.
(Erase heading not required.)

Instructions regarding War Diaries and Intelligence Summaries are contained in F.S. Regs., Part II. and the Staff Manual respectively. Title pages will be prepared in manuscript.

Place	Date	Hour	Summary of Events and Information	Remarks and references to Appendices
	10.10.17	5.30 pm	The Battalion de-bussed at SHRAPNEL CORNER and marched to CANADA TUNNELS where guides of the 11th Royal Warwickshire Regt. were met. These guides took the Battalion as far as the Suffolk Battalion Head-Quarters where guides of the 8th E. Lancashire Regt. took over and led the Battalion to the line. The Battalion Hd.rs. relieved the 8th E. Lancashires with Battalion Head-Quarters at J.20.B.9.2. The left flank rested on the MENIN ROAD. The right flank about J.21.C.0.9. During the way up to the line, especially at MONT SORREL, the Battalion had through very heavy shelling. 7/M. O. W. Bays, and 7/M. E. H. Smallwood were killed. 6 O.R. killed, 5 O.R. wounded. The Battalion remained in the line. The enemy was fairly quiet. No rations arrived. 2 O.R. killed. 7/M. W. M. Chauncy admitted to Hospital.	Reference Sheet GHELUVELT 28 N.E.
	11.10.17		The Battalion remained in the line. Occasionally Battalion Head-Quarters was shelled with light guns. No ration party arrived. 3 O.R. killed.	
	12.10.17		The day passed fairly quietly. 7/M. R. J. T. Irwin was killed. 7/M. E. G. Morgareidh joined the Battalion.	
	13.10.17		Proceeded on leave to U.K. from Base.	

WAR DIARY or INTELLIGENCE SUMMARY.

Army Form C. 2118.

(Erase heading not required.)

Instructions regarding War Diaries and Intelligence Summaries are contained in F. S. Regs., Part II. and the Staff Manual respectively. Title pages will be prepared in manuscript.

Place	Date	Hour	Summary of Events and Information	Remarks and references to Appendices
	14.10.17		It was intimated that the Battalion would be relieved by the 16th Sherwood Foresters, and reconnoitering parties visited Thead-Junction. In the evening the relief was postponed 24 hours. The Battalion on our right sent up the S.O.S. signal during the night, but all remained quiet on our front	
MONT KOKEREELE	15.10.17		The Battalion was relieved by the 17th Hampshire Regt. and was conveyed in lorries to the camp at MONT KOKEREELE. 1 O.R. wounded.	
	16.10.17		The Battalion rested during the day.	
	17.10.17		The men were bathed. The day was spent in general cleaning up.	
	18.10.17		The Medical Officer held an inspection of the men. The Battalion rested.	
	19.10.17		Kit inspections were carried out. "A" Company used the range at R-22-B-5-9 fired.- Quartermaster E.H. Amor to be Honorary Captain 1.7.17 (Authority:- London Gazette 13.10.17)	
	20.10.17		Physical training and general re-organizing of Companies was carried out: the afternoon.	Reference Sheet HAZEBROUCK 5" a.
	21.10.17		The Battalion marched to Hillhoof area South of METEREN via BERTHEN — mentioned	

Army Form C. 2118.

WAR DIARY
or
INTELLIGENCE SUMMARY.
(Erase heading not required.)

Instructions regarding War Diaries and Intelligence Summaries are contained in F.S. Regs., Part II. and the Staff Manual respectively. Title pages will be prepared in manuscript.

Place	Date	Hour	Summary of Events and Information	Remarks and references to Appendices
METEREN	21.10.17		SCHAEXKEN - METEREN. The Battalion arrived about noon. Billets were fairly hut very comfortable.	
"	22.10.17		Programme carried out Training in accordance with S.S. 152. Appendix XIII B. 7/N PH Staff proceeded to 2nd Army Signal School.	
"	23.10.17		The Battalion carried on Training. One officer and 24 O.R. were organised as a sniping class and carried on Training.	
"	24.10.17		Training was continued. Adjutant S. Morans proceeded on 10 days leave to U.K. Lieut. R.G. Williams, Mr A.J. Keiter, H. Telgatt, K.B. Halley? rejoined from IX Corps School. 27 O.R. joined the Battalion.	
"	25.10.17		Battalion carried out a route march. The route was METEREN - OUTERSTEENE, VIEUX-BERQUIN - STRAZEELE - MOOLENACKER - To Billets.	
"	26.10.17		Training was carried out in accordance with S.S. 152. Appendix XIII B. The Commanding Officer inspected the Battalion in Marching Order by Companies.	
"	27.10.17		2/N. E.C. Morpeth and 22 O.R. proceeded to 63rd Infantry Brigade School for course. 5 O.R. joined Battalion.	
"	28.10.17		The Battalion attended Divine Service at 11 a.m. Recreational Training carried out.	

2353 Wt. W2544/1454 700,000 5/15 D.D.&L. A.D.S.S./Forms/C. 2118.

Army Form C. 2118.

WAR DIARY
or
INTELLIGENCE SUMMARY.
(Erase heading not required.)

Place	Date	Hour	Summary of Events and Information	Remarks and references to Appendices
METEREN	29.10.17		Capt. E.G.H. Fenn and 4 other Officers and 223 O.R. proceeded to join the	Reference Sheet 28 N.W.
"	30.10.17		North of YPRES attached to the 10th York & Lancaster Regt. as a working party for roads in the forward area. The details carried on training in Sniping, Lewis Gunnery, and Rapid Wiring. The details of the Battalion left at METEREN and carried on training in Lewis Gun, Sniping, and Wiring.	
"	31.10.17		In addition to the training in Lewis Gun, Sniping &c, an Officers Tactical schemes were carried out, and lectures given by the Commanding Officer.	

B.S. Wasman Capt & Lt.Col.
Commanding 4th Middlesex Rgt.

Army Form C. 2118.

WAR DIARY
or
INTELLIGENCE SUMMARY.
(Erase heading not required.)

4 Middlesex

Place	Date	Hour	Summary of Events and Information	Remarks and references to Appendices
YPRES	1917 Nov 1st to Nov 7		A detachment of 5 Officers and 250 Ranks, worked on forward roads during the period, under Command of O.C. 10th York and Lancaster Regiment, and were billeted in Camp at 1.3.b. During the absence of the above party, various training was carried out, and Special Classes were formed of the remaining junior Subalterns, for training in Bombing, Lewis Gun & Rapid Wiring. During afternoon Lectures by Commanding Officer were given on the following subjects "SALVAGE" "SANITATION" "ORGANISATION OF PLATOONS FOR ATTACK" and "RAIDS". 2/Lt H.F.BACKHOUSE carried out training rapid loading of YUKON PACK with a team selected from the Platoon, with a view to entering a Competition to be held by Brigade on a later date. Rapid wiring instruction was carried out under supervision of Lt. R.F.T. IRWIN. Snipers carried out their usual practice on the Range at under Captain J.N. SCHOLEFIELD. 6 O.Ranks joined Battalion 7-11-17.	METEREN X 22.c.4.2
METEREN			Detachment returned from working on forward roads to previous billets during evening of 7th inst.	

WAR DIARY
or
INTELLIGENCE SUMMARY.
(Erase heading not required.)

Army Form C. 2118.

Instructions regarding War Diaries and Intelligence Summaries are contained in F. S. Regs., Part II and the Staff Manual respectively. Title pages will be prepared in manuscript.

Place	Date	Hour	Summary of Events and Information	Remarks and references to Appendices
METEREN	Nov 8th 1917		Companies under own arrangements made preparations for trenches, whale oil being issued rubbed into feet of the men of their Coy. Lectures on Trench Standing Orders were given during afternoon, and all ranks impressed of the necessity of salvaging every article found lying about, and returning same to Quartermasters Stores for Salvage Dump. 1 Other Rank joined Battalion	
	Nov 9th		Battalion moved to WAKEFIELD HUTS (LOCRE), arriving at destination about 11-30AM. Lieut-Col G.H. Bridgman proceeded to Leave under orders from A.D.M.S.- 3rd Div. (Sick). Captain B.R. Newman Commanded Battalion on line of march. Lieut A.S. Whitlock proceeded to 9th Corps Reinforcement Camp as Instructor during absence on leave of Lt. H.H. Bowen. 2/Lts J.C. Lyall MC, E Edmans, H.M. Champ proceeding to 9th Corps School, were billeted in billets allotted to Brigade in LOCRE for night before reporting to the Corps School. Other Ranks also proceeding to Small Arms School were accommodated for the night at 63rd Brigade School.	

2353 Wt. W2544/1454 700,000 5/15 D.D.&L. A.D.S.S./Forms/C. 2118.

WAR DIARY
or
INTELLIGENCE SUMMARY.

(Erase heading not required.)

Army Form C. 2118.

Place	Date	Hour	Summary of Events and Information	Remarks and references to Appendices
	Nov 10th 1917		Battalion proceeded to Camp at BEGGAR'S REST, situated at N6.d. The march was rather heavy due to continuous showers throughout the day, arriving at destination 2 p.m. The condition of camp was very poor, owing to rain, and some 5 to 6 inches in depth. Upon arrival a working party of 2 Officers & 100 O.Ranks proceeded for work, carrying of R.E. Material from dump to Reserve Line. Captain E.A.W. Fenn proceeded on leave to U.K. Lieut H.T. Bowser proceeded on leave U.K. direct from 9th Corps Reinforcement Camp. 3 O.Ranks joined Battalion.	N6.d
BEGGARS REST CAMP	Nov 11th 1917		During the day working parties were supplied reporting at various points of rendezvous. Major P. Grove White joined Battalion and assumed Command following day. 1 O.Rank joined Battalion. 2Lt L.A.K Stuart proceeded to 2nd Army Central School of Instruction. Duration of Course 6 weeks.	

Army Form C. 2118.

WAR DIARY
or
INTELLIGENCE SUMMARY.
(Erase heading not required.)

Place	Date	Hour	Summary of Events and Information	Remarks and references to Appendices
BEGGARS REST CAMP.	Nov 12/17		Battalion continued to find Working Parties as day previous. 2. Other Ranks Wounded in Action	
" "	Nov. 13		Battalion again supplied Working Parties throughout the day. Captain J.E. Jamieson was detailed as Field Officer for the day.	
" "	Nov 14th		Battalion again carried on with daily working parties around MOLEN DUMP & SPOIL BANK, carrying material for construction of New Reserve Line. Captain & Quartermaster E.H. Amot proceeded on Leave to U.K. 1. O.Rank joined Battalion.	
" "	Nov 15th		Battalion continued to supply working parties as preceding days. 1. O.Rank Wounded in Action (Remained at Duty)	
" "	Nov 16		Battalion again engaged on Working Parties. No Casualties occurred.	
" "	Nov 17		Battalion moved to CURRAGH CAMP, and billeted in hutments, where accommodation was good. Working parties again found by battalion	

Army Form C. 2118.

WAR DIARY
or
INTELLIGENCE SUMMARY.
(Erase heading not required.)

Instructions regarding War Diaries and Intelligence Summaries are contained in F. S. Regs., Part II. and the Staff Manual respectively. Title pages will be prepared in manuscript.

Place	Date	Hour	Summary of Events and Information	Remarks and references to Appendices
CURRAGH CAMP	Nov 17th 1917		Captain F.W. SCHOLEFIELD was detailed as Field Officer of the day. Nothing Party on Completion of work, were conveyed to and billeted by Lorries from BUS HOUSE. Lieut. L.P. Killing, proceeded on leave to U.K. 1 O. Rank Wounded (Accidentally)	
	Nov 18th		2/Lieuts. W.A. BLOY, F.F. MARSHALL & R.I. MILLIGAN, Joined Battalion 18/7.	
	Nov 18th		Battalion at disposal of Company Commanders carried out training including Musketry, Gas Drill etc. Specialist training carried out during the morning. Afternoon devoted to Recreational Training, carried out under supervision of an Officer. Baths allotted to all Companies though-out the day. Clean underclothing issued to all O. Ranks.	
	Nov 19th		Battalion again carried out training Party of N.C.O. & 6 O. Ranks worked under 9th Corps Troops (Details Officer)	
	Nov 20th		Battalion continued training. Specialists doing morning Special attention being paid to bringing up establishment of	

Army Form C. 2118.

WAR DIARY
or
INTELLIGENCE SUMMARY.
(Erase heading not required.)

Instructions regarding War Diaries and Intelligence Summaries are contained in F. S. Regs., Part II. and the Staff Manual respectively. Title pages will be prepared in manuscript.

Place	Date	Hour	Summary of Events and Information	Remarks and references to Appendices
CURRAGH CAMP.	Nov 20th		Lewis Gunners to H Teams per Company. Musketry for Drill also carried out during the morning.	
—	21st		Battalion at disposal of Company Commanders. Continued Training as per previous day. Drill was carried out from 9am to 9-50am. Party of 1 NCO + 6 men supplied for work under Ordnance Officer. O/R Corps Troops CANADA CORNER. No 60281. Pte N. Phillips proceeded to Base under age. (Auth'y Haig 37 Div. A.69. of 9-11-7) Draft of 18 Other Ranks joined Battalion from Of. Corps Reinforcement Camp.	
—	Nov 22nd		Battalion drill was carried out from 9am to 9-50am. Specialist training + musketry for drill continued during the morning. Working parties as under were supplied. 1 NCO + 6 O.Ranks for work under Ordnance Officer. — Of. Corps Troops CANADA CORNER.	

2353 Wt. W2544/1454 700,000 5/15 D. D. & L. A.D.S.S./Forms/C. 2118.

Army Form C. 2118.

WAR DIARY
or
INTELLIGENCE SUMMARY.
(Erase heading not required.)

Instructions regarding War Diaries and Intelligence Summaries are contained in F. S. Regs., Part II. and the Staff Manual respectively. Title pages will be prepared in manuscript.

Place	Date	Hour	Summary of Events and Information	Remarks and references to Appendices
CURRAGH CAMP	Nov 22 1917	—	Working party of 1 Officer + 20 other Ranks for work at BALDOYLE cutting of hides for Water supply. Demonstration at Brigade School attended by all officers. Followed by conference for Commanding Officers.	
—	Nov 23	—	Battalion drill was again carried out from 9am to 9.50am Specialist training, musketry + gas Drill was carried out during the morning, the afternoon being devoted to Recreational training. Parties of 1 NCO + 6 men & 6 Officers + 25 Other Ranks formed by battalion for same as previous day. 2/Lt. G. S. SUTHERLAND, proceeded on Leave to U.K. 2/Lieuts. J. FRANKLIN + G. A. PIERCE, Joined Battalion from 9th Reserve Reinforcement Camp.	
—	Nov 24th	—	Companies carried out preparations before proceeding to trenches. Stale oil being removed + applied to feet of men of their Company. Baths were allotted Companies during the day. 2/Lt. M. G. STANLEY, proceeded to ROYAL FLYING CORPS, on Okeover. Battalion proceed to Kino, by Light Railway, relieving 13th Bn.	
—	Nov 25th			

WAR DIARY
or
INTELLIGENCE SUMMARY.
(Erase heading not required.)

Army Form C. 2118.

Place	Date	Hour	Summary of Events and Information	Remarks and references to Appendices
In the line	Nov 25th 1917		KRRC in front line, one Company in reserve at HILL 60. Relief complete by 9-0 pm. 2/Lt H FELGATE to Hospital (Accidentally Injured).	
—	26th		Battalion in line. Quietness prevailed throughout the day. Patrols sent out during the night. 2 Lt Col. H.A.O. HANLEY MC joined Bn 26/11	
—	27th		Battalion still in line. Situation still quiet. No casualties.	
—	28th		8 Other Ranks Joined Battalion. Battalion in the line. Situation quiet. Towards midnight enemy patrol, rushed one of the posts held by us & 8th S.L.I. One O.Rank Wounded. & 1 Other Rank Missing - believed prisoner.	
—	29th		Battalion in the line, situation still quiet. Companies relieved by support & reserve Companies. "A" & "D" Company holding shell & hole line & posts. Patrols again reconnoitred positions and pillboxes, no opposition was encountered. 1 man missing Major P Grove White proceeded to rejoin 11th Bn. Royal Warwickshire Regiment.	

Army Form C. 2118.

WAR DIARY
or
INTELLIGENCE SUMMARY.
(Erase heading not required.)

Instructions regarding War Diaries and Intelligence Summaries are contained in F. S. Regs., Part II. and the Staff Manual respectively. Title pages will be prepared in manuscript.

Place	Date	Hour	Summary of Events and Information	Remarks and references to Appendices
In the Line	30th Nov 1917		Battalion still in line. Nothing of importance occurred during past 24 hours. Following Officers were invalided to U.K. sick during the month. 2/Lt D.H. Batty, H.A. Gates and H.M. Smyth. 1 Other Rank Wounded.	

H.A. Hanley Lieut Col
Comdg 17th Middlesex Regt.

3-12-17

WAR DIARY
INTELLIGENCE SUMMARY
(Erase heading not required.)

Army Form C. 2118.

4 Trench [?]

Place	Date	Hour	Summary of Events and Information	Remarks and references to Appendices
In the line	Dec. 1.	Sh. 28. T. 32. C.	Bn. still in line (HOOGE BEKE SECTOR) and holding left outpost about R.I.B. C.O's Conference at Brigade to discuss re-manning 37 the outpost line. 2Lt. MARSHALL proceeded to 2nd Army Musketry School	
	2.		Still in line – a quiet day. 1. O.R. killed.	
	3.		Still in line - MAJOR P. GROVE WHITE rejoined from 11th WARWICKS	
	4.		do. A quiet day.	
	5.		Bn. relieved by 10th LOYAL NORTH LANCS, proceeded to billets at RIDGEWOOD by train from SPOIL BANK. Relief complete 8. p.m.	
	6.		Batn. bathed at SIEGE FARM BATHS _ LT. F. C. MORRISON proceeded to 37th DIV. ROAD COY.	
	7.		RIDGEWOOD_ Working parties carried out during the day. 2Lt. T. R. SELFE and 2Lt. F. W. ELLIOTT joined Bn.	
	8.		RIDGEWOOD - Carried on working parties. LTS. F. S. WHITLOCK and	

WAR DIARY
or
INTELLIGENCE SUMMARY.
(Erase heading not required.)

Army Form C. 2118.

Place	Date	Hour	Summary of Events and Information	Remarks and references to Appendixes
	9		J.T.H. HODGSON proceeded on leave. LT. G.S. SUTHERLAND rejoined from leave.	
RIDGEWOOD	10		Bn. carried out working parties. - CAPT. BRODIE V.C. called (Brigade Major) called to say good bye. LT. F.T. MOORAT joined Bn. 2nd LT. P.H. STEELE wounded while 1/0 of working party.	
RIDGEWOOD	11		Bn. on working parties. G.O.C. 37 Division visited camp in the morning.	
RIDGEWOOD	12		REV. DOUGLAS. C.J.E. Chaplain, joined the Bn. Working Parties. 2nd LT. G. N. VINER joined the Bn. from 1st Bn. Middx. appointed ASST. ADJUTANT.	
RIDGEWOOD	13		Lecture by DIVISIONAL GAS OFFICER to officers of Bn. in the morning - in the afternoon Bn. marched via HALFEDAST and LA CLYTTE to CURRAGH CAMP	
CURRAGH CAMP.	14		do. Working parties	
	15		do. By/Brigadier & Brig. Major visited camp in the morning and inspected the model map.	

WAR DIARY
or
INTELLIGENCE SUMMARY.
(Erase heading not required.)

Army Form C. 2118.

Place	Date	Hour	Summary of Events and Information	Remarks and references to Appendices
CURRAGH CAMP	16		All denominations attended church services at 10 am.	
CURRAGH CAMP	17		Two Companys on miniature range during morning – Performance by the Bn. CONCERT PARTY in the evening.	
CURRAGH CAMP	18		Training C & D Coys on range – C.O. and Adjt. attended demonstration at Brigade School – G.O.C. of 37th DIVISION visited the camp during the morning	
CURRAGH CAMP	19		Work done on camp and other camps in the vicinity. C.O.'s conference at Brigade at 4 pm.	
CURRAGH CAMP	20		Work on camp – Officers conference on Trench routine etc. Daily foot treatment against its prevention of Trench foot has been carried out daily throughout this week.	
	21		Bn. paraded for trenches at 12.20 pm and entrained at 1.4 CAMP T. for STOIR BATT. Arrived at STOIR 13 HRR at 2.30 pm and relieved 13th K.R.R. in left (Corkscrew)	
In the line	22		S. Maston quiet –	

WAR DIARY or INTELLIGENCE SUMMARY

Army Form C. 2118.

Instructions regarding War Diaries and Intelligence Summaries are contained in F. S. Regs., Part II. and the Staff Manual respectively. Title pages will be prepared in manuscript.

Place	Date	Hour	Summary of Events and Information	Remarks and references to Appendices
In the line	Dec. 23		Situation quiet. 2nd Lt. POE. U.S.A. Army spent day with Bn.	
	24		do. A German aeroplane dropped down in flames near our lines.	
	25		do.	
	26		do. Heavy (?) snow storms and freezing winds.	
	27		do. Another walk heavily shelled with GAS in the evening. Support Company moved back to MILL 60 owing to the presence of GAS in YSULIER WALK. — The BRIGADE GAS OFFICER – 2nd LT. O'DEA visited the Bn.	
	28		In the line – 2nd LT. CHAUNDY proceeded an Intelligence Course at England. CAPT. SCHOFIELD proceeded an Intelligence Course at IX Corps School. 2nd LT. MINER taking over his Intelligence duties. 2nd LT. SUTHERLAND proceeded on a 10 days Course at IX Corps School.	
	29		Bn. was relieved by the 10th Bn. 40th NORTH HANTS. and moved to dug outs at SPOIL BANK. The relief was completed without a single casualty.	
	30		At SPOIL BANK. 2nd Lt. BENDA joined the Bn. and posted to "A" Coy. CAPT. MARTIN, R.A.M.C. went to Hospital (sick)	

WAR DIARY
INTELLIGENCE SUMMARY

Place	Date	Hour	Summary of Events and Information	Remarks and references to Appendices
	Dec. 31.		SPOIL BANK – The morning was spent by the men, at the BRASSERIE baths and in the afternoon one or two working parties were found. The O.O. and Asst. Adjt. visited the 63rd Bde at RIDGE WOOD and the 112th Bde at LOCK 8 on the YPRES-COMINES CANAL. CAPT. W.A. MILNER R.A.M.C. (T.) joined the Bn. from 50th FIELD AMBULANCE: vice CAPT. MARTIN. R.A.M.C. sick	

5-1-18

A.a. Hunter Lt Col
4th Middlesex Regt

63rd Brigade.
37th Division.

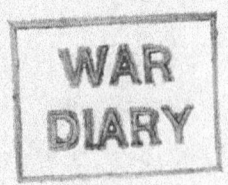

4th BATTALION

THE MIDDLESEX REGIMENT.

JANUARY 1918

Army Form C. 2118
4 Middlesex Rgt 37

WAR DIARY
or
INTELLIGENCE SUMMARY
(Erase heading not required.)

Place	Date	Hour	Summary of Events and Information	Remarks and references to Appendices
In the field	1918 Jan 1st		SPOIL BANK. Working Parties were found by the Bn. Parties of Officers and N.C.O's were sent to reconnoitre various approaches to the front line in case of attack, also positions giving cover and places suitable for strong points. A large magazine dump was placed opposite SPOIL BANK for the use of the Bn. in case of an attack.	
	2		SPOIL BANK. The usual working parties were found also special working parties for the firing of gas blankets throughout the tunnels in SPOIL BANK.	
	3		SPOIL BANK. Working Parties as usual, men still being sent down to the Field Ambulance suffering from the delayed action of mustard gas. 2Lt. HEARMAN and 2Lt. HARRINGTON joined the Bn. on this day.	
	4		SPOIL BANK. Working Parties as usual. A few gas shells were dropped in the vicinity but did not do any damage. Two working parties were delayed and eventually turned back owing to the heavy shelling of tramway tracks and dumps near the front line. Bn. received orders to move to CURRAGH CAMP on the 5th inst.	

WAR DIARY or INTELLIGENCE SUMMARY

Place	Date	Hour	Summary of Events and Information	Remarks and references to Appendices
Little Fish Lake	1918 Jan. 5		SOIL BANK. Working Parties as usual. Bn. moved to CURRAGH CAMP at 2 pm by light railway. Bn. was relieved by 11th WARWICK REGT.	
	6.		CURRAGH CAMP. Working Parties as usual. Severe frost makes transport very difficult.	
	7.		CURRAGH CAMP. Commanding Officer proceeded on short leave to England. A draft of 18 O.R's under 2Lt DEVAH was detailed to proceed to LOCRE and take charge of P. of W. Camp filled with Chinese Labourers. The severe frost still continues.	
	8.		CURRAGH CAMP. No working parties to-day, as the Bn. left this day on XMAS DAY – Snow fell heavily during the night and the whole Bn. was employed during the morning in clearing the roads & entrances to the huts. XMAS Dinners were served at 2 pm, and the various Companies were visited by MAJOR GROVE-WHITE, Acting Adjt and Quartermaster. An impromptu concert was held in the Sergeants mess in the evening.	
	9		CURRAGH CAMP. The C.O visited and inspected all the huts and	

WAR DIARY
INTELLIGENCE SUMMARY
(Erase heading not required.)

Army Form C. 2118.

Place	Date	Hour	Summary of Events and Information	Remarks and references to Appendices
	1918 Jan. 9.		equipment of every man in Bn. Work carried out on improving of the camp and the Steam baths in camp were tested for the first time.	
	10		CURRAGH CAMP. Bathing Parties up the line are resumed — the Steam baths are much appreciated by the men.	
	11		CURRAGH CAMP. Preparations were made for the move into DICKEBUSCH. The Bn. built a magazine hut also fixed window screens for every hut in the camp — Bn. moved to DICKEBUSCH by route march at 12 noon arrived at billets at 1.30 pm. Billets very poor owing to the chilled condition of the village.	
	12		DICKEBUSCH. The day was spent in cleaning the billets which were very dirty and constructing latrines — LT. IRWIN was transferred to the base for defective vision — he had served with this Bn. for a year & a half.	
	13		DICKEBUSCH. Working parties wiring the Corps line — Owing to a sudden thaw the roads are in a very bad condition.	
	14		DICKEBUSCH. Working Parties as usual — owing to the mud the parties have to proceed in Snow boots. The Brigadier General visited the C.O.	

Place	Date	Hour	Summary of Events and Information	Remarks and references to Appendices
DICKEBUSCH	1919 Jan.15.		No working parties to-day. CAPTAIN JAMESON and LT. ANDRAE proceeded on short leave to England. CAPTAIN and LT. proceeded on the 14th inst. Work carried out on billets and clearing away of rubbish. A large amount of salvage was found in the village.	
DICKEBUSCH	16		Working parties proceeded by lorry to the Capra line owing it to the collapse of the railway from the thaw. The Divisional Commander visited the billets of the Bn.	
DICKEBUSCH	17		Working Parties as usual. The Brigade School by-named including 2 Lt. YATES, Lt. ODLING and the R.S.M. B.M. Concert Party gave a concert in the Church Army Hut.	
DICKEBUSCH	18		Working parties as usual, a conference of C. O's of the Brigade and the Brigadier General took place in "Adolpha Offensivo" Mess. B.N. gave a concert for the benefit of the Church Army Hut.	
DICKEBUSCH	19		Working Parties as usual, a drying room was made for the purpose of drying the mens Coats, jackets and puttees. Whilst they returned off working parties. 4 men were killed and 2	

WAR DIARY
or
INTELLIGENCE SUMMARY.

Army Form C. 2118.

Place	Date	Hour	Summary of Events and Information	Remarks and references to Appendices
	1918			
	Jan 19		Wounded on a working party at INVERNESS COPSE, south of the MENIN ROAD. This was the first casualty while the Bn. was up in this area.	
	20		DICKEBUSCHE. Working Parties as usual. CAPTAIN NEWMAN returned from leave. Preparations for move to LA BELLE HOTESSE.	
	21		DICKEBUSCH. Bn. moved at 1 pm by rail to EBBLINGHAM & LA BELLE HOTESSE. STATION and from there by route march to LA BELLE HOTESSE. arriving at billets which were very excellent but comfortable at 5.30 hrs. We were relieved from DICKEBUSCH by 9th EAST LANCS REGT. CAPTAIN SCHOFIELD and LT. ODLING proceeded on leave to England.	
	22		LA BELLE HOTESSE. MAJOR GROVEWHITE and Adjt and Quartermaster inspected all billets. It takes two hours to go round them mounted. Bn. spent the day in cleaning up equipment and improving general turnout.	
	23		LA BELLE HOTESSE. The Bn. had baths at BLARINGHAM and a clean change of clothing. Draft of 85 O.R's arrived, composed of 6 Category "B" men, 13 returned from hospital etc and 66 many boys of about 19 years, will about 3 months training.	

Army Form C. 2118.

WAR DIARY
or
INTELLIGENCE SUMMARY.
(Erase heading not required.)

Place	Date	Hour	Summary of Events and Information	Remarks and references to Appendices
	1918			
LA BELLE HOTESSE	Jan 24		MAJOR GROVE WHITE inspected the Bn during the morning and the remainder of the morning was devoted to Coy & Coy from Training. Football matches were carried out between Companies during the afternoon. The Divisional Cinema gave a two hours entertainment in the Recreation Hut.	
LA BELLE HOTESSE	25		Bn proceeded on route march to LYNDE - SERCUS - WALLON CAPEL and back to billets. Football between the Companies during the afternoon also a cross country run for Headquarters Company.	
LA BELLE HOTESSE	26		Party of 6 OR's proceeded to ARQUES to be decorated by the Army Commander. Lt.Col. H.A.O. HANKEY D.S.O. M.C. returned from short leave to England on 25th inst. A Regain Demonstration was held in the Recreation Hut for Officers and N.C.O's. Off Company Officers & trained under their respective specialist officers. Football between Companies and Platoons during the afternoon.	

T2134. Wt. W708—776. 500000. 4/15. Sir J. C. & S.

Place	Date	Hour	Summary of Events and Information	Remarks and references to Appendices
	1918 Jan 27.		LA BELLE HOTESSE. Puturation Commands instructions were made for the Divisional Commander on Monday. The Commanding Officer & Adjt. inspected all Coys and Readings during the afternoon. Service for all denominations were held during the day in the Recreation Hut.	
	28		LA BELLE HOTESSE. The Divisional Commander, MAJOR GENERAL H. B. WILLIAMS - C.B. D.S.O. of 37th Division accompanied by BRIGADIER GENERAL E. R. CHELLENOR D.S.O. C.M.G. and staff of 63rd Infantry Brigade inspected the Bn. at 12 noon - on a field behind the Transport lines. The Bn. mustered 406 - including officers and men. MAJOR GROVE WHITE and 2nd LT. DEVAR proceeded on Short leave to England. Orest in Rec. Hut & Divisional Entertainers.	
	29		LA BELLE HOTESSE. Commanding Officer and Adjutant inspected the Lewis Gunners on Range - and the Bn. attended a Gas Demonstration during the morning - Inoculation of the Bn. commenced in the afternoon. Commanding Officer had conference with Coy Comdrs. re Training.	1

Army Form C. 2118.

WAR DIARY
or
INTELLIGENCE SUMMARY.
(Erase heading not required.)

Place	Date	Hour	Summary of Events and Information	Remarks and references to Appendices
	1918 Jan 30		LA BELLE HOTESSE. Company Training. All specialists under their respective Specialist Officers. Blankets of the Bn. were disinfected. All the Officers carried out a revolver shoot during the afternoon. Football Match between Officers v. N.C.O's. Result - Draw. MAJOR COURKIETTE proceeded on short leave to England.	
	31.		LA BELLE HOTESSE - Preparations for a demonstration with Contact Aeroplane. Company Training carried out during day and range practices. Football in the afternoon.	

Alexander
Lieut. Colonel,
Commanding A/Bn. Middlesex Regiment.

63rd Brigade.
37th Division.

4th BATTALION

THE MIDDLESEX REGIMENT.

FEBRUARY 1918

WAR DIARY
or
INTELLIGENCE SUMMARY
(Erase heading not required.)

Army Form C. 2118.

Vol 43

Place	Date	Hour	Summary of Events and Information	Remarks and references to Appendices
In the field Loos	1/2/18		LA BELLE HOTESSE. A contact aeroplane was arranged for by Bde. The afternoon but was cancelled owing to unfavourable weather conditions with the result that the majority of the men was wasted. The latter part of the afternoon was taken up on the range. On the afternoon a practice alarm took place, the Battalion being ready to march off 50 minutes from the time of the order being given. Owing to completion took place in the presence of the C.O.	Mission 59
	2/2/18		Coys. bathed at Bethune. Motor 'buses were supplied in the morning, the C.O. judged the platoon games and chose the best for the Bde. Competition. In the afternoon the final for part of B & C Coys. were concluded.	
	3/2/18		Church parade in the recreation hut at 11.30 a.m. Owing to the limited accommodation, only 30 per Coy. could attend.	
	4/2/18		Usual training in the morning. 4 officers attended a demonstration at the Divl. Gympie School. Bde. Transport Competition in the morning in which the Bn. came out first. The following Cabs. under Capt. JAMIESON 2nd Lieut. GOODWIN C.S.M. PINKSON, proceeded to Belgian Croix de Guerre.	

WAR DIARY or INTELLIGENCE SUMMARY

Army Form C. 2118.

Place	Date	Hour	Summary of Events and Information	Remarks and references to Appendices
In the Field	5/2/18		Usual Training by Coys. 2 Officers & 5 NCOs attended a demonstration at Tank Corps Gunnery School. Brigade competition for scouts & runners; the Bn. failed by one mark to receive first place.	Ref. HAZEBROUCK 5A.
	6/2/18		Aeroplane contact plane again postponed at the last moment. Reformening & message writing scheme for Officers. Brigade Board competition in which the Bn. took 2nd place. The 10th York Lancs were broken up & the rates reduced to three Bns.	
	7/2/18		Comrade arranged for the morning could not take place owing to the refusal of the interpreter to open the field to be used, nor be seen by Capt. while the C.O. inspected at 10.30 a.m. The C.O. held a conference of Coy. Commanders to discuss the situation & draft of 300 subjects from the 11 (S) Bn. The Lightning competition resulted: 1st west 50%. Lincoln 25%. Riddlesett 55%. the Bn. there was no protest due to the fact that the Bn. had no signalling officer in Lucerne. In the Role intra-platoon football competition 10.10 Platoon beat the 6 Zoo 11 B. by 3-1. Capt. SCHOFIELD & E. ODLING-SMEE on leave.	
	8/2/18		A Lewis Gun competition was washed out owing to the violence of weather. Draft from 11th Bn. arrived in being & were posted to Coys. Platoon Boxing competition took place in the afternoon. Also Lecture by the Divn S.O. at SERUS was attended by the C.O. & adjt. & other officers. The following officers arrived Capt. H.A. Maynard M.C. Capt. E. Poole, Lt. E.C. Hopfield, 2/Lt. F. Hon., 2/Lt. E.G. Shaker & 2/Lt. J. Hibbert. 2/Lt. F. Simm's 227 O.R.	

2353 Wt. W2544/1454 700,000 5/15 D.D.&L. A.D.S.S./Forms/C. 2118.

Army Form C. 2118.

WAR DIARY
or
INTELLIGENCE SUMMARY.
(Erase heading not required.)

Instructions regarding War Diaries and Intelligence Summaries are contained in F.S. Regs., Part II. and the Staff Manual respectively. Title pages will be prepared in manuscript.

Place	Date	Hour	Summary of Events and Information	Remarks and references to Appendices
On the Field	9/2/18		LA BELLE HOTESSE. Bn. H.Q. competition took place in which the Bn. were not lucky. Bar. held Sports in the afternoon. The C.O. attended a Bde. Conference at Bde. H.Q. The Allouarea Boys gave a good show in the evening and were enjoyed by the Brigadier. Brigadier & Brigade-Major, Experian R.M.C. took over A Coy.	War Ref. Appendix 5A.
	10/2/18		Went training by Coy's. In the afternoon, 10 platoon took the field & the Bn. interplatoon football competition. 9 Cy. R.N.F. The winners proved Lieutenant Corp. PROBY'S & took over C Coy.	
	11/2/18		A football match arranged with the Yeomen at SERCUS, but the latter failed to turn up. Lieut. C.T.S. HOLCOMBE M.C. C/o of the 11th Bn. paid a visit to the C.O.	
	12/2/18		Coy's. were trained for protection against treach- feet. B & C Coys. played a Soccer match which was entered too owing to two back being furnished accompanied for officers. Lieut. Pierce & Lieut. evening. LTS. FENN & MORRISON went on leave.	
	13/2/18		The day was spent by the Bn. in clearing up in readiness for the next day's move to odinq & 2/0. YATES & Jackson Pearson proceeded to Brigade School. LT. MITCHELL to F.A. act.	

J. MITCHELL

Army Form C. 2118.

WAR DIARY
or
INTELLIGENCE SUMMARY.

(Erase heading not required.)

Instructions regarding War Diaries and Intelligence Summaries are contained in F. S. Regs., Part II. and the Staff Manual respectively. Title pages will be prepared in manuscript.

Place	Date	Hour	Summary of Events and Information	Remarks and references to Appendices
In the Field				
LA BELLE HOTESSE	4/2/18	8.45 am	Bazalon proceeded by march route to EBBLINGHEM STA. To entrain for DICKEBUSCH. 2/Lieut. P.W. ELLIOT acted as Entraining Officer.- Bn. left EBBLINGHEM HAZEBROUCK at 11.5 am arriving at DICKEBUSCH at 2 p.m.- Bn. marched to billets in NAPIQUET CAMP.- Lieut. A.N. KAIBER & 2/Lieut. J.E. HARRINGTON went up to reconnoitre Stony Point 1 + 2, E. of MOUNT SORREL.- 2/Lieut. T. DEVAL returned from leave.- 2/Lieut. C.G. SPENDING proceeded on Intelligence Course at Hd. Army School.- Maj. R. GROVE WHITE returned from leave.-	Ref.
DICKEBUSCH	15/2/18		Bn. paraded at 2.50 pm to march to MOUNT SORREL via KRUISSTRAAT HOEK, SUMMER CORNER, TRANSPORT FARM & LOMBSTON SIDING, where guides of the R.R. Regt. (Kildare) Regt. were met, into conducted the Bn. to positions in support to right Bde. viz H.Q. in C. Coy. CANADA TUNNELS, Disp. on MT. SORREL, B Coy at HEDGE ST. TUNNELS, A Coy in Dugouts in SWAN'S BUSY FOREST. Relief complete at 3 p.m.- Companies went into Tunnels 100 strong; the balance proceeding under 2/Lieut. T. DEVAL to ALBERTA CAMP.- 2/Lieut. F.F. MARSHALL accompanied the party to proceed to England on leave.- 2/Lieut. V.R. ROSS appointed Town Major in CANADA TUNNELS.- 2/Lieut. S.R. McCARTHY MO attached Bn. joined from Base.	Ref. Sheet 28.
MOUNT SORREL	16/2/18		Day spent in setting the Tunnels occupies in order & in settling into the new Sector. The Commanding Officer Inspected the Companies & defence dispositions & looked the advanced Points of A Coy. by night.	

2353 Wt. W2544/1454 700,000 5/15 D.D.&L. A.D.S.S./Forms/C. 2118.

Army Form C. 2118.

WAR DIARY
or
INTELLIGENCE SUMMARY.
(Erase heading not required.)

Instructions regarding War Diaries and Intelligence Summaries are contained in F.S. Regs., Part II and the Staff Manual respectively. Title pages will be prepared in manuscript.

Place	Date	Hour	Summary of Events and Information	Remarks and references to Appendices
In the Field MOUNT SORREL	17/3/18		C.O. & Coy. Commrs. proceeded to Transport Lines for dinner. Lieut. Scammell & 20 O.Rs. reported to this Bn. No. 9 Tying Point attending Signalers Course. (Charge). Lieut. G.S. Sutherland reported from Signal Course. (Charge). Capt. C.R. Newman took over duties of 2nd Bn. Imperor. 1 Officer & Coy. recommerced night patrol in Bn. dispositions. (2Lt. SOMERSETT L.)	Ref. Sheet 28.
do.	18/3/18		2Lieut. R.I. MULLIGAN returned from II Corps School. 2Lieut. E.A. HANNING U.S. Army posted to Bn. for instructional purposes.—Considerable activity on the part of enemy heavy artillery this day.	
do.	19/3/18		2Lieut. C. GAPIERCE returned from II Corps Musketry School. Bn. engaged in erecting wire entanglement in rear of Bn. SORREL- CO. 2 Lt. G.S. SUTHERLAND reconnoitred support & right front Bn. (2Lt. SOMERSETT L.) Casualty: 1 wounded A Coy. balloon aw. another.	
do.	20/3/18		Wiring in front Mt. SORREL continued 2 tasks completed. Lts. ANDREWS proceeded to local support for leave. Capt. Greene & 2 Sergeants & other ranks commenced Lewis Box Course with details 51st & other Bdes. from 1 platoon Y block Miniature Rifle at X.19.d.50. 2 Coy. relieved D Coy. left front coy in 8.11.C.K.TR. C Coy. cont. relief ATR SQUARE & Coy. right & that lite book & Coy. support on SENTILL & PALESTINE R TRs. on billets on BASS rob. Relief complete 10.30 P.M.	
do.	21/3/18		Digging commenced on trench from Hd. to B Coy Patrols of O/DONNELL & Pte ELLIOT.— Casualties: 3 killed. 1 wounded. Grayes fell in Wo.2 post. of Q Coy.	

WAR DIARY
or
INTELLIGENCE SUMMARY.
(Erase heading not required.)

Army Form C. 2118.

Place	Date	Hour	Summary of Events and Information	Remarks and references to Appendices
In the Field	22/2/18		O.C. Australian Bath. overnight advised C. of G. to draw cooperation. Hrs. STEWART & ELMORE relieved from Leave. B Coy. relieved by C. Coy. 1 killed 30 M.G.Cans on fatigue relieved by Canadian 118th Bn. making our battalion front for C. of G. B.C.) of Patrols by Hrs. KLAIBER & ELMORE	
	23/2		Divisional General visited Bn HQ. - S.O.S. arrangements ventilated at dusk with green rocket. Patrol by 2/Lt. HOOLIVIN Cancelled. 1 Killed. 2 wounded. 2/Lt. ELLIOT & STEWART did a daylight patrol. Crawling out to an old enemy trench on Road signers 1 edge & obtaining a quantity of information. Visit from Brigade Major.	
	24/2		2/Lts. CHRUNDAY returned from good leave. 2/Lt. POWELL & MILLIGAN went to detail to proceed on leave. 2/Lt. SWAN went down to proceed on Course (Front Duties) Canadiers. 1 wounded. C Coy. at 3 P.M. enemy put down sharp barrage on battalion sector. Patrol by 2/Lt. STEWART.	
	25/2		Enemy repeated barrage at 3 P.M. & apparently attempted raid on right Hist. from B.G.G.S. XXII (Corps) G.S.O.2. 3rd Division of Ree Major Greens White & L. Sutherland went down in attendance to take over Camp Casualties. Relieved by 2/R Lincolns. Bn. marched to billets in Scottish Wood Camp, where the men were comfortably accommodated. Hrs. BLOY, MILLIGAN & POWELL leave to England.	

Army Form C. 2118.

WAR DIARY
or
INTELLIGENCE SUMMARY.
(Erase heading not required.)

Instructions regarding War Diaries and Intelligence Summaries are contained in F.S. Regs., Part II and the Staff Manual respectively. Title pages will be prepared in manuscript.

Place	Date	Hour	Summary of Events and Information	Remarks and references to Appendices
In the Field	26/2/18		Day spent in cleaning up. C.O. attended Conference at Bde. H.Q. Lt. SPALDING returned from Intelligence Course.	
	27/2		Bn. worked on camp. Officers attended bomb exhibition. Capt. MAYNARD M.C. reported to Bde. H.Q. to attend Brigade Major. H. BRANHOUSE took over A Coy. Bn. bathed at Divnl. Baths. L.t MILLIANS returned from Bde. Conference of Coy. Commanders at Bn. H.Q rs at 5.30 p.m. referenced the probability of immediate action (a position stated that the enemy would attack on the morning of the 28th.)	
	28/2		B SUTHERLAND left for 6 month duty tour of England. Details under Capt. SMITH M.C. returned to Bn. covering parties under 2/Lt KRAUSER & 2/Lt MULLINS & 2/Lt MORRICHMAR. 2/Lts PENN & MORYOSEPH returned from leave. 2/Lt PENN took over A Coy. Bn. paraded at 10.15 a.m. to practice forming up on battle formation. D Coy practised for attack of Contemptate.	
			Total Casualties for February 1918: O.R. 5 killed, 14 wounded.	

Heverberley
Lieut. Colonel,
Commanding 4/Bn. Middlesex Regiment.

63rd Brigade.
37th Division.

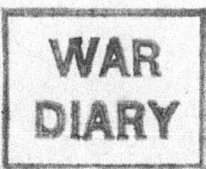

4th BATTALION

THE MIDDLESEX REGIMENT.

MARCH 1918

WAR DIARY or INTELLIGENCE SUMMARY

Army Form C. 2118.

4 Middlesex R

Place	Date	Hour	Summary of Events and Information	Remarks and references to Appendices
In the Field	1/3/18		Bn. relieved 21st Somerset L.I. in CANADA TUNNELS in support. H.Q. and D Coy. in the Tunnels, C on Mt. SORREL, B at HEDGE ST. TUNNEL Ref. Bn. Hd. Qrs. at S.P. 1 & 2. Details remained in reserve 25/3 Map sheet 28. Btn. at SCOTTISH WOOD Camp. Capt. SCHOFIELD remained back for H.Q. Conwe & Lt. WILLIAMS & 2/Lt. PIERCE for leave.	
	2/3/18		Snow fell this day. The men's feet were treated. 2/Lt V.M. HEDLEY joined from F.A. relieved from 182 Bn. Coy. being evacuated at present. Mt SORREL & surrounding area forward.	
	3/3/18		Foot treatment continued. Conference at Bn. H.Q. respecting contemplated raid. Ha RAMBRE proceeded to Jaucourt Tunnel salvage & working parties.	
	4/3/18		Usual routine in support. 18 Lancashire went over. Enemy SOS signal to enemy barrier at night. The night between 4th & 5th about this period difficulty was experienced in carrying out tasks.	
	5/3/18		The Brigadier visited the Battalion in the morning. Bn. proceeded to front line at dusk & relieved 7th Somerset L.I. D,C & A Coys. in front line B Coy. in support. Lt. WILKINS, 2/Lt. PIERCE & Capt. McKAY proceeded on leave to England. Relief complete 11 p.m.	

Army Form C. 2118.

WAR DIARY
or
INTELLIGENCE SUMMARY.
(Erase heading not required.)

Instructions regarding War Diaries and Intelligence Summaries are contained in F. S. Regs., Part II. and the Staff Manual respectively. Title pages will be prepared in manuscript.

Place	Date	Hour	Summary of Events and Information	Remarks and references to Appendices
In The Field	6/3/18		Slight gas bombardment during the morning. Enemy artillery very active. 2Lt. RAY, STUART, Sgt. CLARK & Pte. BUTLER crawled into the enemy lines & captured a Sergt. Major & orderly of the 96 N.R. They were out 4 hours. The Bn. & Lt. STUART in particular, received congratulatory messages from the G.O.C. Division & Brigade.	Shoot 2Lt. J.
	7/3/18		More gas this day. Bn. received warning of expected attack & stood to. Capt VINER returned from leave (9) & took over Adjutancy again. Capt. NEWMAN went down for interview at M.G.O. Hdqrs. to L.Pk. & M.O.Cam went down to detail suffering from Colic.	
	8/3/18		Bombardment of our Trenches from 9.30 p.m. till 5.30 p.m. They then intense & enemy attacked on our left. S.O.S. sent up at 5.30 p.m. & answered in 2 mins. by our artillery who put down a good heavy barrage. Our trenches were badly damaged. Casualties:- No. 1. Pte. HEDLEY killed by Snipers, 10.R killed: 16 wounded: 41, missing: 3. 2 platoons of the SOMERSET L.I. & Hd.Bn. details reinforced at dusk. 3 L.Gs were destroyed. The men behaved splendidly & worked hard during the night to repair the trenches. One direct hit was obtained on Bn. H.Q. but no damage done. The Transport mules arrived at the usual time without interference.	

Army Form C. 2118.

WAR DIARY
or
INTELLIGENCE SUMMARY.
(Erase heading not required.)

Instructions regarding War Diaries and Intelligence Summaries are contained in F. S. Regs. Part II. and the Staff Manual respectively. Title pages will be prepared in manuscript.

Place	Date	Hour	Summary of Events and Information	Remarks and references to Appendices
In the Field	9/3/18		A fairly quiet day. News came that the attack on our left was a complete failure. Br. relieved by 5th Kens. to proceeded to trench position relieving Pte. Somerset vij: H.Q. & D.Coy. in CANADA Tunnels, A.Coy. Mt. SOPPEL, B.Coy. HEDGE ST. Tunnels, C.Coy. R.I.D.R. No. 1 & 2 Strong Points. Mt. SOPPEL was shelled with heavies & gas cover of which penetrated the Tunnels at Bo. Resp'rs etc. were worn. 2Lt. MARSHALL back from leave. 2Lts. SPALDING & MOORWIN proceeded to F.A. for R.F.C. eyesight test.	Ref. Sheet 28.J
	10/3/18		Visit from Brig.-General E. CHALLENOR. The position on Mt. SOPPEL was shelled. Casualties: 1 killed & P.J. DONOVAN. An American Gas Officer, B.R. NEWMAN, was attached to A Coy. for twenty Capt. B.R. NEWMAN took over C Coy. Battn. Provided men for working-parties. Ref. eyesight test, 2Lt MOORWIN passed out the 2Lt SPALDING failed on colour.	
	11/3/18	1	A certain amount of gas-shells on our position. 2Lts ELLIOT & SPALDING & Capt. PROCTER went down for Conv. Lt. FENN & MORJOSEPH to hospital sick.	
	12/3/18		Whitmore to back areas for Cdn. Canteen & on leave in CANADA Tunnel. Usual working-parties provided. D.Coy. relieved C.Coy. in R.I.A.D.R. - Lt. MITCHELL (Gas officer) returned from hospital.	

WAR DIARY or INTELLIGENCE SUMMARY

Army Form C. 2118.

Place	Date	Hour	Summary of Events and Information	Remarks and references to Appendices
In the Field	13/3/18		MT. SORREL. Usual routine in support, cooking & salvage parties provided. 2nd in command proceeded to England for M.G.C. Capt. MAYNARD M.C. from Brigade to Divisional school for course by the O.C. school. Hon. SHIEL, Lieut MULLIGAN back from leave. Capt. JAMIESON & concert party proceeded to SCOTTISH WOOD camp & prepared a show. The whole Battn. was working including the officers, servants who presented a evening party.	Sheet 29
	14/3/18		C Coy under Capt. BR. NEWMAN proceeded to SCOTTISH WOOD to work on right leave the path at ZILLEBEKE BUND were relieved. Usual work.	
	15/3/18		Bn. was relieved by 5th Lincolns & proceeded to Reserve at SCOTTISH WOOD. Bn. travelled by train from MANOR HALT.	
	16/3/18		Usual routine in reserve i.e. work on camp by day & working parties to front line at night. Capt. SCHOFIELD & Lt. MOORAT & Lt. HARRINGTON back from course.	
	17/3/18		Conference of Coy. Commanders about moving arrangements. Maj. P. GROVE-WHITE proceeded to gas course at OXELAERE. Capt. J.P. JAMIESON went to CAPRIS to study methods of dealing with Salvage & unearthen.	
	18/3/18		C.O. proceeded at a F.G.C.M. Battn. to attended a group of gas demonstration by the D.G.O. Hon. BENDA & ELMORE reconnoitred route to left of Centre Battn. Bde. Ht. BENDA answered by a whole while in this mission.	

Army Form C. 2118.

WAR DIARY
or
INTELLIGENCE SUMMARY.
(Erase heading not required.)

Instructions regarding War Diaries and Intelligence Summaries are contained in F.S. Regs., Part II. and the Staff Manual respectively. Title pages will be prepared in manuscript.

Place	Date	Hour	Summary of Events and Information	Remarks and references to Appendices
In the field.	19/3/18		SCOTTSWOOD. Rain prevented work on the camp. The men's feet were treated with castor oil preparator. Chas. BRENNAN proceeded to England to be transferred to M.G.C.	Sheet 27
	20/3/18		The Intelligence Officer attended an Interview with the Divnl. General ref. enfying etc. as N.R.M. 2 detached 50+ from HR now having to work under posters provided	
	21/3/18		Work on camp during the morning. Coy Commander's conference regarding relief. Officers & 1 NCO per Coy & HQ reconnoitred front of Bn. Bn. proceeded by train from VYVERHOEK at 7.30 pm to MAJOR HART Thence by march to front life to relieve 5th SOMERSETS Relief complete midnight disposition: Left- D Coy. Centre- B Coy. Right- A Coy. Support- C Coy. 5th WILTSHIRES & MIDDX relieved our centre & left Coys respectively. 2nd army Boundary General course respectively.	
	22/3/18		The Brigadier & Capt. MAYNARD MO visited Bn. H.Q. Pte 604 STUART, ELMORE & MILLICAN — the MILLICAN was hit by a M.G. bullet & died on the way to the ADS. at CANADA tunnels.	
	23/3/18		Patrol by Lt. STUART to catch a prisoner sighted by enemy. Pte. 916 BAIRD was too weak enemy could see guns.	
	24/3/18		All leave stopped on account of German attack between OISE & St Quentin. Sundry orders received ref. restoration of Divisional front. R.C. Capt. & I.O. spent the morning observing enemy lines. The enemy were quiet except at 47 because	

Army Form C. 2118.

WAR DIARY
or
INTELLIGENCE SUMMARY.
(Erase heading not required.)

Instructions regarding War Diaries and Intelligence Summaries are contained in F. S. Regs., Part II. and the Staff Manual respectively. Title pages will be prepared in manuscript.

Place	Date	Hour	Summary of Events and Information	Remarks and references to Appendices
In the Field.	25/3/18		All were reinspected by O.C. Coy & a report made on it to Brigade. It was detailed to relieve Mr. WEKMAN at Tunnel. Major & Capt. M.G.O. came up to see our position. 2/Lt. BAIRD returned having been stopped at Calais whilst proceeding on leave. Much owing was done. B Coy had a man killed whilst wiring. All officers & ORs returned from course.	HAZEBROUCK S.A.
	26/3/18		Bde Major & G.S.O.3 inspected area. All energies were concentrated in moving this MENOC.	
	27/3/18		Orders received. The entry new Bn. relieve Bn. Bn. & relieve of Hampshire & Land 4/R.Qu. Ber Bn. entrained at SHRAPNEL CORNER & followed to FLETRE marching thence to THIEUSHOEK where billets had been arranged by Mitchell & party. Bn. relieved at 6AM. Transport proceeded by road.	
	28/3/18		C.O. & Adj: rode over to CAESTRE where HQ. the King inspected the entrainment of a Batn. The CO was presented to His Majesty. Valves & other kit was cut down to increase mobility. Lt. MITCHELL & billeting party went on & HAZLE & 28 RANK given charge of Divn. Camp at HAZELE.	
	29/3/18		Bn. paraded at 10AM & marched to FLETRE, embussing there for HOPOUTRE SIDINGS where we entrained & were carried via Hazebrouck, the Train leaving at 12.55 A.M. C Coy. with cookers followed in another Train. Long delays for watering. They then arrived at NOEUDICOURT Team cut to the right of the Batn. Traveled via LILLERS-ST.POL-FREVENT to BOUQUEMAISON arriving at 7.30 P.M. Bn. spent a long stormy harrowing bivouac. The train caused it to get badly Detachment could not be carried out till 3 am owing to congestion of trains in front. Bde School Staff b. Trans. M.G.Bn. joined Bde School Staff who did not rejoin Train until	LENS II.

2353 W⊥ W2544/1454 700,000 5/15 D. D. & L. A.D.S.S./Forms/C. 2118.

WAR DIARY
or
INTELLIGENCE SUMMARY

Army Form C. 2118.

Place	Date	Hour	Summary of Events and Information	Remarks and references to Appendices
In the Field	30/3/18.		After detrainment, Bn was billeted by 2/Lt WILKINS in BOURLEMPTON so that the men could have breakfast. On platoon of "D" Coy entrained the transport. 1 officer & N.C.Os. per Coy L.H.Q. for billeting in HENU. 7 officers & 1 N.C.O. per Coy & H.Q to reconnoitre the kit positions & areas at GOUASTRE & park of JANIN. The tapes reported at 6 a.m. Being the at GOUASTRE where the Brigadier ordered out the arrangements & the party moved back to HENU. The Bath. proceeded by march route via BOISJEAN to HENU where they were billeted, arriving at 10.30am. Casualties 24/3/18.	LENS 11. Sheet 57.
	31/3/18		The C.O. & Signalling Officer & 2 R.O.s per Coy & Transport reported by bus to FONQUEVILLERS to report to G.O.C. 2nd Div. FR Comd Div. FR. C.OM at BITTERMOT FARM. The disposition of the 186th Bde. K.O. at BITTERMOT FARM. The disposition of the 2/4th WEST YORKS. R.B. Bde. in support were taken over. The C.O. & Signalling Officer returned to HENU. The remainder of the replacements remaining in the Line. A number of Easter services were held at HENU.	

Casualties in March 1918:- Officers; killed:- 2/Lt. J.H. HEDLEY
                                              2/Lt. R.I. MILLIGAN
                                    Wounded:- 2/Lt. P. BENDAMIN.

O.R.s: Killed:- 19
          Died of Wds:- 2
          Wounded:- 50

H A Newby
Lt. Col.
Comdg 4th Bn. Middx Regt.

63rd Brigade.
37th Division.

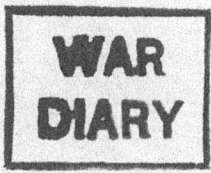

4th BATTALION

THE MIDDLESEX REGIMENT.

APRIL 1918

Army Form C. 2118.

62/37

Vol 45

WAR DIARY or INTELLIGENCE SUMMARY

(Erase heading not required.)

Place	Date	Hour	Summary of Events and Information	Remarks and references to Appendices
In the Field	1/7/16		Bn. relieved 8th Bn. Worcesters, 143rd Inf. Bde, Gen. Division, in support N. of GOMMECOURT. Suffered no cas. to Bn. at FONQUEVILLERS. The Bn. marched from HEBU leaving at 6.30 a.m. & arriving by 11.15 a.m. The Coy Intelligence Officer toured the coln., all the men except 1 platoon of Bn. H.Q. were under cover.	3rd Inf Bde. N.E.
	2/7/16		Details under Major P.GROIKWHITE moved to COISNEUX.	
	3/7/16		C.O. attended conference at Bde Hqrs. at PATIMONT FARM ref. intended attack. Capt. H.A MAYNARD, M.C. took over duties as Staff-Captain. 2nd Lt MARSHALL joined "A" Coy from Details Parties. L.G.O. came up to "A" Lines. 2nd Lt T. SWAN went down to 37 Div. A. R.S. coated watched by the Signaling Officer but operation came over phone as planned.	
	4/7/16		Conference of coll. C.Os. to discuss operations. Shell bombardment of enemy trenches learned. Signaling officers instructed as movements. Intelligence Officer drew rations for and on for Col. TR.	
	5/7/16		Attack by Somerset Yeomanry and 4th Northern Support at 5.30 a.m. had got almost everywhere except in ROSSIGNOL WOOD, but clung doggedly around the attack	

WAR DIARY or INTELLIGENCE SUMMARY

Army Form C. 2118.

Place	Date	Hour	Summary of Events and Information	Remarks and references to Appendices
Tukhe Kale	5/4/18		We tipped some men over original line which told the OC Coy of the Bn. before there were drawn into the line but were not actually engaged. The Co was at Bike Me & the Adj. at Somerset Hotel. The Intelligence Officer then O/Rn CO. TR. & unable to report at HQ of any reinforcements. 9th HARRINGTON Company (Major Speed) k. N. MORRISETT) moved to pontoon & then up the road, they moved later to C Coy HQ & reported to Colonel TROM at Somerset HH. The road reinforced, difficult B Coy were moved back to support at the centre of operation. The other Coys holding the line.	
	6/4/18		A day of rest. The CO & Intelligence Officer temps. could the line. A certain amount of company training was done. Coys. were required to furnish a relief. A quiet day. 9th L. MOORE was killed by a N.C.O. of 13th Bn. K.R.R. & proceed to reserve in Gonne court wood Relief was made very arduous by much heavy rain. Losses are not settled in Tele Car I.	

Army Form C. 2118.

WAR DIARY
or
INTELLIGENCE SUMMARY.
(Erase heading not required.)

Instructions regarding War Diaries and Intelligence Summaries are contained in F. S. Regs., Part II. and the Staff Manual respectively. Title pages will be prepared in manuscript.

Place	Date	Hour	Summary of Events and Information	Remarks and references to Appendices
In the Field	7/4/18		Bn. enjoyed a much needed rest. Felt were rubbed & knees. Knees & refeet got into good working condition again. Congratulatory messages were received from Army & Corps Commanders re operations of 5/4.	
	8/4/18		Baton: Bathed at PONQUEVILLERS. Fives from Brigadier Gen. Commanding meeting ref. next leave.	
	9/4/18		Officers of Regs. & B. at Reconnoitred trenches of 1st ESSEX S. of BUCQUOY. Other Coys. were bivouacked. At daylight Bn. relieved 1st ESSEX. Dispositions. B.C. & Coys. in Front Line, A Coy. in support.	
	10/4/18		Hdqrs. moved to 2 ROSSIGNOL FARM. Great difficulty was found in locating the Coys. owing to blindness & lack of communication.	
	11/4/18		Conference of Brigade Staff & Coo. at B.Hdqrs. re. relief. H.C.O. Intelligence & Signalling Officers recced on invoicing all Coys. Taking 16 Runners.	
	12/4/18		Rossignol Farm. All the morning about 1000 shells mostly heavy. Bn. relieved by 2/5 ROYAL & proceeded to reserve in trenches N. of HEBUTERNE WOOD.	
	13/4/18		Rest & day. C.O. & adj. reconnoitred battle positions in YPRES Line.	

2353 Wt W2544/1454 700,000 5/15 D. D. & L. A.D.S.S./Forms/C. 2118.

WAR DIARY or INTELLIGENCE SUMMARY

Army Form C. 2118.

Place	Date	Hour	Summary of Events and Information	Remarks and references to Appendices
In the Field	14/4/18		Bn. relieved & took over the line. Disposition: A & B in front line. C in support, D in reserve. PWO on guards S. of BIEZ WOOD.	57 D N.E.
	15/4/18		Batn. relieved by 1/5 EAST LANCS. 42nd Div. & marched via SOUASTRE where a cookery provided tea, to HENU. Tents were occupied here.	
	16/4/18		Bn. paraded at 12.10 P.M. & marched to AUTHIE. Tents were erected here in the Chateau Good. Numbers were rather crowded but otherwise comfortable.	
	17/4/18		New Battns. in Active Co. Adj. & 2 i/c B Co. Coy. reconnoitered the forward dispositions to be occupied by the Battn. in case of emergency (people's day). Co. standard scheme (i/rail).	
	18/4/18		Co. Adj. O.i.C. A&D Coy. to & our officers per Coy. recommended purposes his. Co. attended conference at Battn. HQ.	
	19/4/18		Sniping, signalling & Lg. classes began. Coy. practiced themselves & did some hill making.	
	20/4/18		Working party on Red Line (E. of Authie) of 8 officers & 350 men under Capt. F.W. SCHOFIELD. Classes continued.	

Army Form C. 2118.

WAR DIARY
or
INTELLIGENCE SUMMARY.
(Erase heading not required.)

Instructions regarding War Diaries and Intelligence Summaries are contained in F.S. Regs., Part II. and the Staff Manual respectively. Title pages will be prepared in manuscript.

Place	Date	Hour	Summary of Events and Information	Remarks and references to Appendices
In the field.	21/4/18		Parade service C of E in orchard near the Camp. C.O. inspected ½ of the Battn. at 2.15 p.m. C.O. attended conference at Divl. Hdqrs. On 22nd following Officers joined the Battalion: 2/Lt. J. ROSS C Coy. 2/Lt. V. LINDSAY. A Coy. " P. PATER B Coy. " A.M. WILSON. D Coy. " H.R. SUTCLIFFE. A Coy.	Sheet 57
	22/4/18		Clearer (snipers, signallers & L.G.) during the morning. Co 5 p.m. a local conference of Officers & N.C.O's. per Coy. Lt. Hodges. to SOUASTRE whence worked to RETTEMOY to take over dispositions as far as possible of the 15th KOYLI (62nd Div.) They remained in the line.	
	23/4/18		Bn. marched to SOUASTRE halting there for a meal before proceeding to the line where Bn. relieved 15th KOYLI in the front line. (Right Battn. respns. Brigade) Relief complete 12.45 a.m. Dispositions: Bn. Hdqr. at RETTEMOY FARM. B & A in front line. C in support & D in reserve Coy. & Intelligence Officer went round the Bn. front. Coys can only be relieved in darkness.	
	24/4/18		Transport shelled at SOUASTRE. Several arrivals being killed & injured. Coday. went round all Coys. 2/Lt POWELL led a patrol against an enemy M.G. &, in reccey. attempting to rifleit, was killed.	

Army Form C. 2118.

WAR DIARY
or
INTELLIGENCE SUMMARY.
(Erase heading not required.)

Instructions regarding War Diaries and Intelligence Summaries are contained in F. S. Regs., Part II. and the Staff Manual respectively. Title pages will be prepared in manuscript.

Place	Date	Hour	Summary of Events and Information	Remarks and references to Appendices
In the Field	24/4/18		His body was unfortunately not recovered. B Coy. took over the front posts from 5th Somerset L.I.	Ref. 5th D. N.E.
	25/4/18		Details under Maj. Grove-White move from AUTHIE to PAS as part of the Divis. Composite Batn. C.O., Adj. & Brigade-Major reconnoitred line. 2/Lt. SWAN A Coy. wounded by a stick bomb. 2/Lt. PIERCE.	
	26/4/18		Quiet day. Quite a lot of good observation was possible on three places where shots. One man of the 7th Bavarian Inf Regt was identified. Patrols by the CHAUNDY. Two forward posts were established by A Coy.	
	27/4/18		Relieved by the Kiner. & returned to support position. Hdqrs. E.30.d.45.85, C & D front Coys. A in support. B in reserve.	
	28/4/18		C.O. & Adjt. went round the defences. Much work was done on the positions held in evening the N. side of BIEZ WOOD.	
	29/4/18		Bn. Officers spotted a Boche relief near STARE of which our Guns took advantage O.C. A Coy. accompanied the Brigade-Major to the posts established 26/4 & some losses inflicted as to their position. Usual work & wiring done.	

Army Form C. 2118.

WAR DIARY
or
INTELLIGENCE SUMMARY.
(Erase heading not required.)

Instructions regarding War Diaries and Intelligence Summaries are contained in F. S. Regs., Part II. and the Staff Manual respectively. Title pages will be prepared in manuscript.

Place	Date	Hour	Summary of Events and Information	Remarks and references to Appendices
In the Field	30/4/18		Officers sent to FONQUEVILLERS to reconnoitre disposition of 6th BEDS. The T.O. Lt. J.H. HODGSON. MM. was unfortunately killed at FONQUEVILLERS by a shell. 2Lt. SUTCLIFFE came up for duty with A Coy. a draft of 3 ORs also came up.	Gen. Ref. 57. D.
	30/4/18		2Lt. J.E. HARRINGTON returned to duty with the Bn.	

Casualties during APRIL 1918.

Officers: Killed: 6/4. 2Lt. L.E. MOORE.
24/4. 2Lt. T.W. POWELL.
3

Wounded: 30/4. Lt. J.H. HODGSON. MM.
14/4. Lt. H.R. ODLING
25/4. 2Lt. K.T. SWAN.
3

Gassed: 5/4. 2Lt. J.E. HARRINGTON
3. 6/4. 2Lt. F.W. ELLIOT.
8/4. 2Lt. F.C. MORYOSEPH

O.R.s : Killed : 5
Died of Wounds: 3
Wounded : 51
Gassed : 16

Army Form C. 2118.

WAR DIARY
or
INTELLIGENCE SUMMARY.
(Erase heading not required.)

Place	Date	Hour	Summary of Events and Information	Remarks and references to Appendices
In the Field			CASUALTIES during APRIL 1918 (Cont'd.)	
			Officers, admitted to Field Ambulance sick.	
	28.4.18.		2Lt. R.A.K. STUART. M.C.	
	30.4.18.		Capt. F.W. SCHOLEFIELD.	
			APPOINTMENTS.	
	9.4.18.		Capt. H.A. MAYNARD. M.C. — Appointed Staff Captain 63rd Infantry Bde.	
	21.4.18.		Lt. R.E. TAYLOR — Appointed Staff Captain 189th Infantry Bde. & to be Temp. Capt. whilst so employed.	
	22.4.18.		Capt. S. MIRAMS — To 3rd. Division (later.)	
	30.4.18.			

He Hendry Lt. Col.
Cdg. 4th Bn. Middlesex Regt.

63rd Brigade.
37th Division.

4th BATTALION

THE MIDDLESEX REGIMENT.

MAY 1918

Army Form C. 2118.

4 Middlesex R/
56/46

WAR DIARY
or
INTELLIGENCE SUMMARY.
(Erase heading not required.)

Instructions regarding War Diaries and Intelligence Summaries are contained in F. S. Regs., Part II. and the Staff Manual respectively. Title pages will be prepared in manuscript.

Place	Date	Hour	Summary of Events and Information	Remarks and references to Appendices
In the Field	1/5/18		Bn. relieved by 6th Bn. 123rd Inf. Bde. & withdrew to function in & near FONQUEVILLERS as part of Bde. in reserve. O.C. took over command of defence of the village. Major B & D Coys in the village. A Coy in "Snipers' Square" E.24.d. C Coy on the old English front line about E.22 Central.	
	2/5/18		Quiet day. Co. & Oy. reconnoitred defences where we were found to be in course of alteration. A & C Coys stocked in the village.	
	3/5/18		FONQUEVILLERS shelled with 21cm & 15cm shrapnel. A base of one of the former shells dropped on HQrs, but it was that to Bde. The C.O. reconnoitred the defences with the Brigadier & S.O.1. working parties on the neighbouring defences 9 P.M. to 2.30 P.M.	
	4/5/18		2nd in Command Major P. GROVE-WHITE came up from Reinf. Compound Paris for duty. Bnual work done on village defences.	

2353 Wt. W2544/1454 700,000 5/15 D.D. & L. A.D.S.S./Forms/C. 2118.

WAR DIARY or INTELLIGENCE SUMMARY.

Army Form C. 2118.

(Erase heading not required.)

Place	Date	Hour	Summary of Events and Information	Remarks and references to Appendices
IN THE FIELD. 5/5/18				
	6/5/18		Good weather continued during which work on village defences was carried on. 300 Labour Coy. arrived in FONQUEVILLERS to being cadre.	
	7/5/18		A little rain. This day seemed very nervous about the situation owing to the statement of a Boche officer captured, & precautionary measures were accordingly taken. Defensive arrangements of FONQUEVILLERS practically completed. Rations moved to the Church at 9 pm this day being the alleged Boche 'Y' day. The Brigade Staff also arrived in the village.	
	8/5/18		The expected attack failed to materialise. The ZO & 1 Officer per Coy. proceeded to trenches occupied by Support Battal. kept Bde. to take over dispositions. The Coy. officers remained in the line. A small "peaceful" penetration N. of BUCQUOY was carried out by 112 Bde without success. About 29 PWs were were taken & were marched through FONQUEVILLERS.	

WAR DIARY or INTELLIGENCE SUMMARY

Army Form C. 2118.

Place	Date	Hour	Summary of Events and Information	Remarks and references to Appendices
In the Field.	9/5/18		Battn. relieved 10th Royal Fusiliers in support to left Bde. Hdqrs. F.2.C.5.7. 'A' Coy. in 700 yds. of PRUSSIAN AVE. 'B' in 1st LEEDS TR. 'C' Coy. in BRADFORD & HALIFAX TR. 'D' in LEEDS TR. A day of rain had made the trenches muddy. Two Lewis Guns hit by a shell in ESSARTS & two mules knocked out.	Ref. S.T.4.N.E.
	10/5/18		The men cleared up the mud. An O.P. was made in PRUSSIAN AVE. Tour proved very quiet.	
	11/5/18		Usual routine of trench warfare. FONQUEVILLERS was heavily gassed & many casualties caused.	
	12/5/18		Tour continued quiet only counter-battery work being done by both sides. The Brigadier paid a call.	
	13/5/18		Bn. relieved 8th Somersets in left Front Sector. D & C in front line, B & A in support. Bn. Hdqrs. F.2.d. 05.45. Relief was quiet & smoothly carried out.	
	14/5/18		B.C. v A were accessible by day. C Coy. in post winter by night only. Patrols by Lt. WILLIAMS, & Lt. MOORAT. Good observation work was done & targets obtained, remarked on by the Divnl. General. The I.O. liaised with the 2nd Bn. Scots Guards on our left.	

WAR DIARY
or
INTELLIGENCE SUMMARY.
(Erase heading not required.)

Army Form C. 2118.

Place	Date	Hour	Summary of Events and Information	Remarks and references to Appendices
In the Field	15/5/18		Tour continued quiet. Patrol by Lt. MIRAMS & Lieut. CAINE & Roche waterproof was "captured" by the former patrol.	
	16/5/18		Bn. relieved by 2/4th. Duke of Wellington's and Deer marched via FONQUEVILLERS to a point between SOUASTRE & COIGNEUX where the Cookers provided tea & there were waiting. The Batn. was accomodated in tent in the BOIS DE WARNIMONT.	
	17/5/18		Spent in resting & cleaning up. Good weather prevailed. The Brigadier & Bde Major paid a call. Lt. LYAL, McDON & Ingleheart. YATES returned to the Batn. from Divl. wing. 2n. KRAIBER to rest camp.	
	18/5/18		The C.O. attended Conference at Bde. H.Q. Baths at VAUCHELLES. The camp was moved to a better site. Capt. S. MIRAMS returned to the Batn. from Staff Course & assumed command of "A" Coy. The Divl. Band performed in the afternoon. Capt. PROCTER & Capt. MIRAMS leaves with N.Z. Reserve Bde. Conference of Coy Cr.	

WAR DIARY
or
INTELLIGENCE SUMMARY.

Army Form C. 2118.

(Erase heading not required.)

Place	Date	Hour	Summary of Events and Information	Remarks and references to Appendices
IN THE FIELD.	19/5/18		Parade service Camp near the camp at 11 AM. Service also for other denominations. The C.O. reconnoitred the Battn. battle position in the RED LINE. The Bde. Major paid a call. Conference of Coy. Cdr. Wilkins appointed Sports Officer.	
	20/5/18		Battn. paraded for ceremonial drill including all Specialists. Officers from each Coy. reconnoitred RED LINE disposition.	
	21/5/18		Battn. drill in the morning. I.O. reconnoitred route to pit of trenches to be dug by the Battn. Conference of Coy. Cdr. ref. Battery of RED LINE.	
	22/5/18		Bn. marched the RED LINE reporting evence finished at 12.10 PM. Bockerpredation were worn for an hour on this & succeeding days. S.S. 135 under Maj. GROVE-WHITE packed all baggage & cleared the camp. Coys. were in Battle position by 11.30 AM.	

WAR DIARY
or
INTELLIGENCE SUMMARY
(Erase heading not required.)

Army Form C. 2118.

Place	Date	Hour	Summary of Events and Information	Remarks and references to Appendices
In The Field.	22/5/18 (Cont.)		Disposition in REDLINE, B Coy. left front, A Coy. right front, D & C in support. (Bn Hqrs.) at J.8.C.2.2. under a tree.	Ref. Sqt. N.E.
	23/5/18.		The whole Batn. marched to SAILLY-AU-BOIS, to work on new Trenches. Officers & NCOs dug with the men. Batn returned to camp at 1.30 P.M. Lecture to Officers & NCOs by the Corps Cr. (4th) (Sir G.M. HARPER, K.C.B, D.S.O.) Warning received that the Bn. would move forward.	
	24/5/18.		T.O. reconnoitred Hdqrs. of 1st OTAGO Bn. N.Z.R. at windmill J.34.c.2.6. Bn marched to trenches leaving 4 P.M. on reserve to the N.Z. Division occupying disposition of right Bn. in the Purple Line from J.19.c.c. to R.S.Cll. in the order D.B.C.A with Hdqrs. at the windmill. The Reinf. General watched the Batn. marching past at BUS-LES-ARTOIS.	

Army Form C. 2118.

WAR DIARY
or
INTELLIGENCE SUMMARY.
(Erase heading not required.)

Instructions regarding War Diaries and Intelligence Summaries are contained in F. S. Regs., Part II and the Staff Manual respectively. Title pages will be prepared in manuscript.

Place	Date	Hour	Summary of Events and Information	Remarks and references to Appendices
In The Field.	25/5/18		Day spent in settling in, improving bivouacs etc. Baths at BERTRANCOURT were available during the Tour. The C.O. & Adj. went round the lines in the afternoon. This is quite a lengthy task. Training carried on.	Ref: 57.D. N.E.
	26/5/18		Classes in signalling, observing, L.G. etc. The Army Commander (Sir Julian BYNG) & Lt. Genl. Commando (N.Z.) inspected the dispositions & were received at Battn. H.Q. by the Adjt. & Co. who have the pleasure of shaking hands with the General.	
	27/5/18		Quite a lot of shelling on the front of our cabage from 9.2. to 5.7mm probably in connection with the enemy offensive further south. Classes were continued. 2nd Lt MITCHELL to hospital with symptoms of appendicitis. A few shells dropped near Bn HQ after dinner rather disturbing the evening.	

WAR DIARY
or
INTELLIGENCE SUMMARY

Army Form C. 2118.

Place	Date	Hour	Summary of Events and Information	Remarks and references to Appendices
In the Field	28/5/18		A quieter day. Classes were continued. Capt. JAMIESON went down to have his teeth attended to. Capt. E. PROCTER & Capt. B.R. NEWMAN mentioned in Sir Douglas Haig's despatch (Times May 25th). The C.O. made his daily tour of inspection. Day working parties of 320 under the R.E's worked on the defences daily.	
	29/5/18		Quiet day. Classes & firing on Coy. ranges continued. Usual working parties.	
	30/5/18		1 Platoon per Coy. sent down to complete bomb proofing of transport lines. Relieved by 13th. & R.R.C. & withdrew to camp in Authie Wood, & reached billets in by 1am. (31/5)	
	31/5/18		Aeroplane scheme with the afternoon, & attended by all ranks. Aeroplane flew at 500, 1000 & 2000 feet & fired light signals to indicate height. Conference of Coy. Commanders.	

Lt. A.G. MITCHELL killed by an enemy aeroplane bomb at 3rd. Canadian Stationary Hospital, DOULLENS.

WAR DIARY
or
INTELLIGENCE SUMMARY.
(Erase heading not required.)

Army Form C. 2118.

Place	Date	Hour	Summary of Events and Information	Remarks and references to Appendices
In the Field			Casualties during May 1918.	
			Officers: KILLED - Lieut. A.G. MITCHELL. 31.5.18.	
			O.Rs.:	
			Killed :: 4	
			Died of Wounds : Nil	
			Wounded :: 17	
			Appointments etc.	
			7.5.18 - 2/Lt. J.K. ROSS to 63rd. T.M. Battery.	
			4.5.18 - 2/Lt. C.H. HOSKYN to R.A.F.	
			31.5.18 - 2/Lt. A.H. PAYNE to 37 Div. Signal School as Instructor.	

Nathan Lieut.Col.
Comg. 4th. Battalion,
Coldstream Regt.

63rd Brigade.
37th Division.

4th BATTALION

THE MIDDLESEX REGIMENT.

JUNE. 1918

Army Form C. 2118.

4th M[idd]x

WAR DIARY
or
INTELLIGENCE SUMMARY.
(Erase heading not required.)

Vol 47

Place	Date	Hour	Summary of Events and Information	Remarks and references to Appendices
In the Field	1/6/18		Parading at 7.40 A.M. the Batt. proceeded to Training Ground Nr. of AUTHIE. Training being carried out under Coy arrangements. & fair range of musketry & field firing was carried out.	57.D
	2/6/18		Parade Coy Service at 11.30 A.M. by acting E. of Army F.P. In a pastoral match in the evening 8th Lincs Beat 4th M'ddx by 1-Nil. Bombing and Lewis Gun demonstration on training ground by C Coy. Tank demonstration by D Coy. R.G.A. Scale & took place at 11.20 by 112th Bde as Infantry Scout Officers Course. 1 troop of D Coy 15th H Coy. Reg'l to 3 plates to be 1/4 km in rds of war by 2 plates to the Bands & performers in Batt: was followed by the Athenian Boys after dinner. Kit. Scott Lockett	
	3/6/18		Battalion parade at 1.30 P.M. carried Lieut. RE. FM 152 Roy: R.E. order to proceed to move at short notice. Co attended conference at Bde. Hors. Coy. Batt. headed SS 135 detailed. Transport left for BICHEVILLERS (staging only) at dusk.	
	4/6/18			

Army Form C. 2118.

WAR DIARY
or
INTELLIGENCE SUMMARY.
(Erase heading not required.)

Instructions regarding War Diaries and Intelligence Summaries are contained in F. S. Regs., Part II. and the Staff Manual respectively. Title pages will be prepared in manuscript.

Place	Date	Hour	Summary of Events and Information	Remarks and references to Appendices
In the Field	5/6/18		Bathe. Parade 10.15 a.m. to practise attack formation on open warfare on training ground W. of Authieule. Bath. parade at 5.50 p.m. to march into Authie for evening game. The Buses finally arrived about 1.30 a.m. Meanwhile the Coys were detailed to concentrate orchards.	LENS.11 AMIENS.17
	6/6/18		Been practised in Platoon to Picquet acting about T.M. The men were confident & trained in the picturesque country.	
	7/6/18		Coys at the disposal of Coy. Cos. - Conference of Coy. Cos. before tea. Batln. was at two hours notice to move wires repaired. C.O. to H.Q. of Coy. Cos. + Lewis Gun Command attended a lecture on the ground S.W. of PICQUIGNY on advance guard and attack formation by the Brigadier.	
	8/6/18		Coys in Coy. training. C.O. T.O. + O.C. A + C Coys. travelled by Lorry leaving 6.30 a.m. to D/R. + St-FUSCIEN to see the rear areas of the French 37th Division. Parties were conducted by French Staff officers. Lorries returned via Amiens.	

2353 Wt. W2544/1454 700,000 5/15 D. D. & L. A.D.S.S./Forms/C. 2118.

Army Form C. 2118.

WAR DIARY
or
INTELLIGENCE SUMMARY.
(Erase heading not required.)

Instructions regarding War Diaries and Intelligence Summaries are contained in F. S. Regs., Part II and the Staff Manual respectively. Title pages will be prepared in manuscript.

Place	Date	Hour	Summary of Events and Information	Remarks and references to Appendices
IN THE FIELD	9/6/18		Evening to prepare to move at 5.30 am. Owing to enemy attack between MONTDIDIER & NOYON. Alarm cancelled at 7am. Parade Coy. service at 10.45 am in castle grounds. Lecture to officers of the Bde. by a R.A.F. officer on aeroplane work.	AMIENS 17.
	10/6/18		Parade at 8.30 am. March outside previous to embus in French lorries & proceed to LOEUILLY. Bath & educational lectures during evening to officers of French troops. L/S WILLIAMS acted as interpreting officer.	
	11/6/18		Coy. & a party of officers reconnoitred area of R. NOYE between JUMEL & COTTENCHY.	
	12/6/18		Parade 7am. March to ORESMAUX where Bn. was billeted. Good accommodation here. H.Q. in CHURCH acted as visiting officer.	
	13/6/18		Batt. parade for training. Training ground allotted by Corps on arrangement by Brigade near SHORTLEY WOOD. Pogramme of work to be carried out by the Brigade	

Army Form C. 2118.

WAR DIARY
or
INTELLIGENCE SUMMARY.
(Erase heading not required.)

Place	Date	Hour	Summary of Events and Information	Remarks and references to Appendices
IN THE FIELD	14/6/18		Batt. Steve. Battn. paraded at 5.30 a.m. & marched to assembly position near the Bois de Sommets. The Bois 24 Battalion were heavily attacked & taken at 8.30 a.m. The hour of zero. Namdin attacked & supported by the 6 Tanks. The enemy represented by the 136 rifle Command. by Major P. Grove & his officers & Censors at 1 p.m. & to conference of the General followed with Battn. officers.	AMIENS 17.
	15/6/18		Battn. paraded at 7 a.m. & marched to locality where it was situated (Cpl. G. T. Devil) being returned. Co. Vr. O. recounted. The billeting was done by P.K. Luvro. Battn. at Tronville & Amiens-Roye Road. At 9.45 a.m. between Branches to Rumigny where it was billeted.	
	16/6/18		2 other Lancs recon. Recommoutred Ansmeett position in Bois de Boves. Battn. returned to hir billet. Training - ground allotted. Attack Scheme referred. Conference of Coy. Commanders.	
	17/6/18		Attack scheme on envelope at Rumigny retained by Coys. & Batt. Commander. Coys. & Battn. Commander Recommoutred Averaly position in Bois de Boves & bridges over the Noie & Avre.	
	18/6/18		Training by Companies. Conference of Coy. Commanders at Batt. H.Q. after tea.	

Army Form C. 2118.

WAR DIARY
or
INTELLIGENCE SUMMARY.
(Erase heading not required.)

Instructions regarding War Diaries and Intelligence Summaries are contained in F. S. Regs., Part II and the Staff Manual respectively. Title pages will be prepared in manuscript.

Place	Date	Hour	Summary of Events and Information	Remarks and references to Appendices
In the Field.	18/6/18		Battn. training in the morning. Demonstration by 1 & D Coys. of tactical moves to Order reference to Training. Baths left PERNOIS 10.45 a.m. being relieved by a French Battalion. 2 Battalion 5e Regiment. Bn. marched to PLACHY-BUYON. I.T.O. & an Guide arranged to act as guides for the Advance parties. Arrived PLACHY 6 a.m. 20/6/18	Ref. AMIENS.17 LENS.11
	20/6/18		PLACHY-BUYON. In Coys. Battns. in open order & running. Inter Coy's Platoon Sports were held at 5.30 p.m. at watering P Coy beat the rest by 2-1. Hawk offers from the R. Corps made an hour & report from Cadets duty in England.	
	21/6/18		Battn. marched off at 2.30 a.m. to an Assembly position near PLACHY Station. Entraining completed by 10 a.m. Train left at 10.25 a.m. & travelled via AMIENS/DOULLENS, arrived at MONDICOURT. A march to camp near COURCELLES. Completed by noon. Accommodation comprises Nissan huts & bell tents.	
	22/6/18		Firing in A.R.A. Platoon competition of the Coys to decide on the platoon Int. Officer reconnoitred Bn. Battle position in Sector Line N. of CHATEAU LA HAIE outside the FONQUEVILLERS/SOUASTRE Road.	

WAR DIARY or INTELLIGENCE SUMMARY

Army Form C. 2118.

Place	Date	Hour	Summary of Events and Information	Remarks and references to Appendices
In the Field	22/6/18		Bn. now filling double scale of G.H.Q. Reserve (3 hours notice) to rejoin XXII Corps) & left Reserve Division IV Corps.	LENS 1-11, 57.D. N.E.
	23/6/18		Coft. Service 10.45am. ARA Brigade Competition won by 16 Platoon. at Fozzare. Baton. beat Str. tenor. 3-Mk. A v B Coys. tested at 9.9s. Conference of Coy. Commanders 7 P.M. 10 Officers per Coy. & 1 N.C.O. Platoon to reconnoitre ABLAINZEVELLE Sector. (2/HA. KOPJ.)	
	24/6/18		Evidence of "Spanish" influenza began to appear especially amongst the officers. C.H.Q. & Hd. Batted at P.P.S. Int. Officers proceeded to HQ. HERKOSKI to arrange details of relief. Conference of C.O.'s en H.Q. hrs. at 10 am & Coy. Commanders at 10.30 am.	
	25/6/18		Parade 7.30 PM. March via SOUASTRE & WILLOW PATCH "A" to relieve 11th KOYLI. Relief completed 4.30 A.M. Delay owing to Baltn. being relieved at the last moment. Disposition:–	
			Left Front Coy. D Coy. Capt. A. KAISER took
			Right – – C Coy. over C Coy. Capt. E.
			Left Support Coy. B Coy. PROCTER being sick.
			Right – – A Coy.
			Batn. Hdqrs. F.2. at 05.50.

Army Form C. 2118.

WAR DIARY
or
INTELLIGENCE SUMMARY.
(Erase heading not required.)

Place	Date	Hour	Summary of Events and Information	Remarks and references to Appendices
IN THE FIELD	26/6/18.		Quiet day. The C.O. went round the lines in the morning. HUBBARD sick with influenza. Many cases of this there are in the Bats. Previously arranged the Officers & NCOi. & Sergeants of C Coy. went down this day.	57.d. N.E.
	27/6/18.		Some shelling of BADEN BADEN where gas projectors were installed. Capt. MIRAMS, Capt. SMITH MC & Capt. MOORAT sick and removed to the base. Lt. LYNN & 2/Lt. CHUNDY down sick (influenza). Lt. DEVAR returned from Special Leave to England & came up to G.O.C. Brigade paid a call at Bunkers. duty over C Coy. Capt. KAIBER sick but remained in the line.	
	28/6/18.		Fairly Quiet. 2/Lt. Yate to duty from Bde. School owing to scarcity of officers.	
	29/6/18.		2/Lt. ANDREWS up from Bde. School. Capt. JAMIESON & 2/Lt. Yates down sick (influenza). 16 platoon D Coy. won Divn. R.R.A. Competition. (under Sgt. STOREY). Mr. R.R.K. STUART granted leave to S. Africa. R.R.A. Comp. Scores.	
	30/6/18.			

Score by Lts.   16 pln   2 pln   6 pln
Protection   HR 16 det   1/1 Hen Zt 13 AR Bde.
                  63rd Bde   112 & 73 Bde 111 AC Bde
                   147   128   148
                    86   2,126   102
                     -         142   44
                   86   23   58
                   233   90   206
                              216

Score by Lts.
Protection
Score by divi.
Protection
Total.

2353 Wt. W2544/1454 700,000 5/15 D. D. & L. A.D.S.S./Forms/C. 2118.

Army Form C. 2118.

WAR DIARY
or
INTELLIGENCE SUMMARY.
(Erase heading not required.)

Place	Date	Hour	Summary of Events and Information	Remarks and references to Appendices
In the Field	30/6/18		Casualties during JUNE 1918.	

Officers: Killed. Nil.
Wded. Nil.
Sick. 5/6. 2/Lt. G.A.Pierce
" V.J. Ross
" H.R. Sutcliffe
2/6. Lt. L.W.Andreae
25/6 Capt. E. Procter
Lt. E.H. Fenn
2/6. P. Pater
2/6. 2/Lt. Cyraine
" V.H. Baird
2/6. Lt. R.G. Williams
" V.C. Lyle MC. Dem.
" 2/Lt. H.M. Chundy
30/6 Capt. J.P. Jamieson
2/Lt. P.S. Yates

O.Rank: Killed. 3.
Wded. 19.
Sick. 140.

Appointments &c.
Lt. F.F. Moorat to be additional H. capt. 30.5.18
2/Lt. P.J. Klaiber to do. 1.6.18
2/Lt. G.A. Pierce from F.A. 22/6.
Lt. L.W. Andreae from hospital in England 29/6.
Lt. F.C. Morrissey to England M.G.C. 9/6.
2/Lt. P.H.P. Wilson to hospital 9/6. (Diag: Shell-Shock (W))

Reinforcements — 62 O. Ranks.

30/6/18

[signature] Lieut. Col.
Comg. H.P. Battalion
Middlesex Regt.

63rd Brigade.
37th Division.

4th BATTALION

THE MIDDLESEX REGIMENT.

JULY 1918

WAR DIARY or INTELLIGENCE SUMMARY

Army Form C. 2118.

July 1918   4 Middlesex Regt

Place	Date	Hour	Summary of Events and Information	Remarks and references to Appendices
In the Field	1/7/18		Relieved by 3rd Lincolns & Border to Hutments. Disposed as follows: H.Q. in ESSARTS A Coy in front line B " in support C " in Gonnecourt Tr. Right D " in " " Left (Suspended) (Lincolns) Artillery Support to	Ref 57 D 9 SE 4 & NE
	2/7/18		A Coy. billeted in ESSARTS covering/party formed under R.E. for work on defense & dugouts.	
	3/7/18		HQ. Coy. bathed. Capt. N. Smith MC. on short leave to PARIS. Capt. the Rgt. of D Coy. Lt. Royle, C Coy officers Capt. Mackin's MC Coy officers Sergt Major 2nd Lt. for repatriation let off. H.Q. FOUNQUEVILLE.	
	4/7/18		2nd Lieut L. ANDRENE reported from Rgt. base. V. Hvy. took over B Coy. to ANDRENE bodies & D. Ye Lindsay rejoined filter police & Rgt posted to C. Coy. Re-Org. at 10m (1918) 200 gas shells fell near	
	5/7/18		B & D Coys. Ironville (Green Cross 4) a few Casualties received. The CO has a narrow Escape of Gas shell bursted for a few secs near to SONSTRE. Lt R.GROVE	
			Remarks: A & B Coys relieved C & D Coys respectively C & D Coys withdrew to ESSARTE.	

WAR DIARY
or
INTELLIGENCE SUMMARY.
(Erase heading not required.)

Army Form C. 2118.

Place	Date	Hour	Summary of Events and Information	Remarks and references to Appendices
In the Field	6/7/18		Usual working parties. MG was rather heavy and the enemy's one pounder being heard.	Ref. Std N.E.
ESSARTS	7/7/18		Relieved by 10th Royal Fusiliers. The Brigade withdrawn to Divisional reserve. HQrs Hebe Hedge. Reconstruction Battalion HQrs in the Z (old Boche line). A Coy in ESSARTS at disposal of Left Brigade. B Coy in RUM TR. C & D in BEER TR at the disposal of Right Brigade.	
	8/7/18		Working parties furnished (whole Battn.) HQ CUCUMBER reports from hospital.	
	9/7/18		Quiet day. Usual working parties.	
	10/7/18		Maj. GROVE-WHITE took over temporary command of the HERTS at RETTEMOY FARM. Battn. relieved by 2nd LONDONS and went to VALLEY CAMP, SOUASTRE. Very comfortable huts. Bn expected down for one week before going in for another 5 days.	
	11/7/18		Coys bathed. Intelligence officer sent down to No 59 Coy. Stood down in connection with air photos etc.	

WAR DIARY or **INTELLIGENCE SUMMARY.**

Army Form C. 2118.

Place	Date	Hour	Summary of Events and Information	Remarks and references to Appendices
In the Field SOUASTRE	12/4/18		All Coy's front on range near HENU (excluding H.Q.) one Officer per Coy. Remainder to have to take over from 1/1st Herts (Right Battn Right Bde). Takings over Officers reconnoitred the portion of Battalion front between BIENVILLERS & N. of FONQUEVILLERS. Battalion relieved 1/1st Herts in the line. Dispositions Battn Hdqrs KETTEMOF FARM. A Coy. left front, B Coy right front (between DUCQUOY & BIEZ WOOD) C Coy in support. & D Coy in reserve.	Ref STATE
	13/4/18			
	14/4/18		6. HODGES took over Transport 2/Lt ELMORE took over as duties of Gas Officer from 2/Lt WILKINS M.C. The Coy. inspected the dispositions. Quiet day. 9.15 HERDING joined the Batta & was posted to C Coy. H.Q. shelled heavily & 1 man killed Gibson by Capt S. MIRAMS.	
	15/4/18			
	16/4/18		Rain during the night. Caused the trenches to be in a very bad condition. Patrols by the respective Co's. LINDSAY	
	17/4/18		Co's Conference at Bn. H.Q. D & C Coy's relieved A & B Coy's respectively & ANDREAE to England to M.G.O.	

WAR DIARY
or
INTELLIGENCE SUMMARY
(Erase heading not required.)

Army Form C. 2118.

Place	Date	Hour	Summary of Events and Information	Remarks and references to Appendices
In the Field	18/7/18		A Coy relieved by A Coy 8th LINCOLNS & proceeded to SOUASTRE to practise for proposed operation. 2/Lt ELMORE proceeded on a gas course. Lt WILKINS MO temporarily doing Lt's duties. Return by 2/Lt LINDSAY and Frederickson. Patrol by 2/Lt LINDSAY and Frederickson came under fire.	Ref 57d.N15
	19/7/18		Been retired from ROSSIGNOL WOOD on our right. Front Coy (B+C) pushes out patrols to ascertain whether he had retired on our front but they met with strong resistance establishing the fact that he was reserved stationary on our front. Casualties — 2 killed & 7 wounded (OR).	
	20/7/18		Battalion relieved by 8th Sea. Lives & withdrew to support KEEPS in PIGEON WOOD. C & D Coys in PURPLE LINE (GOMMECOURT TR.) B Coy in OMITECOURT TR.	
	21/7/18		Coy went to SOUASTRE to inspect training for raid. Officers taking part in raid formed from 1/Lt & 2/Lt CAINE B Coy & Lt K.R.S.	

Army Form C. 2118.

WAR DIARY
INTELLIGENCE SUMMARY.
(Erase heading not required.)

Report on Raid carried out by 4th Battn Border Regt. night July 23/24 1918.

Place	Date	Hour	Summary of Events and Information	Remarks and references to Appendices
In the Field	23/7/18		The raiding party consisted of 4 officers & 114 O. Ranks (including R.C. & stretcher bearers) divided to follow:- The party entered at Jump off tape about 9:30 pm & arrived at PIGEON WOOD about 10 pm. Here they connected with guides (1 in AYRELLE AVE) & the party moved off about 11:30 pm by platoons to the line. The right was led by Pte Smith to an exact point taken from the 4th Battn Emblem & came to the detonating shelter. The 4 Parties came out at 12:10 to await 12:50 am & after beating away with Bangalore Torpedoes, etc. were in positions by 11:30am. The Barrage commenced punctually at 1 am & not before could the noise of an engagement be heard. The firing off & movement of the Barrage of the infantry- No 1 Platoon (Right) Sergt C.H. REANEY — The Barrage commenced at 1:45 am & was excellent. Officers about 3 sets of enemy were encountered & 3 sets of enemy were not front as came out of our barrage at the time. — Some of our Infantry were seen in the sunken road leading over in front of the wood & amongst the enemy troops & disorganised. I got the platoon on the left not worth of remote. Pte ELLIS & went through & killed with the bayonet. That out. The enemy were in a very disorganized condition. 6 prisoners were taken. One of the enemy having surrendered with a M.G. The remainder of the gunners & was forced to capture together.	Ref. Sket. N.E. 1:20000

Army Form C. 2118.

WAR DIARY
or
INTELLIGENCE SUMMARY.
(Erase heading not required.)

Place	Date	Hour	Summary of Events and Information	Remarks and references to Appendices
In the field	22/7/17		*[handwritten entries illegible due to faded scan]*	

WAR DIARY
or
INTELLIGENCE SUMMARY.

Army Form C. 2118.

(Erase heading not required.)

Place	Date	Hour	Summary of Events and Information	Remarks and references to Appendices

to the one of our (i.e. British) Lewis Guns with magazine attached. I then got my bombing party & proceeded to A.T. when up a C.T. there we found several dugouts, three of which were found to be No. 27. No enemy were met, but like other dugouts the signal to return went up, & we came back through the dugouts & found that the Bangalore Torpedoes had not been used, so Pte. NICHOLS & myself fired them, one on a shelter, the other on a dugout. There was no enemy M.G. fire. The enemy trenches were lined with the exception of the front. We were seen from Burgerna and packed up and returned to the Scarborough.

No. 2 Platoon under Mr. BACKHOUSE (Capt. CARR) "Backhouse" damage done to trench was the register, and & good at Bangalore to first the left 4 platoon of the Bangalore torpedo put into leading trench was on his lure of (?) and on direction are ???? hard. The got ??? and the group was large out up to be covered to ??? N. of the sunken trench, but as ??? could not be ??? ???? hollow & overgrown & does not appear to have been used at all as the enemy was twenty (20) along which & also seeing men on right who found along to this point & first as might, and developed here by No. of Coopers.

HQ Lieut PAYNE's section was not dropped here of the search. He reports a cop of Cooper's Lamps

WAR DIARY or INTELLIGENCE SUMMARY

Army Form C. 2118.

Place	Date	Hour	Summary of Events and Information	Remarks and references to Appendices

a large crater about 1.2d. x 5.30. Thought to be occupied about 70+.5 of this trench we struck a nest of low wire knee high which was badly damaged. The cottage whatever 30+ further on we crossed the 2nd trench which was also occupied. About 6" deep. but of course to be only dug out. We found a section dated October 9 from NETT was dropped into 3 dugouts which were found. Two endeavoured to explore but what did not appear to be weld the excavated 1. No 5. down and a Platt regained the woodwork. These were found two empty or one face. Three with Germans were in. The dugouts. One or two old British water-proof sheets were found in bad condition. The Column then ran into a thick belt of flax & barbed wire coming in a bad state which was covered where the aid of the Torpedoes "y.15+ further on was the free trench. This was reached the very narrow, about 5' deep. Parties were sent both ways. The got into touch right & left. On alight up of our Lysers out P bombs. There was no sign of the enemy but a few shots were seen by unit/colour steel belmet of some sort. So, the retreated legged over rear of the column returned by the self out before have been seen or enemy. The whole fire in front of our TR.

No. 3 Platoon, 2nd Lieut. F.F. MARSHALL: (Right Centre).

Our Barrage was effective, Barrage opened, & at 3am plus 3 the Platoon moved forward the Trench was crossed no resistance being met of the road. A section remained on the road & the remaining 3 moved on a plan conception were as found about 15 ft in front of the Trench & this was easily trampled down. The Trench was entered at L.2.a.37.10. One section worked to the left & two to the right. At L.2.a.35.10. there was a fort in the Trench & here the two sections separated, one working to the left & the other to the right, clearing the Trench as far as the first communication from L.2.d.25.02 in a S.E. direction. The dug outs at L.2.a.37.10 was forced with Mills Grenades & the next was cleared down with Mills Grenades, all shelters were destroyed. No bomb or SAA was thrown up the A.G.M. dump at Y.R.d.37.10 was not deep, but very well made (about 6'). No enemy M.G. fire or rifle fire was encountered. On the attempt to get on to the "Tape", attack was brought forward along the "Tape", attack was brought up by the last man of No. enemy was seen at all. The platoon suffered no casualties.

No. 4 Platoon. 2nd Lieut. A.S. YATES. (Right)
At 1.45 A.M. a very effective barrage was put down by our artillery, but unfortunately a T.M. dropped short into the first company of the platoon inflicting severe casualties. The angle of explosion had a demoralising effect but well in the sights of the men that they immediately closed up & filled up out of the trench. 3 rifts of men were observed N of the road. The first two, being rather thin & carried out with one section, the 2nd rifts of Hungarians(?) to a gap. On making the sunken road, we of the Lewis gun several bits of wire but these did not cause very much of delay, men facing the flank & de-loved us to get between about 100 yards & another bits of the enemy trench, at about L.2.a.26.10, were on a Chinese harganel(?) on what we was through the gap, when the urgency to return was to ut in 32.20 to 32.20 The Lewis gun officer on the road to our front and alked to bring up his army & we made goods it was occupied. There were 4 officers & many men but these advanced for some time. No enemy were encountered. There was a little m.g. fire from around L.2.a.3x27(?)

WAR DIARY or INTELLIGENCE SUMMARY

Army Form C. 2118.

Place	Date	Hour	Summary of Events and Information	Remarks and references to Appendices
			The Company expressed their satisfaction at the excellence of the barrage. About two new MGs were firing short over G post. The Battalion on right left cooperated to divert the enemy's attention. Dummy figures were raised opposite left battalion. Plenty of damage appeared to be done (Route L2 & STALINCOURTS on the right sent back two heavy parties along OAK & WASP trenches to engage the enemy post reported there. The Artillery fire which was to have cracker was stopped at 2.38 — fixed from the report centre at L.2.d. 30.45. a. We have had one officer wounded & one man. The signal for Barrage was 30 minutes. Right Barrage (on road near Fosse from the report centre (a road near junction of the Gretton road to the O in road. There was also some fire from the NO Five all guns. Having been told of a marked feature of enemy apparently held the house either side.	

Army Form C. 2118.

WAR DIARY
or
INTELLIGENCE SUMMARY.
(Erase heading not required.)

Instructions regarding War Diaries and Intelligence Summaries are contained in F. S. Regs., Part II. and the Staff Manual respectively. Title pages will be prepared in manuscript.

Place	Date	Hour	Summary of Events and Information	Remarks and references to Appendices
			what few enemy there were were obviously in a very demoralised condition. The raiding party returned to their dugouts in LA BRAYELLE AVE & were checked & moved down but tea & food. After a rest the parades on small parties to SOUASTRE for baths etc. The enemy barrage which came down about Zero plus 10 was weak & the right flank. The raiding party was accompanied by anyone in CLIFF TR until all telephone wires had been observed to be at Zero plus 5 from the trenches of BUCQUOT N. CLIFF TR. Casualties Officers :- Capt. SMYRK'S O.Rank. killed.—	
			R.P. Leaved &.2.a. 37.60.	
			wounded (R.king) — 4 wounded — 1 Total: 13	
			Killed — 7	
			(sgd) H.A. HAMLEY Lt. Col. Cdg. H.O Batt. Leicester Regt.	
			29/7/18	

(Copy)

P. P. & L., London, E.C.
(A10266) Wt W5900/P713 350,000 7/18 Sch. 52 Forms/C2118/16.

Army Form C. 2118.

WAR DIARY
or
INTELLIGENCE SUMMARY.
(Erase heading not required.)

Instructions regarding War Diaries and Intelligence Summaries are contained in F. S. Regs. Part II. and the Staff Manual respectively. Title pages will be prepared in manuscript.

Place	Date	Hour	Summary of Events and Information	Remarks and references to Appendices
IN THE FIELD	24/7/18		Rest day after the raid	Ref: STOSNE
	25/7/18		Report on raid sent in. Capt MOORAT took over D Coy & R G WILLIAMS joined D Coy	
	26/7/18		Battalion relieved 1st/13th KRRC & proceeded to reserve. H.Q. in B&D Coys at SOURSE Coys Coys in the Chateau a little S.W of FONQUEVILLERS RD. Heavy rain hindered relief. 2Lts B E GOODWIN & H E HODGKINSON joined the Battalion	
	27/7/18		Quiet day. The C.O. attended a M.G. demonstration at H.Q. 16th Div. Lt Col LANCE M.C. the Bde 2nd day 2 Lts A H ZENN rejoined the Battalion from PERONNE(?)	
	28/7/18		On a Sunday. Battle in the area General Pete Coys first in the morning making L.G practice the afternoon. Total of all counting 2 parties 627 men R W SHORT joined the Battalion	
	29/7/18		2Lt B Coys relieved C/A Coy in Frontline Sector —	

WAR DIARY
or
INTELLIGENCE SUMMARY.
(Erase heading not required.)

Army Form C. 2118.

Place	Date	Hour	Summary of Events and Information	Remarks and references to Appendices
In the Field	3/7/18		Squadron stayed during the morning. 10 Canadians to the Battalion. Lt. R.G. Williams to England - R.A.F. Maj. P. Grove-White took over command from Lt-Col. H.A.C. Harvey D.S.O. M.C. who proceeded (morning 3/7) to England for 6 mos. tour of duty as Deputy Asst Cmdt Cadet School near the Gas School. Force up in VALLEY CAMP.	
	3/7/18		An A. Hodgkinson who has been away sent to the Bath by mistake returned to Base. The Intelligence Officer in-a-a-hugr. Lt. R? (Lt Scott, Right Baker) to take over inspection & issue of respirators & passes to Monteurbons in VALLEY CAMP Relieved Offr Je. Lt. J.Hibbard - about leave to England.	

Army Form C. 2118.

WAR DIARY
or
INTELLIGENCE SUMMARY.
(Erase heading not required.)

Instructions regarding War Diaries and Intelligence Summaries are contained in F. S. Regs., Part II. and the Staff Manual respectively. Title pages will be prepared in manuscript.

Place	Date	Hour	Summary of Events and Information	Remarks and references to Appendices
In the Field	31/7/18		Casualties during July 1918	
			Officers died Capt. S. Mearns 23/7	
			Other ranks killed 11	
			wounded 29	
			Died: 2	

31-7-18

4TH BATTALION,
MIDDLESEX REGT.
No. BK 1382
Date 19/8/18

E.J.H. Roberts
Major
O.C. 4th Battn
Middlesex Regt.

63rd Brigade.
37th Division.

4th BATTALION

THE MIDDLESEX REGIMENT.

AUGUST 1918

WAR DIARY
or
INTELLIGENCE SUMMARY.

Army Form C. 2118.

4 Middlesex Ry
August 1918

Place	Date	Hour	Summary of Events and Information	Remarks and references to Appendices
In the Field	1/8/18		Officers of Advance Corps B+C went up to take over on the morning. Batt. relieved (Btt. Bath. Right-in-Line) left Helen (Piece of Bucror) Batt. HQ at 51.6.57. Front 1.20.000. Capt. A (Capt) + D (Rugby) Companies C (Capt) + B (Capt) 2/Lt. J.K. SELFE appointed Bolagus Haste Officer and continually of work on the Brigade Front. Following reinforcements went out: 2/Lt. H. BACKHOUSE to Rest Camp St MARY. " J.E. HARRINGTON } 3rd. Army School. " A.S. YATES }	Ref. STAIRS 1.20.000
	2/8/18		2/Lt. A.R. BURCH to Hospital (influenza). The C.O. & Bde. Major visited the Posts. Heavy rain rendered the condition of the trenches very bad. Attention paid particularly to evening.	
	3/8/18		Continued wet but quiet. Pte. BUTLER & 2OR did good work in patrolling BUCQUOY by day. Night patrol by Mr. F.F. MARSHALL.	
	4/8/18		A daylight patrol of 2/Lt. R.W. SEABY, Pte. BUTLER, 2 men got to the Boche outposts & perfect a M.G. but was discovered before they could get it away. They suffered no casualties. 2/Lt. H.F. BOWSER (D) rejoined from sick leave. 2/Lt. G. PRITCHARD (B) joined the Batt. from Ballon Coy Capt- F.F. MOCRATT to Hospital (P.U.O.) Capt. A.J. KLAIBER	

Army Form C. 2118.

WAR DIARY
or
INTELLIGENCE SUMMARY.
(Erase heading not required.)

Instructions regarding War Diaries and Intelligence Summaries are contained in F.S. Regs., Part II. and the Staff Manual respectively. Title pages will be prepared in manuscript.

Place	Date	Hour	Summary of Events and Information	Remarks and references to Appendices
In the Field	4/8/18		Assumed Command of "A" Coy. 2/Lt. F.R. Smith to hospital. The Intelligence Officer having met with the 8th Somersets (Support Bn) to take over dispositions.	Ref. 5th Div. N.E
	5/8/18		Battalion relieved by 8th Lincs & withdrew to support Bn. Hdqrs. Sausage Rise, 'D' Coy Essarts, 'B' Coy Gommecourt Tr., 'C' & 'B' in Halifax & Bradford Tr. Relieving relief.	
	6/8/18		Lt.Col. W.B. Molony, 9th Royal Lancaster Regt. arrived to take command of the Batn. Major P. Groves-White proceed to depositon. Lieut. C.A. King (A) & Lieut. F.G. Nutton (B) & Lieut. F.H. Meacham (D) joined the Batn. The period continued calm.	
	7/8/18		Quiet day. Our Coys continued to be exclusively engaged in working-parties. Capt. Jamieson & Capt. Proctor went down to attend a Court martial. A test was made of firing with Black Gogga for night firing practice. These were not found to be being successful. B.G.G.S. 4th Corps (B.G. Parker) visited Hedge.	

D.D. & L., London, E.C.
(A10260) Wt W3300/D713 250,000 2/18 Sch. 52 Forms/C2118/16.

Army Form C. 2118.

WAR DIARY
or
INTELLIGENCE SUMMARY.
(Erase heading not required.)

Instructions regarding War Diaries and Intelligence Summaries are contained in F. S. Regs., Part II. and the Staff Manual respectively. Title pages will be prepared in manuscript.

Place	Date	Hour	Summary of Events and Information	Remarks and references to Appendices
In the Field	8/9/18		Force continued quiet. The whole Battalion continued to occupy and work parties.	Ref. Stone
	9/9/18		Bn. relieved 8th Lancs. in the left Front Sector (Apps to ABLAINZEVELLE). Dispositions:— H.Q. TOP TR. A 21 d 05. 50. Front Coy. B + C (TOP TR) Support Coy. D (TOP TR) HQ. NUTTON to hospital. The CO. took command of Bn. during temporary absence of the Brigadier (on a course). Maj. P. GROVE-WHITE assumed temporary command.	
	10/9/18		The CO. & 2i/c visited the posts by day by comm: eng. up ABLAIN TR.— The enemy attempted to hold the Somerset left flank (on our right) at 3.15 A.M (8/9/18) but was unsuccessful. The Brigade Major paid a call.	

WAR DIARY or INTELLIGENCE SUMMARY

Army Form C. 2118.

Place	Date	Hour	Summary of Events and Information	Remarks and references to Appendices
In the Field	11/3/18		The enemy was very quiet in the forward area. Shelling was practically nil and T.M. activity was much below normal. LT. CHIPPERFIELD and 2 O.R. proceeded to PARIS on leave. CAPT JAMIESON proceeded to SUSSTRE so promised/found. The acting-Brigadier COL MOLONY visited the trenches in the afternoon. LT STONE M.O.R.C. relieved CAPT MIHER R.A.M.C. who proceeded to IV CORPS R.E.	
	12/3/18		Enemy continued quiet. C.R.E. visited BN. H.Q. DIV. CMDR. also visited BN. H.Q. later in the morning with the DIV INTELLIGENCE OFFICER. The enemy was very quiet and let all our observation guns out. Good work to the barrage opened by the 2nd __ CAPT. JAMIESON returned from SUSSTRE. A few gas shells fell near BN. H.Q. about 9.38 P.M. An intensive artillery duel occurred at O Cot acheroy 18 in the left front acly and a relieving o in the night front.	
	13/3/18		The enemy was reported to be relieving troops on our front. APHS were set out and enemy outposts were some distance from the same position. A C.O.'s conference was held at the time H.Q. in the afternoon. The O.O. (MAJOR GRUBE-WHITE) light on __ __ the enemy rendezvous at A sqn. H.Q. at 5:15 P.M.	

WAR DIARY or INTELLIGENCE SUMMARY

Army Form C. 2118.

Place	Date	Hour	Summary of Events and Information	Remarks and references to Appendices
	15/8		Regt. prepared to force their way into the enemy main line of resistance during the morning with one platoon. 2/Lt. TURNER's platoon attempted to effect an entrance into the enemy line at TRENCH S.5. No troops were put down at ZERO and it was decided to make another attempt at 2.35/1.57 pm. At 5.15 a very isolated barrage was put down and the platoon advanced under cover of a few smoke shells but were unable to get past the enemy wire. The party had to return. Lts. MOLONY and CAPT. MAYNARD M.C. came to Bn. HQ. for orders.	Appendix E
	16/8		Quiet day. The brigade major visited HQ. in the afternoon. 2/Lt. LINDSAY to FM., Lt. LYON to DOUBLERS for an interview with R.A.F. Lt. BOWSER, Major HAY and 2/Lt. SELFE to UK. on leave.	
	17/8		C.O. to Bde. for conference in the afternoon. Quiet day. Bn. relieved by 10 R.F. and took over from 13 KRR at VALLEY CAMP SOUASTRE.	
	18/8		The commanding officer returned from Bde. The C.O., CAPT. PROCTER and CAPT. SMITH M.C. and LT. WILKINS M.C. reconnoitred	

Army Form C. 2118.

Army Form C. 2118.

WAR DIARY
or
INTELLIGENCE SUMMARY.
(Erase heading not required.)

Instructions regarding War Diaries and Intelligence Summaries are contained in F. S. Regs., Part II. and the Staff Manual respectively. Title pages will be prepared in manuscript.

Place	Date	Hour	Summary of Events and Information	Remarks and references to Appendices
	19/5		The right sector of the Div. front. Orders were received that the 39th Div. were to attack at an early date. A Div. conference was held at HANNE'S CAMP on the morning of the C.O. held a conference with coy cmdrs. at 2.30 P.M. the BH. relieved the 13 R.F.F. in right sub-sector. BH. HQ. RETTEMOY FARM. Dispositions A coy. left front B coy. right front D coy. support C coy. reserve. Signal arrangements were made for the attack and all officers reconnoitred the ground.	
	20/5			

Army Form C. 2118.

WAR DIARY
or
INTELLIGENCE SUMMARY.
(Erase heading not required.)

Instructions regarding War Diaries and Intelligence Summaries are contained in F. S. Regs., Part II. and the Staff Manual respectively. Title pages will be prepared in manuscript.

Place	Date	Hour	Summary of Events and Information	Remarks and references to Appendices
In The Field.	26/8/18		Bn. spent the day in resting & fitting up to CHIPPERFIELD Dugout from leave. 2/Lt. SELFE rejoined from leave to England & took command of "D" Coy.	
	27/8/18		The Co. congratulated the men on the recent successful operation & read out a message from G.O.C. IV Corps. 2/Lt. F.R. SMITH rejoined from hospital & posted to "B". R. GROVE 2/Lt. HARRINGTON proceeded to England on short leave. Work continued on Cotters Kilvenies.	
	28/8/18		Day spent in organised salvage work to clear the area. Squares L.12. & G.7 allotted to the Batn. a large amount of stuff was collected, sorted & loaded & dumps	

WAR DIARY or INTELLIGENCE SUMMARY

Army Form C. 2118.

(Erase heading not required.)

Place	Date	Hour	Summary of Events and Information	Remarks and references to Appendices
In the Field	29/8/18		Work of salvage continued. The C.O. attended a CO's conference at Divisional HQ. Arrival of Lt. Grant. Draft of 172 O.R.s (incl. 55 to "C" Coy, 55 to "C", 40 to "D") joined the Battn. Lt. E.S. DASHFIELD Lt. T. MARSHALL Lt. J.B. BUCKNELL Lt. R.F. McFADDEN	Ref. 57.C.N.W.
	30/8/18		A Contest amongst officers of holding out a H.M. gun was experienced this day, two teams of officers being successful. Lt. T. DEVAL returned from leave. 2/Lt. A.S. YATES Lt. J.C. LYAL M.C. D.C.M. proceeded to "A" Coy. R.A.F. to England to Engineers	
	31/8/18		An attack scheme on a M.G. nest was carried out by the Battn. during the morning. Practice musketry & field on the range. Capt. A.J. KLAIBER proceeded on ordinary leave to England. 2/Lt. A.S. YATES Temp. Commander "A" Coy. An officers' revolver shooting practice was held after tea.	

Army Form C. 2118.

WAR DIARY
or
INTELLIGENCE SUMMARY.
(Erase heading not required.)

Instructions regarding War Diaries and Intelligence Summaries are contained in F. S. Regs., Part II. and the Staff Manual respectively. Title pages will be prepared in manuscript.

Place	Date	Hour	Summary of Events and Information	Remarks and references to Appendices
In the Field	31/8/18		Casualties & Appointment. Aug. 1918.	
			Officers: Killed – 2/Lt. H.F. BACKHOUSE 25.8	
			D.o.W. – Capt. F.E. MOORAT 24.8	
			Wounded – " J.P. JAMIESON 25.8	
			Lt. E.A.H. FENN 21.8	
			2/Lt. R.W. SEABY 22.8	
			" J.H. BAIRD 23.8	
			" F.H. MEACHAM 23.8	
			" B.E. GOODWIN 24.8	
			" A.J. HURDING 24.8	
			" H.E. HODGKINSON 25.8	
			" W.A. BLOR 25.8	
			11	
			O.Ranks: Killed 33	
			Wounded 233	
			Gassed 20	
			Missing 13	
			(6 killed) 299	
			Total: 310	
			Officer A/Dk etc.	
			2/Lt. A. HODGKINSON to Base. Struck off Strength 31.7	
			Lt. P.P. BURCH to FA 2.8	
			2/Lt. W. HUTTON " 9.8	
			" G.A. KING " 15.8	
			2/Lt. P. PATER " 17.8	

WAR DIARY
or
INTELLIGENCE SUMMARY.

(Erase heading not required.)

Army Form C. 2118.

Place	Date	Hour	Summary of Events and Information	Remarks and references to Appendices
In the Field	31/8/18		Officers sick etc.	
			2Lt. G. PRITCHARD to F.A. 22.8	
			- V.C. LINDSAY to do 29.8 (promoted temporarily at duty 25.8)	
			Appointments etc.	
			Lt. Col. W.B. MALONY (9th. Royal Lancaster Regt.) Took command of the Battn. 6.8.	
			Capt. S. MIRAMS awarded M.C. 7.8.	
			Capt. R.N. SMITH M.C. to U.K. 250 for 6 months Tour of duty.	
			Lieut. V.C. LYAL M.C. Dcm. to U.K. 30.8	
			13625 Pte. CLARKE. F. D Coy. R.A.F.	
			204065 " RAMS. H. D " Awarded M.M.	
			43663 " ROWE. H. A " " M.M.	
			1229 " BUTLER. R.M. M.M. D Coy " M.M.	
			360 Serg. CLARKE. M.Dunn. D Coy " Bar to M.M.	
			1229 Pte. BUTLER. R.M. now D Coy " do	
			13047 Serg. REANEY. C.H. A Coy " do	
				Bar to M.M.
				D.C.M.
			31.8.18.	W.B. Malony Lt. Col.
				Cmdg. 1/7 Bn. Middlesex Regt.

4th. BATTALION MIDDLESEX REGIMENT.

Account of Operations - 21.8.18 to 25.8.18.

The Battalion was in the assembly position one hour before zero which was 4.55 a.m. on the 21.8.18. The enemy carried out slight harassing fire on our positions and added a few gas shells, but did not hinder our assembly. It was a clear night with a bright moon, but towards morning a ground mist appeared and thickened as zero hour approached. This was rather serious because it greatly hindered our four tanks and the result was that they were unable to co-operate with the Battalion during the attack.

The objective of the 63rd. Brigade was the high ground East of BUCQUOY and the attack was made with the 4th. Middlesex on the right and 8th. Somerset Light Infantry on the left with the 8th. Lincolnshire Regt. in support to the Brigade. Two Companies of the 13th. Royal Fusiliers were attached to each of the attacking Battalions for carrying purposes. Companies went over in Two waves, the first to capture and consolidate the objective and the second to pass through and form an outpost line.

"B" Company was on the right under Capt. SMITH, M.C.
"C" Company in the centre under Capt. PROCTER.
"D" Company on the left under Capt. JAMIESON.
"A" Company was in Support under Capt. KLAIBER.

Battalion Headquarters moved to an advanced position at 1.30 a.m. and Lt.Col.MOLONY and the Signalling Officer went forward to an observation post just before zero.

Considering the fog, which obliterated all land marks, the advance was conducted splendidly.

"B" Company on the right advanced on a compass bearing, a M.G. on their right opened fire, but was silenced by Cpl. HASWELL, who gallantly rushed in and killed the men at the gun.

"C" Company worked round South of BUCQUOY and gradually forced their way up trenches which were held by M.G's. Cpl. ONYETT and Cpl. JARVIS rushed these posts. 2/Lieut. HODGKINSON went through the centre of BUCQUOY and pushed up to the enemy advanced post, where he took several prisoners.

"D" Company on the left had a stiff time in BUCQUOY as the tanks were not able to function as arranged. A Strong Point put up a great fight with T.M's. and M.G's., but was rushed by Capt. JAMIESON and Sgt. PERRY and 3 or 4 men. They got to the final objective about 5.45 a.m. capturing in all about 50 prisoners and killing a large number.

Shortly after the objective was captured, the enemy barraged it heavily.

An advanced report centre was established at a derelict tank in "C" Company's objective to which a telephone line was laid shortly after the Companies had taken the objective.

The total captures of the Battalion were 115 prisoners, 7 M.G's. and 2 T.M's.

The 5th. Division went through the Brigade in splendid style, and the Battalion set about the consolidation of the objectives.

The two Companies of the 13th. Royal Fusiliers were withdrawn during the afternoon and replaced by two Companies of the 8th. Lincolnshire Regiment.

The following special order was sent to Companies by the Commanding Officer :

"I wish to convey my hearty congratulations to all ranks on splendid way the attack was carried out yesterday. The dense fog making all cohesive action and keeping touch and direction extremely difficult. All dificulties that were met were swept away without delay and the road cleared for the 5th. Division. I greatly regret the loss of Cpl. Kent

/and

and L/Cpl. Curry and those who lost their lives during and after the action."

Capt. JAMIESON proceeded to Field Ambulance for an Anti-TETANUS injection, and rejoined Battalion the following day.

On the 22nd. Aug. the men were rested as much as possible during the day and S.A.A. etc. was made up from organized dumps. About 3 p.m. a warning order was received that the 37th. Division was to attack on the afternoon of 23rd. with the 112th. Brigade on the right and the 111th. Brigade on the left, supported by the 63rd. Brigade.
Objectives:- ACHIET-LE-GRAND and BIHUCOURT.

The ground North of LOGEAST WOOD was reconnoitred by Major GROVE WHITE and one officer per Company during the afternoon.

The Brigade moved to assembly positions North of LOGEAST WOOD during the night, where final preparations for the attack were made.

Battalion Headquarters moved to a point about 700 yards North of ABLAINZEVELLE on the COURCELLES Road.

The barrage opened at 11 a.m. 23.8.18 and the Brigade advanced in Support, 4th. Middlesex Regt. on right, 8th. Lincolnshire Regiment on left with 8th. Somerset Light Infantry in reserve.

The enemy put down a fair barrage of 4.2's, 5.9's and H.E. shrapnel, but the Battalion advanced with few casualties until it neared ACHIET-LE-GRAND. A certain amount of M.G. fire was also encountered from the direction of GOMMIECOURT.
Order of Companies:- "A" left front and "B" right front.
"C" Support and "D" Reserve.

The Battalion advanced as arranged and consolidated a line about 500 yards East of the ARRAS-BAPAUME railway. The enemy kept up a heavy barrage in the vicinity of ACHIET-LE-GRAND and sent over a large proportion of gas-shells in the village itself.

About 5.30 p.m. orders were received to push on just beyond BIHUCOURT. "A" and "C" Coys. were to work around South of BIHUCOURT and "D" Coy. to go around by the North of the village and all Companies would then connect up in front. "B" Company at this was rather split up and parts of it went with the other 3 Companies.

Companies advanced about 500 yards but met heavy M.G. fire. The 8th. Somerset Light Infantry came forward and took up a position in the trenches between BIHUCOURT and ACHIET-LE-GRAND. The Battalion then withdrew to their original positions and the night was spent in reorganizing Companies and consolidating.

Flank liaison was established and a defence organized. A section from each Company was sent to the BRICKWORKS to carry up supplies of S.A.A. etc.

Battalion Headquarters was situated in a old Signal Office on the East outskirts of ACHIET-LE-GRAND.

Capt. F. F. MOORAT was mortally wounded early in the morning of 24th. and died shortly afterwards.

Orders were received early in the morning that the Brigade was to advance on BIEFVILLERS in conjunction with the New Zealanders, the 4th. Middlesex being in support to the 8th. Lincolns on the left and the 8th. Somerset Light Infantry attacking on the right. Owing to the lack of time Companies could not be assembled by zero and 8th. Somerset Light Infantry went on with the New Zealanders, eventually the order was cancelled and the Battalion was ordered to push on as soon as possible to aid the Somerset L.I., who had reached BIEFVILLERS. The Battalion moved off about 1 p.m. - "A" Company to be in close support to Somerset L.I. and New Zealanders, who were holding BIEFVILLERS.
"B" Company to occupy trenches just West of BIEFVILLERS and "C" and "D" Companies to form a protective flank facing North East.

About halfway between BIHUCOURT and BIEFVILLERS Battalion Headquarters was established in a railway tunnel by "C" and "D" Companies.

In spite of heavy shelling Companies reached their positions with few casualties.

BIEFVILLERS and the valley West of it was heavily shelled all the afternoon, and the shelling became even more intense at night. Orders

2.

Orders were received about 7.30 p.m. that the 63rd. Brigade was to advance on the left of New Zealand Division and occupy high ground on the BAPAUME-ARRAS Road, South of the MONUMENT. 8th. Lincolns were to support 4th. Middlesex, and 8th. Somerset L.I. were to move in rear, echeloned to the left. The attack was planned, but shortly afterwards these orders were cancelled and fresh orders arrived about 1 a.m. 25.8.18.

The new orders were that the attack would be on a two Battalion front, the objective being the BAPAUME-ARRAS Road, North of the MONUMENT, Lincolns of left and 4th.Middlesex on right with Somerset L.I. in support.

Battalion Headquarters moved to dugout in Hollow Road just West of BIEFVILLERS, where the new plans were communicated to Company Commanders.

Great credit was due to all Officers, N.C.Os. and men for getting to their assembly positions in time in spite of the constant shelling.

Zero hour was 5 a.m., a heavy fog greatly impeded the attack & made direction hard to maintain. After slight loss of direction Companies reorganized and attacked QUARRIES where 60 prisoners were captured.

During the attack there were many acts of individual heroism, with the result that the objective was captured about 6.30 a.m.

Captures - 80 prisoners, 13 Machine Guns and 1 Heavy T.M.

2/Lieut. H.F. Backhouse was killed and Capt. Jamieson was wounded during the attack.

Capt. PROCTER and Capt. KLAIBER worked hard reorganizing the Battalion and were ably assisted by 2/Lieut. J.C.LINDSAY, who with a small party captured a M.G. post on the BAPAUME-ARRAS Road.

Flank liaison was established with the New Zealanders on the right and the 111th. Brigade on the left.

The Battalion consolidated captured positions throughout a heavy barrage and the reorganization was completed.

The Battalion was relieved by a Battalion of the 5th. Division and withdrew to ACHIET-LE-PETIT.

During these operations the Battalion suffered the following losses:-

	OFFICERS.	OTHER RANKS.
Killed........	2. Capt. F.F.MOORAT. 2/Lieut.H.F.BACKHOUSE.	25.
Wounded.......	9. 2/Lieut.J.H.BAIRD. " F.H.MEACHAM. " B.E.GOODWIN. " A.J.HURDING. " H.E.HODGKINSON. " W.A.BLOY. Capt. J.P.JAMIESON. Lieut. E.A.H.FENN. 2/Lieut. R.W.SEABY.	213.
Missing.		25.

63rd Brigade.
37th Division.

4th BATTALION

THE MIDDLESEX REGIMENT.

SEPTEMBER 1918

4 Middlesex Regt
63/5

WAR DIARY
or
INTELLIGENCE SUMMARY.
(Erase heading not required.)

Army Form C. 2118.
September 1918.
Vol 50

Place	Date	Hour	Summary of Events and Information	Remarks and references to Appendices
En Bs Field	1/9/18.		Training continued on the range & practice attack. The Lt/Gun carried to gives Section Coy. passed back to the Div.res. T.Cos. were given practice with 297-bombs. (Boars).	Ref. 57 C
	2/9/18		Orders received that the Bn. will relieve the 5th Division. Maps distributed & divisional salvage work continued.	
	3/9/18		Prepared to move. Bn. marched to ACHIET LE GRAND & ARRIVED there at 3.30 p.m. & was made for tea. Thence to march on. Moved via BEUGNY & FREMICOURT. Bn. relieved 1st Royal Warwicks (13th Bde). Bn.HQ. being in I.23.6 & the Coys distributed nearby.	
	4/9/18.		12th Bde conference pushed on enemy of 63rd Bde. in support. Bn on left, 56 Bde on right. A Coy. in front, B Coy. in support, C & D in reserve. Bn.HQ. moved to I.19.d.4.0 Thence to I.20.c.0.0. Bn. moved up on the right of A Coy. Wounded prisoners were	

Army Form C. 2118.

WAR DIARY
or
INTELLIGENCE SUMMARY.
(Erase heading not required.)

Place	Date	Hour	Summary of Events and Information	Remarks and references to Appendices
In the Field	4/9/18		Brought in a large amount of energy gas shell over the area.	Ref 57.c.NE & SE
	5/9/18		Co. attended conference at Bde. H.Q. 63rd Bde relieved N.Z. left Bde. in the line. Taken on support. Bn. H.Q. in railway cutting at P.2.d.45.50. A & B Coys in front line P.3.a.& c. C & D in support in sunken lane in P.2. d d.6. A lot of shelling during the night.	
	6/9/18		Lt. HODGES returned from leave. 2/Lt. CHAUNDY went on leave. Coys. attached to different Bns. A & D to relieve Coys to 8th Somersets advance through HAVRINCOURT WOOD.	
	7/9/18		2/Lt ANDREWS returned from leave. At 6 a.m. A Coy. moved to V.35.a. & B Coy. to PAUPER TR. (P.10.B) C & D moving up to their late positions late on. B	

WAR DIARY or INTELLIGENCE SUMMARY.

(Erase heading not required.)

Army Form C. 2118.

Place	Date	Hour	Summary of Events and Information	Remarks and references to Appendices
In the Field	7/9/18		Coy. moved to P.11.6 & C.Coy. to PAUPER TR. 2 of our aeroplanes dropped a dozen lamp bombs in our line with great accuracy.	Ref. 57c NEUSE
	8/9/18		Bn. H.Q. moved to J.35.d. (Sunken road). B Coy. moved up to J.36.d. D Coy. moved up to J.35.d.	
	9/9/18		Fairly quiet day. Bn. HQ. advanced to Q.R.6.c. 5.9. C & D Coys. moved up to our horizon & went up to take over front line from Q.9.a.2.2 to Q.3.6.3.0 from Sh. Somerset. D Coy on left C Coy on right. A Coy. moved up to support to HUBERT TR. Henry beverage along Oxford Valley. Q.8.a.9.6. Lt. MARSHALL J 12 S.R. casualtied. Advanced Bn. H.Q. established near CRAYTON CROSS at P.P.a. 05.60.	

WAR DIARY
or
INTELLIGENCE SUMMARY.

(Erase heading not required.)

Army Form C. 2118.

Place	Date	Hour	Summary of Events and Information	Remarks and references to Appendices
In the Field	10/9/18		Patrols were pushed out N. & S. of TRESCAULT under 2/Lt. McFADDEN & Lt. DASHFIELD respectively. The latter patrol encountered resistance & Lt. DASHFIELD was wounded. 3 men were wounded. "C" Coy relieved "B" Coy in the front line.	Ref. S7.C. N.E.Y. S.E.
	11/9/18		Day opened quietly but shelling became severe towards dusty. 9/Lt. Bon was relieved by 2/Lt. KRRC (11th Bn) & took over to Billets around the ruin of VELU Chateau.	
	12/9/18		Meeting of Coy. Commanders in H.Q. mess at 3.30 p.m. The C.O. dined with the G.O.C. Posti: Capt. ROW proceeds to D. Coy (relieving). 2/Lt. A.E. STAFFORD — to "C" (command) Draft of 25 O. Ranks arrived.	

WAR DIARY
or
INTELLIGENCE SUMMARY.

Army Form C. 2118.

Place	Date	Hour	Summary of Events and Information	Remarks and references to Appendices
In the Field	13/9/18		The day was taken up with coy. parades, inspections and bomb proofing of huts. Lt. CHIPPERFIELD proceeded to England on leave. The enemy continued to shell the neighbourhood of VELU WOOD with H.V. guns but no casualties resulted.	
	14/9		Coys. fired on the Bn. rifle range in the morning. An inter-platoon football competition was started in the afternoon. Each platoon furnished a team of six men.	
	15/9		Church parade at 11.30 AM in charge of VELU WOOD. Semi-finals of football competition were played in the afternoon. The enemy bombed and shelled the camp at night but did no damage. One of our night-flying 'planes brought down a seven-seater enemy 'plane in flames near BEUGNY amidst great cheering from a large group of spectators. 2/Lt. HODGKINSON and 2/Lt. LINDSAY rejoined from hospital.	
	16/9		The finals of the inter-platoon competition were played in the morning, 12 platoon winning from 15 platoon. The Bn. moved off at 1.30 P.M. to relieve 13 K.R.R. as Bn. in immediate support to BDE. in the line. The relief was carried out by daylight, coys. being spread along the	

WAR DIARY
or
INTELLIGENCE SUMMARY.

Army Form C. 2118.

Place	Date	Hour	Summary of Events and Information	Remarks and references to Appendices
	17/9		E. edge of HAVRINCOURT WOOD. D coy. were fairly heavily shelled at night - casualties 1 killed & wounded. C coy. on right. B coy, A coy on left and D coy in a quarry about 500x in front. 2/Lt. LINDSAY was awarded the M.C. the C.O. and I.O. lived / with his o/ the front line bns. during the evening. Bn. H.Q. was situated at BUTLER'S CROSS - Q.3.b.3.2. The C.O. and I.O. reconnoitred the ground and visited coys. in the morning. Coy. officers liased with front line Bns. in case we should be called to counter-attack. Quiet day. MAJOR BIGGS and the G.S.O.1 of DIV. called at Bn. H.Q. during the afternoon.	57e NE SE
	18/9		The ESSEX and FUSILIERS attempted to clear a pocket of the enemy but met with slim resistance. Orders were received that we would relieve the 1st HERTS. on night 18/19 but the relief was postponed until the night 19/20. Later in the day at 5:30 PM the Boche opened a heavy barrage along the whole front and many low flying airoplanes circled HAVRINCOURT & rgmt came in that -	

WAR DIARY
or
INTELLIGENCE SUMMARY.
(Erase heading not required.)

Army Form C. 2118.

Place	Date	Hour	Summary of Events and Information	Remarks and references to Appendices
	19/9		The Boche had broken through but this were found to be false. BN. HQ. stood to for two hours. It was later that the attack had been magnificently repulsed by the HERTS and the DIV. on the left and about 40 prisoners were left in our hands. CO. and I.O. reconnoitred the front. Our mid sector. Advance parties were sent up to take over in the morning. BN. relieved at night. B coy. left front A coy. right front C coy. in support and D coy. in Reserve, BN. HQ. remaining in the same place. The Brigadier and brigade major visited the BN. in the afternoon.	
	20/9.		C.O. and I.O. went about the line early in the morning. Two of our aeroplanes were brought down behind the Boche lines after a serious dog fight. The Brigadier held a conference at BN. HQ. at noon. The 1/8 MANCHESTERS arrived and would take over our BN. dispositions. CAPT. KLAIBER and CAPT. MIRAMS M.C. rejoined the BN. The former took over command of A coy and the latter acted as an advance party to take over	

WAR DIARY
or
INTELLIGENCE SUMMARY.
(Erase heading not required.)

Army Form C. 2118.

Place	Date	Hour	Summary of Events and Information	Remarks and references to Appendices
	21/9		as second in command during the absence of MAJOR GROVE & MAJOR WHITE who proceeded to England on leave earlier in the morning.	57c NE 57c SE
	22/9		The C.O. and company commanders of the 1/5 MANCHESTERS came to BN. HQ. to arrange details of the relief. The day passed quietly and the MANCHESTERS arrived on time. The relief was carried out quietly and the BN. proceeded to huts W. of LE BUCQUIERE where the night was spent.	
	23/9		The BN. had dinners and moved off at 1.20 P.M. Order of march HQ. A.B.C.D with usual intervals between companies. The C.O. went to BDE. to reconnoitre the corps line defences and went from there to our new quarters at LA BARQUE. It started to rain when the BN. was just E. of BAPAUME and the march was finished in a downpour. BN. settled in billets at 5.30 P.M. The C.O. and CAPT. MIRAMS MC. reconnoitred two ranges for the BN. details from BN. HQ. and cos. bathed during the	

Army Form C. 2118.

WAR DIARY
or
INTELLIGENCE SUMMARY.
(Erase heading not required.)

Instructions regarding War Diaries and Intelligence Summaries are contained in F. S. Regs., Part II. and the Staff Manual respectively. Title pages will be prepared in manuscript.

Place	Date	Hour	Summary of Events and Information	Remarks and references to Appendices
			Morning. Brigne was very pleased to hear that the following decorations for the good work done by the battalion during the 21st and 26th of August, had been awarded by the C in C.	
			D.S.O.	
			LIEUT-COL. W.B. MOLONY	
			T/LT. (A/CAPT) J.P. JAMIESON	
			BAR TO M.C.	
			T/LT. J.C. LINDSAY, M.C.	
			M.C.	
			TEMP. CAPT. E. PROCTER	
			" T/LT. (A/CAPT) A.J. KLAIBER	
			D.C.M.	
			NO. 4567 CPL. A.H. ONYETT. C COY.	
			" 14822 SGT. F. PERRY. D "	

Army Form C. 2118.

WAR DIARY
or
INTELLIGENCE SUMMARY.
(Erase heading not required.)

Place	Date	Hour	Summary of Events and Information	Remarks and references to Appendices
LA BARQUE	24/9		The morning was spent by Companies in inspection of kits, equipment and clothing. The men were accounted for excellent billets, each man having a wire bed, tables in small groups to stand in. Companies worked and being in small groups the Divisional Concert Party gave entertainments. The "Barn Owls" Divisional Concert Party gave a performance in LA BARQUE THEATRE at 6 pm. The show was a great Bn. entertainment and was very much enjoyed.	
LA BARQUE	25/9		Companies bathed at the THULLOY baths throughout the day. One Company was detailed for work on unloading MISSEN HUTS in the vicinity. The Bn. paraded outside Bn. HQrs to see Brigadier General who was had orders to take up an appointment at G.H.Q. being Generally arrived up at 12.30 pm and in a few well chosen words told the Bn. how sorry he was to leave us complimented us on our recent successes and wished us the best of luck in the future. The C.O. then thanked the General and called for three cheers for which were roaringly given. The General spoke to	

(A10266.) Wt.W5300/P1715 750,000 2/18 Sch. 52 Forms/C2118/16.
D, D, & L., London, E.C.

WAR DIARY
or
INTELLIGENCE SUMMARY.

Army Form C. 2118.

(Erase heading not required.)

Place	Date	Hour	Summary of Events and Information	Remarks and references to Appendices
	26/9		his speech, presented the prize medals won by a platoon of "D" Company in an A.E.G. competition held in June. Only eight of the original platoon were present, the remainder of the medals were sent to the home addresses. The C.O. held a company commanders Conference on prospect training after the parade.	
			LA BARQUE Training of all ranks was carried out during the morning. The Drums played selections in the morning in front of B. Bn. Hd. Qtrs. the collection were afternoon was carried out by small parties of ranges was granted to the following men throughout the day. The Military Medal was presented to the following men for conspicuous gallantry and devotion to duty near HARI'COURT on 8/10th Sept. No. 205260 Sgt W. NORTHCOTT "C" Coy " 50537 R.S.M. BEARD (Honours) " 6944 Sgt G. TAYLOR " do	
	27/9		LA BARQUE Training of under Company arrangements. Schemes in "the Platoon in the Attack" were carried out. also range practices, special attention being paid to classification.	

WAR DIARY or INTELLIGENCE SUMMARY

Army Form C. 2118.

Place	Date	Hour	Summary of Events and Information	Remarks and references to Appendices
LA BARQUE	28/9		Training under Company arrangements. All Company moved through a Lookers by Chariot for the purpose of testing the S.R's. Enemy aeroplanes were fairly active during the night but did not drop any bombs in the area. A Revision Deloway was made for use of the Bn. A return was given in the afternoon by the Divisional Observation officer on the Souvenirs Reservation Room on the lake on the Authigh of educating groups by means of the Groups Albums and Lectures being delivered. Groups taken up on leave being uniformly delayed. One Company marched off on leaving anything to an area	
LA BARQUE (SUNDAY)	29/9		The Bn. attended Church Parade at 10.15 am in LA BARQUE THEATRE, owing to the small size of the theatre it was not possible to find seating accommodation for everyone. A bright and observation competition was held during the afternoon which interesting points regarding the use of camouflage were brought out. The S.O. fired a range of shots 50 to 70 Yards. S.G.S. BALDWIN M.A. Capt. During the evening warning orders were received to be ready to move to the forward area.	

Army Form C. 2118.

WAR DIARY
or
INTELLIGENCE SUMMARY.
(Erase heading not required.)

Place	Date	Hour	Summary of Events and Information	Remarks and references to Appendices
LA BARQUE	30/9	6.30 a.m.	Bn. moved to NEUVILLE-BOURJONVAL, leaving LA BARQUE at 6.30 a.m. and arriving at NEUVILLE at mid-day, marched via BEAUENCOURT — VILLERS-AU-FLOS — HAPLINCOURT — BERTINCOURT — and thence cross country. Owing to insufficient transport being supplied, blankets were left behind on a dump & the Bn's transport rather crowded were quite food. General and staff called during the day and informed us another move the following day to Q.16 area (quarries over trenches)	

WAR DIARY
or
INTELLIGENCE SUMMARY

Army Form C. 2118.

Place	Date	Hour	Summary of Events and Information	Remarks and references to Appendices
In the Field			Casualties and Appointments September 1918	
			Officers — Killed — NIL	
			Wounded — Lt. E.S. DASHFIELD	
			Lt. L.T. MARSHALL	
			O. Ranks Killed — 9 (2 L. Gassed)	
			Wounded — 43 (3 (wounded) at duty)	
			1 Wounded & missing	
			Missing — 2	
			Missing believed Wounded	
			Total 57	
			OFFICERS SICK 2/Lt A.R. SMITH	
			O. RANKS " 63	
			MISCELLANEOUS 2/Lt H.W. CRAYDEN proceeded on	
			23/9/18 and was posted to "A" Coy.	

W Willoughby Lieut. Colonel.
Commanding 1/7 Bn Middlesex Regiment.

63rd Brigade.
37th Division.

4th BATTALION

THE MIDDLESEX REGIMENT.

OCTOBER 1918

4 Battalion
Army Form C. 2118. 63/37

WAR DIARY
or
INTELLIGENCE SUMMARY.
(Erase heading not required.)

OCTOBER — 1916 Vol 51

Place	Date	Hour	Summary of Events and Information	Remarks and references to Appendices
In the field	1/10		BN. moved from NEUVILLE to Q.16.a area. BN Adjce having a Quarry and the Companys in Trenches & Shelters. Two of our Balloons were brought down in flames and the occupants escaping by parachute. Enemy aircraft active during the night, bombs been dropped in HAPPINCOURT area. Tents arrived during the afternoon supplementing the few accommodation available. The men are still without their Blankets and the nights are very cold.	
	2/10		O.C. No 6 Company reports that a shot if fired from under the Company's camp might set him on fire and that the range was shorter than they think and he had therefore given orders that you life was not to be taken but that you give way if attacked on the change that the enemy may not know if your life were feared that they might try to do so. As to the M.O. I think Bruce and notice of more O.C.M.H of 1 Officer 2 W.O. & WATNABY and C.C. Godfrey and in the evening of October 3rd & CR 48 C.S. M3	

WAR DIARY or INTELLIGENCE SUMMARY

Army Form C. 2118.

Place	Date	Hour	Summary of Events and Information	Remarks and references to Appendices
	3/10		@ 16.0. Hrs. the C.O. inspected the draft in marching order. About 6.30 p.m. the enemy began an intense bombardment & followed up with an attempt to capture our line. They had some local success being temporarily successful in the capture of Stamford & Copthorne in Sh. I [illegible]. An immediate counter attack by Capt. Blakely's Coy. with L.G.[illegible] & [illegible] drove the enemy [illegible] (WCTOR) & recaptured from the enemy. Lt (NCTOR) CHIPPERFIELD returned from leave.	
	4/10		@ 16.C. C.O. attended Coy commanders conference at Bde HQ. Bn. W.N.O. was also present. Flag & Aero flare practice was carried out by Bde at 3–4 P.M. A Band Pte. (1 [illegible]) Rfn. was heard playing in Company Mess RFA.	154 Bde RFA
	5/10		@ 16.C. Training consisted of half an hour @ Bde Hdqrs. Bn. of Company training and a great deal of [illegible] death chair intermixed. An [illegible] ordered at 5.45 pm was quickly & smartly carried out by the area inspected by Brig. Gen. VINCER & MIO H. 9 pm & arrived & around trenches and shelters however ranked and short leave to England 2/LTE ENMORE himself an Army School.	

WAR DIARY
or
INTELLIGENCE SUMMARY.
(Erase heading not required.)

Army Form C. 2118.

Place	Date	Hour	Summary of Events and Information	Remarks and references to Appendices
VILLERS BOCAGE	6/10		On today's march from a Regiment to ____ into billets near the railway. C.O. Adjt & Coy Cmdrs reconnoitred the front line during the afternoon. Bn at half an hour's notice to move. Enemy aeroplane very active during the night. Bomb was dropped ____ near to Nº on ____	FRANCE SHEET 57
VILLERS PUICH	7/10		C.O.'s conference at Bde HQrs. Bn ordered to be at GRAND DE LESCAUT at 01.00 hrs on the 8/10/18. Bn started afternoon 7th hrs found Bn on the east of ____ at 01.00 hours and bivouacked in the vicinity of VAUCELLES COPSE. A ___ ordnance dropped at HQ in afternoon. B ____	
	8/10		___ moved on left of ____ W. side of BASSE UX ____ to ____ attached to the 11th F ____ to arrive at D ____ about ___ and ___ from L. Gd. ___ were ____ by M. G. ___ from ____ GUILLEMIN FARM, long ____ rifle ___ and ___ from sent into ____ at ____ numerous bridges of ammunition, ___ considerable resistance 2nd ___ hoisted 1st SOMERSETS ___	

WAR DIARY
or
INTELLIGENCE SUMMARY.
(Erase heading not required.)

Army Form C. 2118.

Place	Date	Hour	Summary of Events and Information	Remarks and references to Appendices
In the Field	9/10		The LINCOLNS did a night attack and the division on the right front — Cavalieries [Officers] — Lt. H. E. HOOKHAM — VILRE STAFFORD-BELL and Lt. Col. RYAN — 4th O.R.S. All had been taken in advance to line E. D. HARCOURT — 732 [Centre] to the right for the Battalion. Lt. HARCOURT was 4th in Command and in support. The march led to CAUDRY and the Bn. moved into fields at HARCOURT. The day was spent in HARCOURT at midnight the Bn. moved to LIEMY to support the attack of the 46th Div. on CAUDRY.	
	10/10		The Bn. in the night attacked ordered to form up as fast as possible. They were greatly helped by smoke. Liaison was difficult on the right but it worked out alright in [...] On [...] of the CHURCH of SANS was found [...] right of the SEILLE 5th [...] for [...] the attack on [...] Lnt ACLERMONT indicated when the attack would start CHURY they secured a most important [...] armed [...] and were stated no more [...] no in the [...] of carrying the [...] Major [...] was quite intact with [...]	

WAR DIARY
or
INTELLIGENCE SUMMARY.
(Erase heading not required.)

Army Form C. 2118.

Place	Date	Hour	Summary of Events and Information	Remarks and references to Appendices
Br. H.Q. Viesly	11/10		They [illegible] army moved up to [illegible] the lines and Coy were detailed two platoons [across] the river, showing to Coy there was a certain amount of shelling but [illegible] not sufficient to cause [illegible]. The C.O. and Capt. VINER reconnoitred the very high ground [illegible] [illegible] to VIESLY CHATEAU about 11.00 hours. Was spent in preparation for the attack on the following morning. The [illegible] shelled the CHATEAU every 10 mins but only slightly damaged the buildings and no casualties resulted. [illegible] and [illegible] and [illegible] until at 16.00 hrs at 04.00 hours on the 12.10.18.	

WAR DIARY or INTELLIGENCE SUMMARY

Army Form C. 2118.

Place	Date	Hour	Summary of Events and Information	Remarks and references to Appendices
In the Field	12/10		Bn. details moved to CAUDRY. Where the billets were cleaned up in anticipation of the arrival of the Bn. The Boche had left the houses in even a more filthy state than he usually keeps his billets. A good working party of the men to arrange the billets. The operations carried out by the battalion on this day are attached.	
	13/10		The Bn. was settled in billets about 06.45 hours owing to the scarcity of mechanical transport it was impossible to get the men's packs and blankets up but the billets were quite good and the men settled down to a well-earned tolup Taylor sent lit- food. The Brigadier visited Bn. HQ at 35 RUE D'ANDRÉ early in the afternoon. A company commanders conference was held in Bn. HQ mess at 15.00 hours to discuss the recent operations.	
	14/10		A divisional conference was held in Bn. HQ mess at 10.00 hours, the divisional commander presiding. 2/Lt H.T. BUSH joined the Bn. as a reinforcement. A dinner in honour of CAPT. E. PROCTER M.C. who was about to proceed to	

WAR DIARY
or
INTELLIGENCE SUMMARY.
(Erase heading not required.)

Army Form C. 2118.

Place	Date	Hour	Summary of Events and Information	Remarks and references to Appendices
	15/10		England for six months rest, was given at HQ. mess. The following Junior were present CAPT. PROCTER. M.C., CAPT. FITZGIBBON, CAPT. NEWMAN and CAPT. MAYNARD. M.C. The Brigadier was to have addressed the Bn. but this was cancelled owing to rain and he said the men in their billets. CAPT. PROCTER. M.C. proceeded to England. A draft of 35 casuals including 2 C.S.M'S. reported. Companies spent the day cleaning up and holding the usual usual inspections.	
	16/10		The C.O. addressed all the officers and N.C.O.'s on the recent operations in the morning. The following officers joined as reinforcements:— 2/Lt. W.H. LYNCH, 2/Lt. A.L. NORMAN, 2/Lt. ABERNETHY. MAJOR GROVE-WHITE lectured the officers on the prismatic compass in the evening. The Brigadier and 2/Lt. FORREST (Bde. S/Offr.) dined with HQ. 2/Lt. PIERCE rejoined from leave to England.	
	17/10		The Bn. paraded at 09.30 hours. and practiced deploying from roads. A company commanders conference was held in HQ. mess after the parade. At 14.30 hours the C.O.	

Army Form C. 2118.

WAR DIARY
or
INTELLIGENCE SUMMARY.
(Erase heading not required.)

Place	Date	Hour	Summary of Events and Information	Remarks and references to Appendices
In the Field	18/10		took a riding class for officers which was much appreciated. The afternoon was spent in cleaning up for the inspection by the Divisional General on the following morning.	
			The Battalion paraded outside billets in CAUDRY at 10.00 hours and marched to the ground selected for the inspection. The whole Bde. was inspected during the morning. 8th LINCOLNS at 10.00 hours, 9th SOMERSETS at 10.30 hours and 10th MIDDLESEX and 63rd BDE. TRENCH MORTARS at 11.00 hours. The Battalion formed up in mass with H.Q. on the right, A coy and drums and stretcher bearers in rear of the Battalion. The Divisional Commander walked around and inspected the men and seemed quite pleased with the general appearance of the Battalion. While he inspected the T.M.B. the Battalion was formed in a square in preparation for a short address. The G.O.C. reviewed the fighting through which the Battalion had done since August 21 and complimented the men on their splendid record. He visited the transport lines afterwards and expressed his appreciation of the hard work of the transport as shown in the good condition of all the animals. In the afternoon the Intelligence	

WAR DIARY
or
INTELLIGENCE SUMMARY

Army Form C. 2118.

Place	Date	Hour	Summary of Events and Information	Remarks and references to Appendices
In the Field	19/10		Officers attended a demonstration of German wire obstacles and how to overcome them. Major Prof. Süttle conducted a night march by compass for all officers in the evening. The following officers joined as reinforcements:- Lt. A. ANDERSON (A Coy.) 2/Lt. M.V. LITTON (A Coy.) 2/Lt. J.H.D. BALDOCK (B Coy.)	
	20/10		Very dull day. Training under company arrangements was carried out until 11:00 hours, from then until 13:00 hours the Bn. practised attack formations. During the afternoon classes were held for stretcher bearers and Lewis Gunners. The Officers' riding class was continued. A church parade was held in the Barn OWLS Stable for the Wesleyans. A Presbyterian Church was attended. To special Thanksgiving service partly in French and partly in English was held in the Barn church. The weather continued dull.	

Army Form C. 2118.

WAR DIARY
or
INTELLIGENCE SUMMARY.
(Erase heading not required.)

Place	Date	Hour	Summary of Events and Information	Remarks and references to Appendices
Dr. Highfield	2/1/10		Owing to rain, all ranks were indoors. Lieut. Col. W.F. Moberly, D.S.O., M.C., for England for a visit amongst sick and wounded. Whilst all ranks were sorry to see Major P. Snow going, they were delighted that a large proportion of the battalion's friends were among the last few months due to his tireless energy and good leadership. Chosen as friend as usual the afternoon. Capt. T. Gunman dined with H.Q. Company training was carried out until the afternoon. Classes as usual in the afternoon. The C.O. inspected the newly arrived drafts. The morning. At 17.00 hours a demonstration of how to load a limber was given outside the men's bond. CAPT. H.H. NEWSUM M.C. joined the bn. as second in command. A reg. commanders conference was held in HQ. mess at 17.30 hours. Capt.	

WAR DIARY
or
INTELLIGENCE SUMMARY.
(Erase heading not required.)

Army Form C. 2118.

Place	Date	Hour	Summary of Events and Information	Remarks and references to Appendices
In the Field	23/10		Chipperfield dined with H.Q. Orders were received that Bn. was to march & will take over the line from the 8th Div. on the following day and 2/LT A.G. PIERCE proceeded to Y.IESLY with `a' billeting party. Bn. paraded at 09.30 hours. Order of march H.Q.A. R.C.D. Details remained in CAUDRY under CAPT. NEWSUM. M.C. the Bn. settled in billets at 18.30 hours. As the advance had now resumed that morning the C.O. and I.O. reconnoitred the forward areas during the afternoon and company officers reconnoitred the crossings of the river SELLE	

WAR DIARY
or
INTELLIGENCE SUMMARY.

Army Form C. 2118.

Place	Date	Hour	Summary of Events and Information	Remarks and references to Appendices
In the Field	24/10		Bn. paraded at 06.45 hours with kits & returned to VIESLY CHURCH and marched to BEAURAIN via BRIASTE. Three companies were billeted in the town and C coy. boy shelters in an orchard. Bn. had dinners and paraded again at 15.30 hours to move forward and relieve the 111th BDE. in support. The Bn. relieved the 13 K.R.R.'s with Bn. HQ. in NEUVILLE and coys. in shelters and sunken roads on E. and S.E. outskirts of the village.	57b NE 51a SE
	25/10		The C.O., coy. cmdrs. and I.O. reconnoitred the forward area in the morning. Coys. spent the day in musketry/training and sabotage. The platoon of B coy. were moved into billets in NEUVILLE.	
	26/10		Coys. trained during the day - musketry and Lewis gun. Men were allotted to coys. for salvage and parties were sent out. Capt. E.H. AMOR visited the Bn. after an enjoyable leave and stayed to lunch. Lieut. E.E.IMORE who had also recently rejoined from leave and taken over the duties of assistant adjutant, came to tea.	

WAR DIARY
or
INTELLIGENCE SUMMARY.
(Erase heading not required.)

Army Form C. 2118.

Place	Date	Hour	Summary of Events and Information	Remarks and references to Appendices
In the Field	27/10		The usual company training was carried out. The gunners had erected spray baths at Bn. HQ and one coy was bathed in the morning. Orders were received that the 83rd Bde. would relieve the 112th Bde. in the line that night. The Bn. was to be in support with SOMERSETS on the left and LINCOLNS on the right-front sectors. The Bn. relieved the 13th ROYAL FUSILIERS in support by daylight. Three coys. and Bn. HQ. were in SAKESCHES and one coy. (A) in machine trenches X 9 a. CAPT. NEWSUM M.C. and CAPT. AMOR inspected the Bn. in the afternoon.	5/78 4/E 5/A S/E
	28/10		The C.O. visited coys. LT. SUTHERLAND rejoined from six months tour of duty in England. Coys. carried on with training and baths. Very fine weather.	
	29/10		A coy. were heavily shelled with gas shells in the early morning and were compelled to wear their gas masks for 3 hours. The C.O. visited A coy. in the morning. CAPT. NEWSUM MC rejoined the Bn. from S.S. 135" details	

WAR DIARY
or
INTELLIGENCE SUMMARY

Army Form C. 2118.

Place	Date	Hour	Summary of Events and Information	Remarks and references to Appendices
In the field	29/10		[illegible faded handwriting]	59 A S.E.
	30/10		The programme was for the Bn to go to the afternoon. [Lt] Fraser was wounded. The C.O. and 2nd in C. went to the CHISSIGNES to arrange the relief. HQ & Thompsons in CHISSIGNES to arrange. Owing to the line being cancelled the plans — [illegible] — carried on the afternoon — [illegible] — that night ...	
	31/10		SOMERSETS right of the act — the Bn moved up to HQ & B & D and I.O. arrived with the [illegible] — on the night of the 30th and were taken to the effect that the relief would take place. That night the Bn HQ was at 11:50 hours in CHISSIGNES. B and C coys in support, a line — [illegible] — line mS & D coys in the Villages and A coy in Machine Gun x 9 central railway D coy in reserve [illegible]	

WAR DIARY
or
INTELLIGENCE SUMMARY.
(Erase heading not required.)

Army Form C. 2118.

Place	Date	Hour	Summary of Events and Information	Remarks and references to Appendices
			The following officers joined and quitted the Bn. during the month of October 1918	
			LIEUT-COL. W. B. MOLONY DSO - To ENGLAND for six months tour of duty.	23.10.18
			CAPT. H. W. NEWSUM. M.C. - attached to "C" Coy.	
			CAPT. E. PROCTER MC - To ENGLAND for six	16.10.18
			2/LT. A. E. NORMAN - Reinforcement	16.10.18
			2/LT. H. W. CLOYDEN - to F.A.	5.10.18
			2/LT. J. T. ROSS - rejoined from F.A. - 26.10.18	
			2/LT. F. F. MARSHALL - reinforcement - 1.10.18	
			2/LT. F. W. WARTNABY - " - 1.10.18	
			LT. L. BROOKS - " and to base (Unfit.) 5.10.18 - 29.10.18	
			2/LT. H. T. BUSH - "	14.10.18
			W. H. LYNCH - "	16.10.18
			A. E. NORMAN	
			D. S. ABERNETHY - "	16.10.18
			V. HAYES - "	18.10.18
			M. V. LITTON - "	18.10.18
			J. H. D BALDOCK - "	16.10.18

Army Form C. 2118.

WAR DIARY
or
INTELLIGENCE SUMMARY.
(Erase heading not required.)

Instructions regarding War Diaries and Intelligence Summaries are contained in F. S. Regs., Part II. and the Staff Manual respectively. Title pages will be prepared in manuscript.

Place	Date	Hour	Summary of Events and Information	Remarks and references to Appendices
			2/Lt. G.W. HAWKINS - JOINED BN. - 25.10.18	
			W.H. RANDALL - do - 25.10.18	
			H.A.J. VAUGHAN - do - 25.10.18	
			A.H.B. ELLEY - do - 25.10.18	
			E.G. IRWOOD - do - 25.10.18	
			A.H. MARKS - do - 25.10.18	
			F.J. DAVIES - do - 25.10.18	
			CAPT. G.N. VINER - KILLED IN ACTION - 14.10.18	
			2/LT. A.G. ANDREWS - DIED OF WOUNDS 14.10.18	
			W.J. TURNER - KILLED IN ACTION 12.10.18	
			R.F. McFADDEN - do - 13.10.18	
			CAPT. A.J. KLAIBER MC - WOUNDED IN ACTION - 12.10.18	
			LIEUT J.B. BUCKNILL - do - 15.10.18	
			2/LT J.L. SELFE - do - 12.10.18	
			H.C. LINDSAY MC - do - 13.10.18	
			H.F. HODGKINSON - do - 9.10.18	
			A.E. STAFFORD - do - 9.10.18	
			LIEUT A. ANDERSON - JOINED BN. - 17.10.18	
			F.W. ROUSE - do - 30.10.18	

A.J.Groom-Watt Major
Commanding
4/7th Bn. Middlesex Regt.
31.10.18.

WAR DIARY
or
INTELLIGENCE SUMMARY.
(Erase heading not required.)

Army Form C. 2118.

Place	Date	Hour	Summary of Events and Information	Remarks and references to Appendices
			The MILITARY MEDAL was granted to the undermentioned NCO's and men on 21.9.18 in conspicuous gallantry & devotion to duty during the operations from August 21st — 26th 19.18.	

```
No. 52985   Cpl   H. JARVIS        — C Coy
   53276    Pte   J. DAMS          —  "
   81130    L/Cpl T.C. EVANS       —  "
   165130   Sgt   C. CHANNON       — B
   209254   Cpl   D. LAKE          —  "
   4871     Pte   H. KINGSLEY      — B
   52999    Sgt   H. LESLIE        — A
   129694   Sgt   J. COLLINS       — A
   87121    Pte   G. SYKES-SEY     — B
   54119    Pte   W. SPENCE        —  "
   1-808    Cpl   P. BARCLAY       — D
```

Ref. Sheet-57B N.E. 1/20,0 00.

12.10.18.

NARRATIVE OF BATTLE.

Orders were received that the advance was to be continued on 12th.Oct.1918. The objective of the 63rd.Inf. Bde. being the high ground in E.26 and E.19. Zero hour was at 05.00 hours and the Battn.attacked with "D" Coy. on left, "B" Coy. in the centre, "A" Coy. on the right, & "C" Coy. in support. The support Coy. was to follow at a distance of 800 yards to mop up the Rly. Line and to help consolidate the main line of resistance. Battn. H.Q. was at J.6.a.

The barrage opened at Zero, and was good on the right of the Battn.front although not so good on the left. The attack divided itself into two phases, i.e. the capture of the Rly. and the capture of the final objective.

The Battn.encountered heavy M.G. fire at the start both from the flank, especially from BELLE VUE, and from the Rly. line in front. This M.G. fire checked the advance but the centre Coy., under 2/Lt.H.M.CHAUNDY, opened 10 rounds rapid fire which demoralised the enemy and he abondoned his M.GS. This enabled the attack to proceed and the Rly.line was gained by the centre Coy. and the right Coy. Rifle fire was opened on the retreating enemy and considerable execution was done. Sgt.HARRIS of "A" Coy. discovered a Boche Officer and his Orderly hiding in a tunnel under the Rly. and followed them, killing them both.

The advance from the Rly. to the final objective was carried out without resistance. 4 M.Gs. under did excellent work, firing on the retiring enemy from positions on the ridge. The next ridge could easily have been captured at this time if troops had been available. The enemy afforded many excellent targets. These were taken advantage of by our men.

The left Coy. encountered the heaviest M.G. fire from BELLE VUE. Its plan of attack was completely upset by the failure of the assault of this place. The nest of M.Gs. there kept up a continual fire and it was found to be impossible for the Coy. to get forward. 2/Lt.BLOY who was on the right of the left Coy., succeeded in crossing the Rly. line with one section and took up a position on the high ground on the left of "B" Coy. The remainder of the Coy.were forced to form a defensive flank in M.19.c. Sgt. PERRY did some excellent sniping, killing two Boche Officers at 500 yards range.

The Support Coy. crossed the River, after passing through the enemy barrage, and sent one platoon forward to fill up the gap between the centre and left Coys. The other three platoons echeloned to the left to protect the flank from the North.

When the enemy discovered that the attack was not being pressed he returned to the high ground in E.27. and E.21. and pushed small parties of men down the Rly. from BELLE VUE. He opened fire from these positions on our men consolidating.

At 15.00 hours the enemy opened a heavy barrage along the front concentrating somewhat on the right. The Division on the right retired. Shortly afterwards our men were ordered to withdraw to the line of the Rly. The barrage did not touch our position and when the attacking Infantry appeared they were met by M.G., Lewis, and rifle fire. Heavy casualties are known to have been inflicted on his troops.

Owing to infilade M.G. fire it was found to be impossible to hold the Rly. and our men withdrew to the Sunken Road, through D.30.b and E.25.c. Here a line was organised and posts pushed out about 200 yards East of the road. Patrols were pushed forward to the Rly. when the capture of BELLE VUE was reported, but the Battalion was relieved before a line could be organised there.

Casualties.
 Officers.
  Killed.
   CAPT. G.N. VINER
   2/LT. W.J. TURNER
  Wounded.
   CAPT. A.J. KLAIBER M.C.
   LIEUT. J.B. BUCKMILL
   2/LT. J.C. LINDSAY M.C.
   2/LT. J.L. SELFE
   2/LT. A.G. ANDREWS (died of wounds 14.10.18)
  Missing (Since Reported Killed)
   2/LT. R.E. McFADDEN.
 Other Ranks.
  Killed - 19
  Wounded - 95 (3 since died of wounds)
  Missing - 15
  Wounded and missing - 1
  Missing believed prisoners - 2
  Gassed - 1.

63rd Brigade.
37th Division.

4th BATTALION

THE MIDDLESEX REGIMENT.

NOVEMBER 1 9 1 8

WAR DIARY
INTELLIGENCE SUMMARY
(Erase heading not required.)

4 Middlesex Regt
November 1918

Place	Date	Hour	Summary of Events and Information	Remarks and references to Appendices
	1/11		the C.O. and Capt. NEWSUM tried with moments in the morning and from that worked to sight to which was the only part of the enemy could get to in daylight. C. and party were in open country and could only be reached under cover of darkness. The enemy snipers i.e. SCESHOT were very alive and observant and Vickers guns making any observation of the enemy impossible. The enemy were very quiet on the whole and it appeared to be as if the Boche guns he had were kept the full time and rifle & machine gun fire was in the afternoon. CAPT. NEWSUM visited the posts at night.	57 A S.E.
	2/11		Another quiet day. Our guns harassed the enemy day and night and there was light shelling in reply in the morning and at front. Day the front coy. of the Bn. just was re-organised at night. In company of NEW ZEALAND troops relieved B coy. & others and our 3rd column of CHISSIGNIES. The platoon C.O. coy. relieved the billets of the MAIRIE. This was accomplished at 11 p.m. and it was a 8 inched front.

Army Form C. 2118.

WAR DIARY
or
INTELLIGENCE SUMMARY.
(Erase heading not required.)

Place	Date	Hour	Summary of Events and Information	Remarks and references to Appendices
In the Field	3/11		The en remained inactive. Patrols were sent out [illegible] on the following morning no attempt be [illegible] or on the morning by the en and it is believed the enemy have to [illegible] on our front. The platoon [illegible] at nightfall [illegible] the III the Brigade were relieved as authorised for 2 [illegible] three companies and I coy [illegible] to a camp of Inglewood at SH ESQUEIRS Or. No 3 of [illegible] [illegible] in the line of BRASSIGNES	ERASE
	4/11		Bn encountered no [illegible] at 12 30 hours orders following engaging received to proceed to help the Canadians [illegible] of having reached the [illegible] at [illegible] the advance and nearly up to the order, Bde [illegible] the Bns [illegible] and advanced at 20.30 hours [illegible] to relieve the [illegible] Bde in Belgium [illegible] relief not being [illegible] the Bns [illegible] in reserve [illegible] [illegible] are attached [illegible] in advance [illegible] [illegible] our [illegible] our [illegible] [illegible] were [illegible] sent off [illegible] CAPT. NEWSUM	

Army Form C. 2118.

WAR DIARY
or
INTELLIGENCE SUMMARY.
(Erase heading not required.)

Place	Date	Hour	Summary of Events and Information	Remarks and references to Appendices

Place	Date	Hour	Summary of Events and Information	Remarks and references to Appendices
	6/11		settled in by now that Lt. W.G. CHAPMAN M.C. was the only officer left at NEUVILLE and that no news could be received from Major GROVE + Lieut WHITE. He and his company (originally in support) had thrown out defensive flanks and it was impossible to get the guns off. However, he and about 115 men held on by himself to fight just four unwounded men. He answered during the day + during the night held all through the day. Company was till the early morning of the 7th when the commanders conferred and decided to leave. At 17.30 hours the company CAPT. NEWSUM M.C. signalled to 8 LINCOLNS who had joined the 8th YORKS on our right that he would retire at 18.30.	AZ.59/5.F
	7/11		Owing to rain companies formed to battle. The C.O. until each company during the morning and the conference at 18.30	

Place	Date	Hour	Summary of Events and Information	Remarks and references to Appendices
H 59 S.E.				H 59 S.E.
	8/11		The divisional commander held a CO's conference at [?] and [?] and made [?] the afternoon. The weather cleared about 09.00 hours and companies carried out a training programme on the Bn. training area. A party of 40 men under 7/LT. A. H. MARKS proceeded to the forward area for salvage, and burying of dead. The G.O.C. 65th Inf Bde. inspected the Bn. line transport at 14.30 hours. Lt named after the inspection started and companies marched off as soon as they were inspected. The Brigadier and Bde. Major dined with H.Q.	
	9/11		Companies spent the morning drilling and on the range and the afternoon on games and recreational training. The drums beat retreat at 16.00 hours on the road outside Battalion H.Q. All subaltern officers were told to join the drums in the afternoon.	

WAR DIARY
or
INTELLIGENCE SUMMARY.
(Erase heading not required.)

Army Form C. 2118.

Place	Date	Hour	Summary of Events and Information	Remarks and references to Appendices
In the Field	10/11		...stated that the Bde. would move on to CAUDRY in the morning day. An advance party proceeded to CAUDRY under CAPT. WILKINS to arrange billets. The Bn. paraded for divine service in the village green at 10.00 hours. In the afternoon the Corps Commander was to have presented medal ribbons but this parade was cancelled.	51 ASE 57 5ME
	11/11	08.10	The Bn. marched to CAUDRY passing X.25.b. 93.93. Route — NEUVILLE — VENDEGIES — BEAURAIN — MAROU — BELLEVUE — BRIASTRE — BETHENCOURT — CAUDRY. The billets were quite good with the exception that they had not been in-habited since the Boche left and consequently were in a filthy condition. The Bn. was billeted in the RUE D'EGALITE. The news that the armistice had been signed was received on the line of march and cheered wildly by the men. The Bn. was settled in billets at 14.00 hours.	

WAR DIARY
or
INTELLIGENCE SUMMARY.
(Erase heading not required.)

Army Form C. 2118.

Place	Date	Hour	Summary of Events and Information	Remarks and references to Appendices
In Field	12/11		The Bn. spent the day cleaning and scrubbing equipment and in drilling. The drums beat retreat outside Bn. H.Q. in the RUE D'AVESNES at 16.00 hours. C and D Coys. played football in the afternoon, D Coy. winning 2-1.	57.5
	13/11		Company sires at the absence of Company Commanders present medal ribands in the square outside the HOTEL DE VILLE at 14.30 hours. He O.C. conferred the Grand Cordon from the Bde. and CAPT. F.W. WARTHABY commanded the guard from the Bn. (40 men). The weather continued clean and fine although rather cold.	
	14/11		Companies carried out training in the morning including an hour's route march & gymnastics. The march to Germany the afternoon was spent in recreational training.	
	15/11		Training was carried out until 11.30 hours when the battalion went on a route march via BETHENCOURT. The usual games took up the afternoon.	

Army Form C. 2118.

WAR DIARY
or
INTELLIGENCE SUMMARY.
(Erase heading not required.)

Place	Date	Hour	Summary of Events and Information	Remarks and references to Appendices
Aldershot	15/11		[illegible handwritten entry regarding parade at Aldershot]	
		10.15	hours. [illegible] was given by the C.O., 2nd [illegible] not [illegible] a lecture on education. [illegible] attended	
	17/11		The Bn. paraded and marched over to [illegible] at 09.00 hours and moved to the church parade. It was found that [illegible] A.B. C and D companies had gone to first [illegible]. The inter-company football match was played in the afternoon between B and D Coys. After this [illegible] D Coys. [illegible] won the match.	
	18/11		The C.O. held a Co. commanders conference at HQ at 09.00 hours. The battalion paraded at 10.30 for ceremonial drill on the football ground. There was a ceremonial parade for the Bde. in the afternoon in preparation for the inspection by the B.O.C. on the following day. The weather was fine but cold during the morning.	

WAR DIARY or INTELLIGENCE SUMMARY

Army Form C. 2118.

Place	Date	Hour	Summary of Events and Information	Remarks and references to Appendices
Rouen	19/11		at 09.00 hours. The C.O. had an N.C.O.'s conference at Bn. HQ. CHOURT. The final game of the inter-Coy. football was played in the morning Coy. won 2-0. In the afternoon the battalion was inspected at 13.15 hours by the G.O.C. The turn-out was pronounced by the G.O.C. to be excellent. The weather was fine and the men throughly enjoyed the inspection.	Bn. No. 573 CHOURT
	20/11		Companies spent the morning in company drill, bayonet training and musketry instruction. An N.C.O.'s class was also formed under the R.S.M. paraded at 10.30 hours. A recruits' class was also formed under C.S.M. WARNER M.C. In the afternoon the officers challenged the sergeants to a game of football but the game was a draw 1-1.	
	21/11		The Bn. less 'C' Coy. paraded for ceremonial at 11.00 hours on the football ground. 'C' Coy. were employed for the day in cleaning the town. The N.C.O.'s and recruits' classes paraded as usual. The drums beat retreat outside Bde. HQ. at 16.00 hours. CAPT. FRY re-joined the Battalion— bringing the colours with him.	

WAR DIARY
or
INTELLIGENCE SUMMARY.

(Erase heading not required.)

Army Form C. 2118.

Place	Date	Hour	Summary of Events and Information	Remarks and references to Appendices
In the Field	21/11		for the review by the G.O.C. The Bn. paraded at 09.30 hours to march to ground and, after the inspection, marched past the Divisional Commander. The whole division was on parade. The Bn. was the only bn. to have colours on parade. "C" coy. played the 673rd Bde. Trench mortars in the second round of the Bde. football competition. "C" coy. won 3-nil.	S75
	22/11		Coys. spent the morning in bombing, bayonet & specialist training. The N.C.O's & recruits class paraded as usual. 1 Officer & 2 O.R. attended a lecture at the Divisional Y.M.C.A. by the Divisional P.Coy. Education Officer, the subject being "Demobilization & Reconstruction". The afternoon was devoted to football & running off heats for the Batt. Sports.	
	24/11		The Battalion paraded for Divine Service at the Barn Cwts theatre at 10 a.m. In the afternoon Cpl. Bird representative to hear a lecture delivered by Professor Adkins of Sheffield University on "German War Aims". The rest of the Bath. devoted the afternoon to sports.	
	25/11		During morning Coys. were at disposal of O.C. Coys for training. In the afternoon "C" Coy played S.L.I. Ilkal Team 2-1. The Coy is now champion Coy in the Brigade.	

WAR DIARY
or
INTELLIGENCE SUMMARY.

Army Form C. 2118.

Place	Date	Hour	Summary of Events and Information	Remarks and references to Appendices
In the Field	26/11		During the morning Coys were at disposal of O.C. Coys until 11 hrs. Subsequently representatives of all Coys, making about 200 in all, attended a lecture at 11.30 hours by Prof. Adkins in the Y.M.C.A., the subject being "Belgium". The Origin of the War. During the afternoon "A" Coy and "C" Coy ran a cross-country race.	57 B
	27/11		The Battalion less "D" Coy who were at Bulho, paraded for Brigade Route March. The Batt. returned at about 12.30 hours. The Batt. was the only one on the march to have no men fall out. During the afternoon representatives from Coys attended a lecture by Prof. Adkins in the Bear Garden. Recreational training was also carried out.	
	28/11		At 11.30 hours a lecture by Prof. Adkins on the "Y.M.C.A." the subject being "U.S.A. & Japan". Owing to bad weather no recreational training was possible during the afternoon. The new Batt. Mess was used for all officers for the first time at lunch today.	
	29/11		During the morning Coys were at the disposal of the O.C. Coys for training etc. There were no parades during the afternoon.	
	30/11		Q.O.C. Coys paraded at 9.30 hours, in drill order, & was addressed by the G.O.C. 63rd Inf. Brigade, on the subject of D.D.'s Botanical activities in the British Army.	

WAR DIARY
INTELLIGENCE SUMMARY

Army Form C. 2118.

Place	Date	Hour	Summary of Events and Information	Remarks and references to Appendices
Lichfield	30/11		During the afternoon the Battn. Football team visited Lichfield & played the 1st Battn. Middlesex Regt. The friends' victors by 2 goals to 1. The commanding officer was the second in command of the 1st Middlesex — a 11 furlongs flat horse race.	57 B
	30/11/18			

W. G. Chapman Lt Colonel
Cmdg
4"B"n Middx Regt.

63rd Brigade.
37th Division.

4th BATTALION

THE MIDDLESEX REGIMENT.

DECEMBER 1918

WAR DIARY or INTELLIGENCE SUMMARY.

Army Form C. 2118.

4 Manchester
Middlesex
December 1918

Place	Date	Hour	Summary of Events and Information	Remarks and references to Appendices
2 IN F.R. HAUSSY	1/12	10.45 hours	The Batt. moved to the HAUSSY area moving Via BRIASTRE - BELLEVUE - SOLESMES. The Batt. was settled in billets at 14.25 hours.	
VILLERS-POL	2/12		The march was continued to-day the Batt. moving to VILLERS-POL Via MAISON BLANCHE - VERTAIN - PONT À PIERRE - BEAUDIGNIES - ORSINVAL. The Batt. was settled in billets at 13.45 hours. The billets consisted chiefly of huts & shell shattered houses.	
	3/12		The morning was spent in meeting & cleaning up. During the afternoon Officers & O.R. from all Coy lined the road on the outskirts of ORSINVAL & saw H.M. the King who was passing to troops in this area.	
	4/12		The morning was spent in lectures in billets. The day being very rainy. At about 17 hours H.M. the King passed through the Western outskirts DORSINVAL.	
	5/12		Coy. parades for arms & platoon drill until 11.30 a.m. References 9 + R 13. 1. "D" Coy attended Shortland Class at 10.30 hours.	
	6/12		Class in shorthand for "C" H.Q. Coy. platoon & arms drill. "B" Coy officers & Sgt played Rest of City during afternoon.	

Army Form C. 2118.

WAR DIARY
or
INTELLIGENCE SUMMARY.
(Erase heading not required.)

Instructions regarding War Diaries and Intelligence Summaries are contained in F. S. Regs., Part II. and the Staff Manual respectively. Title pages will be prepared in manuscript.

Place	Date	Hour	Summary of Events and Information	Remarks and references to Appendices
In the field VILLERS-POL	7/12		Corps under O.C. Corps during morning. Some football was played during the afternoon.	Valenciennes 1/100,000
	8/12		Batt'n paraded for Divine Service at 10.00 hours in the Concert Barn near "A" Coy billets.	
	9/12		Drill under O.C. Coy's until 11.00 A.M. At 11.00 hours Lt. Palmer M.V.O. delivered a lecture in the Concert Barn on "The importance of India". During the afternoon in spite of unpropitious weather, a rugby practice was held.	
	10/12		Corps under O.C. Corps for drill etc. Three shorthand classes were held during the morning.	
	11/12		Corps under O.C. Corps for drill etc. Educational Activities under Coy arrangements from 11.30–12.30. Three French classes were held during the morning. "D" had "A" by 4–1.	
	12/12		Batt'n parade for Ceremonial drill was abandoned owing to rain. Class in boot keeping & elementary English continued as usual.	
	13/12		"C" & "D" Coys these halted this morning. "A" & "B" were engaged in fitting equipment. At 11.30 hrs Major Grove White delivered a most illuminating lecture on "India". At 14.30 hours a conference was held to discuss proposed classes in advanced English Literature	

Army Form C. 2118.

WAR DIARY
or
INTELLIGENCE SUMMARY.
(Erase heading not required.)

Instructions regarding War Diaries and Intelligence Summaries are contained in F.S. Regs., Part II. and the Staff Manual respectively. Title pages will be prepared in manuscript.

Place	Date	Hour	Summary of Events and Information	Remarks and references to Appendices
In the Field	14/12		The Batt. commenced to march to the area to be occupied in Belgium moving to the LOUVIGNIES area. The Batt. moved off at 11.55 hours marches by the following route:- Cross roads 1 mile N. of ORSINVAL – WARGNIES LE - GRAND - ST WAAST LA VALLÉE – BAVAY. The Batt. reached its destination at 15.45 hours & was quickly settled in fairly comfortable billets.	Valenciennes / 100,000.
SOUS-LE-BOIS	15/12		March resumed. The Batt. moving to the SOUS-LE-BOIS area, moving off at 10.45 hours and marching via road junction 150 N. Y.L. in LOUVIGNIES – LA LONGUEVILLE – DOUZIES. The Batt. also absorbed 147 filled in one huge building. It was billeted by 14.30 hours.	
	16/12		Day spent in resting, cleaning up. All staff officers were of the opinion that the marching of the Batt. was easily the best in the division.	
GRAND-RENG	17/12		Batt. resumed its journey, moving to GRAND RENG area, starting at 9.25 hours marching via MAUBERGE – FAUBOURG DE MONS-ELESMES – VIEUX RENG. The Batt. was billeted by 13.00 hours.	
RESSAIX	18/12		The march was resumed today, the Batt. moving to the RESSAIX area via ROUVEROY – GIVRY – ESTINNE AU MONT – BINCHE. The Batt. was billeted in very good billets by 15.00 hours. Although the march was in very wet weather & was the longest the Batt. has done, nobody fell out.	NAMUR / 100,000
COURCELLES	19/12		March resumed today, the Battn. moving to the COURCELLES	

WAR DIARY or INTELLIGENCE SUMMARY

Army Form C. 2118.

Place	Date	Hour	Summary of Events and Information	Remarks and references to Appendices
	20/12		After marching at 09.10 hours and marching via MORLANWELZ - CHAPELLE to HERLAIMONT, and then everywhere nearing with acclamation. The battalion was settled in billets by 13.15 hours	Manuev 100,000
REVES	21/12		The day was spent in resting & cleaning up. The last stage of the march was commenced today, at 09.30 hours the Batt. moving to the REVES area via GOSSELIES-LIBERCHIES. The colours were carried during the march. The companies were very pleased yet was about 16.00 hours before the men were finally settled in billets. Batt HQ & "A" Coy were billeted in the village of REVES itself, B & D Coy in SART-A-REVES, & "C" Coy at WATTIMEZ	BROSSELS 1/100,000
	22/12		Day was spent in resting, cleaning up & preparing for Xmas	
	23/12		Day spent in resting & preparing for Christmas. The battalion was the best in the brigade for the whole series of marches.	
	24/12		Coys still engaged in cleaning up & decorating their billets for Christmas.	
	25/12		Christmas Day. Ample preparations had been made to provide Xmas dinners for the men. In addition large issues were requisitioned turkeys, chicken, geese, etc. however	

Army Form C. 2118.

WAR DIARY
or
INTELLIGENCE SUMMARY.
(Erase heading not required.)

Instructions regarding War Diaries and Intelligence Summaries are contained in F. S. Regs., Part II. and the Staff Manual respectively. Title pages will be prepared in manuscript.

Place	Date	Hour	Summary of Events and Information	Remarks and references to Appendices
Field	25/12		From the villages the dining halls were profusely decorated. The C.O. & Adj. commenced a tour of Companies at about 14.00 hours. The men thoroughly enjoyed themselves, & everything ran smoothly. The transport & men D.M. Store had their dinner in the Evening & spent a very merry time. The C.O., 2nd in Command & Adj. of 6-S.R.1 paid a visit to the Battn during the afternoon of congratulating the C.O. on the Battn having gained first place in the Brigade for marching.	BRUSSELS 100,000
	26/12		The day was spent in reading & recreational training the Sgts of "HQ" "A" Coys held their dinner at 19.15 hours.	
	27/12		Morning, Coy's were at disposal of O.C. Coys for 1 hour educational work & recreational training.	
	28/12		This morning 16 Officers & 20 O.R. per Coy attended a lecture at FRASNES by Colonel Bourne, the subject being "Forest Surgeons for Settlement in ex-Service men".	
	29/12		Coys paraded at varying hours in the own villages for Divine Service. During the afternoon the Battalion played the 9th Bn N. Staffs at football the result was 5-3 in our favours. A very strong wind rather spoiled the game.	
	30/12		Coys under Coys arrangements during the morning. It now became	

Army Form C. 2118.

WAR DIARY
or
INTELLIGENCE SUMMARY.
(Erase heading not required.)

Place	Date	Hour	Summary of Events and Information	Remarks and references to Appendices
Field	30/12		Known that this Battalion gained Second place in the division for marching & march discipline, during the advance into BELGIUM.	Ref. BRUSSELS 1/100,000
RÊVES	31/12		Training under Coy arrangements in Musketry, physical training and educational work, was carried out during the morning. In the afternoon the Battalion played the 37 D.A.C. at football and a well contested game resulted in a draw of 3 goals each.	
	31.12.18.			

S. G. Chapman
Lt Colonel
Commanding 4th Bn
The Middlesex Regt.

4 Middlesex   Army Form C. 2118.

January 1919

WAR DIARY
or
INTELLIGENCE SUMMARY.
(Erase heading not required.)

Instructions regarding War Diaries and Intelligence Summaries are contained in F. S. Regs., Part II. and the Staff Manual respectively. Title pages will be prepared in manuscript.

Place	Date	Hour	Summary of Events and Information	Remarks and references to Appendices
RÊVES	Jan 1		Companies under O.C. Coys for musketry, Physical training & education	BRUSSELS 100,000
	Jan 2		Companies under O.C. Coys for drill & education & training. 1 Officer & 19 O.R. per Coy attended a lecture on "Agriculture & its prospects" at FRASNES-LES-GOSSELIES.	
	Jan 3		Coys under O.C. Coys for bayonet fighting, Physical training and education.	
	Jan 4		Company commanders inspected billets. Inter educational training was carried out. In the afternoon the Brigade played the 112th Brigade at rugby. The latter won by 14 points – nil. Capt Pillow M.C. Capt Satchwell & Lt F. referee'd the Battalion side.	
	Jan 5		10.45 Run. 9 the afternoon the Battn. played the 8 S.L.I. in football, ground very sodden. Coys drew by 9–0.	
	Jan 6		Coys under O.C. Coys for musketry, education.	
	Jan 7		Coys under O.C. Coys for inspections & education. "A" & "C" Coy on the R. Brabançon "B" Coy on the French Revolution & Napoleon "D" Coy heat at poisons. Lecture part 2.	

C in C.B. Sir N. Holroyd for R. & R. Education

Army Form C. 2118.

WAR DIARY
or
INTELLIGENCE SUMMARY.
(Erase heading not required.)

Instructions regarding War Diaries and Intelligence Summaries are contained in F. S. Regs., Part II. and the Staff Manual respectively. Title pages will be prepared in manuscript.

Place	Date	Hour	Summary of Events and Information	Remarks and references to Appendices
BEVES	Jan 9.		Corps. races at The district & Corps Commander for Evening. 2/Lieut. H.M. GIBBONEY and 3/Lt. J.E. HARRINGTON and awarded the Military Cross. No. 15405 Sgt. HARRIS and 1529 Cpl. BELL M.M. were awarded the D.C.M.	
	Jan 10.		Corps Kewal under Corps Commander. Physical and Bayonet Training, Education. The Transport Officers Left The Battalion for Dunkirkington. Capt. H.W.M. POTTER M.C. Lieut. T. FORBES, Lieut. F.W. RODIE 2/Lts. H.A.L. VAUGHN, E.G. INWOOD, W.A. BLOY, E. ELMORE, J. ROSS and 26 O.R.	
	Jan 11.		Training was continued under Corps arrangements. The Football [?] 1st R. Hants. Regt. 2/Lts. 30ns of Ammunition followed. The result was a draw — no goals being scored.	
	Jan 12.		Band Parade at 11:45 hrs. The remainder of the day was all in preparation.	
	Jan 13.		Training was carried out under Corps arrangements.	
	Jan 14.		Usual Infantry Drill and Education was carried out. The 1914-1915 [?] Ribbons have been issued to all ranks who have qualified.	
	Jan 15.		Recreational Training in the afternoon.	

Army Form C. 2118.

WAR DIARY
or
INTELLIGENCE SUMMARY.
(Erase heading not required.)

Instructions regarding War Diaries and Intelligence Summaries are contained in F.S. Regs., Part II. and the Staff Manual respectively. Title pages will be prepared in manuscript.

Place	Date	Hour	Summary of Events and Information	Remarks and references to Appendices
REVEL	Jan 16		Training was continued under Coy. arrangements. A Coy. played C. Coy. at Football. In the afternoon. Result a draw — each lot scoring 1 goal.	
	Jan 17		Platoon, Section, Drill and Gas drill were carried out. Lieut. A.M. ANDERSON billeted in the Battle of WAR— The remainder of the day was spent in Regimental Training.	
	Jan 18		Inspection of Billets and usual Training was carried on with.	
	Jan 19		Divine Service was held at 10:30 am. The following Officers were detailed to join the Battalion:- Capt. S. CHIPPERFIELD, 2/Lt. G.A. PIERCE and also 5 F.O.R.	
	Jan 20		The Battalion attended a Lecture by Lieut. Col. APPLIN D.S.O. at FRASNES-LES-GOSSELIES.— Subject Demobilization at Reconstruction. B & D Companies were amalgamated. 2/Lt. Capt. T. DE VAL in command.	
	Jan 21		The usual Training was carried out under Coy arrangements. Recruits' Training was carried out in the afternoon.	
	Jan 22		Captains carried out a tactical cross-country run in the morning. In the afternoon games were played in the Training in the morning. The Battalion were the 63rd If. Lieut. A.M. ANDERSON and 2/Lt. A.H. BELLEY and I.H.D. BALDOCK joined the Battalion along with 22 O.R.	
	Jan 23		Training in the morning. Coy arrangements. Afternoon games were played.	

WAR DIARY
or
INTELLIGENCE SUMMARY.

(Erase heading not required.)

Army Form C. 2118.

Instructions regarding War Diaries and Intelligence Summaries are contained in F. S. Regs., Part II. and the Staff Manual respectively. Title pages will be prepared in manuscript.

Place	Date	Hour	Summary of Events and Information	Remarks and references to Appendices
REVES.	Jan 25		The Commanding Officer inspected C. Coy. The Battalion worked at until noon [on] arrangements. Recreational Training and games were played in the afternoon. 14 O.R. demobilized.	
	Jan 26.		Church Parade was held at 11:30 hrs. The remainder of the day — rest.	
			The "EMMA EX" Exam. is performed. This was brought attention by all ranks.	
	Jan 27.		Drill, Recreational Training and Education was carried out. There was played in The afternoon.	
			30 O.R. was demobilized. C.S.M. SNURAMS M.C. proceeded on leave to U.K. En route FRANCE 1919	
	Jan 28.		Platoon Inspections and Cross-country runs were carried out in the morning. Recreational Training and games in the afternoon.	
	Jan 29.		The Battalion attended a Lecture by Capt. GUEST at FRAMES-LES-GOSSELIES. Owing to bad weather no Co's of companies, the Battalion could not play the football match with 1/5th Bn. Rifle Bde.	
			Platoon Inspections, Drill and Recreational Training was carried out. 46 O.R. demobilized.	
	Jan 30.		Platoon Inspections were carried out. The Commanding Officer and Adjutant attended a conference at 6.30 of 98/Bde. H.Q. The "EMMA EX" under the management of Lieut. A.A. BURCH goes on to improvement at Bde Headquarters at MOUTAIN LE VAL.	

C. G. Chapman
Lieut.-Colonel,
Commanding 4/Bn. Middlesex Regiment.

63rd Inf. Bde.

Forwarded herewith please, War Diary of this Battalion for the month of February.

[signature]
Commanding 4/Bn. Middlesex Regiment.

Army Form C. 2118.

WAR DIARY
or
INTELLIGENCE SUMMARY.
(Erase heading not required.)

February 1919

Instructions regarding War Diaries and Intelligence Summaries are contained in F. S. Regs., Part II. and the Staff Manual respectively. Title pages will be prepared in manuscript.

Place	Date	Hour	Summary of Events and Information	Remarks and references to Appendices
Rues.	Feb 1		The parade to practice the presentation of colours was abandoned on a/c of the weather	
	Feb 2		The Battalion marched to Frames and took part in the practice of the parade for to-morrow	
	Feb 3		The Batt. marched to Frames and took part in the 13th ceremonial parade when King's Colours were consecrated by the Senior Chaplain of the 37th Div. and presented to the 5th & 13th Somerset Light Inf. and the 5th & 13th Lincolnshire Reg. by the Corps Commander. The Div¹ Commander was also present.	
	Feb 4		Platoon inspection and Recreational training	
	Feb 5		The B^n attended a lecture at Frames by Lt Comdr Everard R.N. on the work of the navy.	
	Feb 6		Training under Coy arrangements	
	Feb 7		The 13th attended a lecture at Frames by Rev G. E. Martin on the "League of Nations"	

Army Form C. 2118.

WAR DIARY
or
INTELLIGENCE SUMMARY.
(Erase heading not required.)

Instructions regarding War Diaries and Intelligence Summaries are contained in F. S. Regs., Part II. and the Staff Manual respectively. Title pages will be prepared in manuscript.

Place	Date	Hour	Summary of Events and Information	Remarks and references to Appendices
Rews	Feb 8		The B^n was engaged in clearing snow off the football ground	
	Feb 9		Divine service was at 10.30 hrs.	
	Feb 10		The men detailed for the Army of Occupation have enlisted by the C.O. Medal ribands were presented by Lieut Colonel at Bronne to recipients in the 63rd Inf. Bde. The recipients from the 4th & 13th middx Regt were. Second Lieut J.E. Harrington M.C. 13769 Sgt a Harris D.C.M. 6549 Sgt W Giddings M.M. 290524 Sgt a Lake M.M.	
	Feb 11		The Bm attended a lecture at Bronne by the Brigadier on the Malay Peninsula. The B^n won the Div^l Guard mounting competition at Gosselies.	
	Feb 12		The 13th paraded in the square at Rews and the Brigadier presented a cup for winning the 13th Brigade country run which was won on the 23.1.19.	
	Feb 13		The 13th attended a lecture at Bronne by the Div^l C.O. on the	

WAR DIARY
or
INTELLIGENCE SUMMARY.
(Erase heading not required.)

Army Form C. 2118.

Place	Date	Hour	Summary of Events and Information	Remarks and references to Appendices
	Feb. 13		"Battle of Waterloo". Lt. A.M. Andrews and 2/Lt J.W.D. Baldock conducted a party to England for demobilization.	
	Feb. 14		"A" Coy was inspected by the Brigadier in the square at Reeds. "B" Coy training under Coy arrangements. 2/Lt J.R. Harrington M.C. conducted a party for church the England.	
	Feb. 15		Training under Coy arrangements.	
	Feb. 16		Divine Service was at 09.30 hrs. Major Kay and Capt Sutherland M.C. proceeded to England.	
	Feb. 17		Training under Coy arrangements. Lt Col Chapman proceeded to England on leave. Capt Putnam M.C. took over command of the Bn.	
	Feb. 18		Platoon inspections and education.	
	Feb. 19		Platoon inspections, drill and education.	

Army Form C. 2118.

WAR DIARY
or
INTELLIGENCE SUMMARY.
(Erase heading not required.)

Instructions regarding War Diaries and Intelligence Summaries are contained in F. S. Regs., Part II. and the Staff Manual respectively. Title pages will be prepared in manuscript.

Place	Date	Hour	Summary of Events and Information	Remarks and references to Appendices
Reux	Feb 20		The C.O inspected stores and men for the Army of occupation at 11.00 hrs on the "B" football ground at Sart-a-Reux.	
	Feb 21		Platoon inspections and education.	
	Feb 22		The C.O inspected "A" Coy at 10.30 hrs at Reux and "B" Coy at 11.30 hrs on the football field at Sart-a-Reux. The following N.C.O's were awarded the M.S.M. 89337 S/Sgt Burden G. 95249 L/Cpl Millar J.R } vide supplement to London Gazette Jan 18th 1919	
	Feb 23		Divine Service was at 10.30 hrs.	
	Feb 24		Platoon inspections, drill and education	
	Feb 25		Platoon inspections, drill and education. Lieut-Col G.F. Chapman VC was today married in London to Miss M. Knox Little.	
	Feb 26		Platoon inspections, drill and education	

WAR DIARY
or
INTELLIGENCE SUMMARY.

(Erase heading not required.)

Army Form C. 2118.

Place	Date	Hour	Summary of Events and Information	Remarks and references to Appendices
Rusco	Feb 26		Inter Company football competition. "B" beat "A" 1-0.	
	Feb 27		Inter Company football competition. "A" beat "B" 5 goals to nil.	
	Feb 28		Final match. A Coy beat B Coy 5 goals to nil. Platoon inspections, drill and route march.	

3/3/19.

Commanding 4/Bn. Middlesex Regiment.

www.ingramcontent.com/pod-product-compliance
Lightning Source LLC
Chambersburg PA
CBHW08085823 0426
43663CB00013B/2574